DARK REALITIES

America's Great Depression

Wyn Derbyshire

Published by Spiramus Press Ltd,
102 Blandford Street, London, W1U 8AG.

© Wyn Derbyshire, 2013

ISBN

978 1907444 77 7 Hardback

978 1907444 78 4 Paperback

British Library Cataloguing-in-Publication Data.

A catalogue record for this book is available from the British Library.

Printed by Berforts Information Press

Cover illustration: "Jobless Men Keep Going" (John E. Allen, Inc.), in the Franklin Delano Roosevelt Library and Museum collection

For Andrew, Anjna and Elora

About the author

Wyn Derbyshire originally trained as a research chemist, gaining a PhD from the University of Cambridge before qualifying as a lawyer. Now a partner at City law firm SJ Berwin LLP, he has for many years been interested in the history of finance and business.

He is the author of *Six Tycoons - The lives of John Jacob Astor, Cornelius Vanderbilt, Andrew Carnegie, John D Rockefeller, Henry Ford and Joseph P Kennedy.*

He lives in St Albans, Hertfordshire with his wife and daughter.

Contents

Table of abbrevations

AAA	Agricultural Adjustment Administration
AFL	American Federation of Labor
CCC	Civilian Conservancy Corps
CIO	Committee for Industrial Organisation (later the Congress for Industrial Organisation)
CWA	Civil Works Administration
FERA	Federal Emergency Relief Administration
FTP	Federal Theater Project
FWP	Federal Writers Project
NIRA	National Industrial Recovery Act
NAACP	National Association for the Advancement of Colored People
NRA	National Recovery Administration
NUSJ	National Union for Social Justice
NYA	National Youth Administration
PWA	Public Works Administration
REA	Rural Electrification Agency
RFC	Reconstruction Finance Corporation
SEC	Securities and Exchange Commission
TERA	Temporary Emergency Relief Administration
TVA	Tennessee Valley Authority
UAW	United Auto Workers
UTW	United Textile Workers Union
WPA	Works Progress Administration

Chapter 1 The Birth of the Twenties

"My God, this is a hell of a job! I can take care of my enemies all right. But my friends, my God-damn friends, they're the ones that keep me walking the floor nights!"
President Warren Harding (1865 – 1923)

From Wilson to Harding

For many Americans, the miseries of the years of the Great Depression were compounded by their rosy memories of the decade that preceded it – the Roaring Twenties. That decade occupies a special place in America's folklore, as the era of Prohibition and gangsters and bootleggers, as the years of jazz and flappers and fun, and as a time when it seemed that peace and material progress could never end. It was a period when many ordinary people believed fervently in the benefits of capitalism and business, that a gleaming, self-sufficient and above all a superior America could stand aside from the rest of the world and all of its troubles, and that the bad days would never come again. That was a fantasy of course, but an exceptionally beguiling one, and when it was abruptly shattered in the weeks of October 1929, and it became clear over the months that followed that the good times had gone, perhaps forever, the shock to many Americans must have been profound.

But before the bad days came the good days. Historians, economists and politicians still argue over exactly when the phenomenon of the Twenties began, but as good a time as any is mid-day on 4th March 1921, a cold but bright day in Washington DC, and as good a place as any is the East Portico of the Capitol Building. For that was the time and place of the inauguration of the 29th President of the United States, Republican Warren Gamaliel Harding. By then, most of the ingredients of the Twenties were in place, and for many the party had already started.

Harding's reputation has not fared well in the hands of historians. Indeed he is frequently regarded as one of the worst Presidents of all time. But that is with the benefit of hindsight and is a judgment that is at least open to some debate. At the time of his inauguration, he was extremely popular, having triumphed over his Democratic opponent James Cox at the Presidential polls in 1920, and gaining the largest popular vote until then recorded in the process.[1]

Born in 1865 (the first President to have been born after the end of the American Civil War), Warren Harding had originally been a small town publisher in Ohio before becoming involved in first state and then national politics. Elected a US Senator in 1915, for several years he attracted relatively little attention outside his home state before being approached by a number of powerful backroom Republicans with a view to securing his candidacy for President in an effort to resolve a deadlock between other would-be Republican nominees. The story is told that they asked Harding if he had anything in his personal history that might cast a shadow over his nomination, the Republican Party or the office of the President, and that he went into another room, thought deeply for a while, and then emerged to announce that he had no flaws.

In fact, he had several, including a secret mistress and an illegitimate daughter whom he never saw. He was also weak, ineffective and easily led (probably one of the reasons why the political king-makers in the smoke-filled backrooms had been eager to secure his candidacy), and his principal attribute was an ability to make himself seem like a decent, likeable and ordinary man. His speeches were famous for their lack of eloquence, and were the subject of merciless ridicule by unsympathetic journalists. To some extent, he was aware of his flaws, and towards the end of his life he said of himself: *"I am a man of limited talents from a small town. I don't seem to grasp that I am President."* Nevertheless, for the time being he was President, and at a time when the country was in a state of political and economic transformation.

By the early 1920s, America had already established herself as the world's economic superpower. Although, January 1920 had seen the onset of a sharp post-war slump that eventually led to more than five million workers being unemployed and a 47 percent fall in stock market prices as measured by the

---

[1] Cox's running mate and candidate for the Vice Presidency in the 1920 presidential election was Franklin D Roosevelt. Unsuccessful Vice-Presidential candidates have often faced political obscurity; fortunately for the history of the world, FDR managed to avoid this fate.

Dow Jones industrial average index between November 1919 and August 1921, by the time of Harding's inauguration, there were signs that the country was beginning to pull out of its economic malaise and was heading into calmer and more benign financial waters. Admittedly, America's economic prosperity was not distributed evenly between its citizens. Urban incomes were on average considerably higher than those of workers in rural areas, and workers in the northern states tended to be better paid than those in the South, where the economic damage sustained during the Civil War, and as a consequence of the failure to industrialise in the decades that followed, was still evident. Farmers everywhere suffered from the onset of a long term decline in the value of agricultural produce (and land) which would persist into the 1940s, and since over half of the country's farmers were located in the southern states, this exacerbated the North-South wealth divide. African Americans, especially those in the South, suffered most of all from poverty, disease, lack of opportunity and politicised and social racism, and many lived in conditions little better (if at all) than their ancestors had endured in the years before the abolition of slavery.

Nevertheless, thanks to the efforts of men such as Andrew Carnegie, J D Rockefeller, Henry Ford and many others in the decades leading up to the First World War, America's industrial strengths, and particularly the might of America's steel, oil, chemical and automobile industries, far exceeded those of her foreign rivals, both in terms of production and innovation. Moreover, the First World War had allowed America to gain advantages in other fields. Loans granted to the allied nations[2] in the opening years of the War had helped to consolidate America's position as the leading creditor nation, giving immense advantages to her financiers and bankers and allowing Wall Street to oust the City of London from its traditional position as the centre of the world's financial systems. And America's participation in the First World War (albeit that her entry was, at least to the eyes of European allies, somewhat tardy) coupled with the debateable but widely held view that it was America's entry alone that had secured victory for the Allies, had for many people in the world

---

[2] These included France, the United Kingdom, and its Empire and Commonwealth, Italy, Belgium and, until 1917, Russia.

given America an image of decency and chivalry. This view of America persisted into the 1920s notwithstanding that American popular opinion had swung sharply in favour of isolationism following the end of the war.

This swing to isolationism – strongly fuelled as it was by the attitude of many of the two million servicemen of the American Expeditionary Force returning from Europe after the end of the war – had already helped to undermine the efforts of Harding's predecessor Woodrow Wilson to create a new worldwide political framework that would (he had hoped) make future wars impossible. Wilson had travelled to Europe to attend the Versailles peace conference at the beginning of 1919 on a tide of goodwill, convinced of his own moral superiority but sincerely determined to do all he could to help the suffering peoples of Europe following the collapse of the Central Powers at the end of the war. Alas the goodwill did not persist. Firmly believing in the principle of self-determination for individual nationalities, and conscious of the need to secure a just peace, Wilson found many of his ideas rejected by the politicians of his European allies. It seemed to Wilson that the Allies were more concerned about securing economic reparations from Germany for the damage the European allies had sustained during the war (and to enable them to pay off the war loans they had received from America, which the Americans were now loudly demanding should be repaid) rather than pursuing the noble but arguably naïve proposals of the American President. The Allies (especially France) were also determined that any peace treaty should ensure that Germany would never again be in a position to threaten her neighbours. Wilson felt that too much was being demanded from Germany, a view that was shared by the renowned British economist John Maynard Keynes, who felt so strongly about the matter that he resigned from the British peace delegation and returned home. Eventually, after much argument, a peace treaty was agreed at Versailles and imposed on the former belligerent nations, but it was a pale reflection of what Wilson had hoped to achieve. It was also a treaty which left many signatories (most notably of course, but not exclusively, Germany) feeling profoundly ill-used and dissatisfied, and eventually the ill feelings it generated would be used to sinister effect by the Nazis.

Coupled with the peace treaty were Wilson's proposals to establish a League of Nations through which he hoped the nations of the world could discuss and resolve international difficulties. The League was established; however, during the six months that he had spent in Europe, Wilson had effectively lost control of his Government back in the United States, and on his return he found he was unable to persuade Congress (more sensitive than Wilson to the growing domestic calls for isolationism) that America should join the League. Without American involvement, the League was ultimately doomed, and although it did achieve several successes in the early years of its existence, it rapidly declined into an international irrelevance.

President Wilson never really recovered from the rejection of his ideas in Europe and in Congress, and the remainder of his administration was effectively a failure. On 2nd October 1919 (at the height of his battle with Congress to secure American membership of the League), he suffered a stroke, the details of which were withheld from the public. For the remainder of his term, he was barely able to function as President, and would probably have had little choice but to resign save for the efforts of his wife Edith, who in her own words effectively assumed a "stewardship" of the Presidency in a manner not envisaged by the US Constitution.

Consequently, the Inauguration Day of Warren Harding found the general American public increasingly unwilling to see America engaged in the affairs of other nations. This wariness as regards foreign matters was exacerbated by their suspicions of socialism and the rise of communism in Russia, coupled with fears that the Bolshevik "contagion" could spread to the United States thanks to the presence of large numbers of immigrant workers. A number of anarchist bomb attacks (including one against the home of US Attorney General A. Mitchell Palmer on 3rd June 1919, and another in the heart of Wall Street on 16th September 1920 which killed 28 people and injured 200 more) helped to fuel those fears. In addition, the summer of 1919 saw an outbreak of race riots in a number of US cities (partly fuelled by an influx of half a million workers from the South, many African Americans, seeking work in northern cities) including one in Chicago that left 38 people dead and which added to the general sense of social unrest. The authorities responded with a series of crackdowns and raids on the activities of anarchists, socialists and union organisers, perceived or real, with a view to deporting as many of them as possible. Helping to co-ordinate many of the raids was one of Palmer's principal assistants, an eager young man called J Edgar Hoover, later to find fame (or infamy) as Head of the FBI. In fact, the majority of the people seized in the raids were legitimate US citizens, most of whom were innocent of any wrongdoing and eventually released, though not before many of them had been brutally treated by the authorities. After the attack on Wall Street, there were no further bomb attacks and the raids ceased, thanks in part to increasing concerns in Congress as to the methods being used by law enforcers. Nevertheless, widespread suspicion of radicals and of organised labour generally continued for much of the 1920s.

Above all, the American people at the time of Harding's inauguration longed for a return to the comforting apparent certainties that had sustained them in the days before the War. Harding, for all his faults as a President, managed to tap into this mood perfectly, promising America a return to "normalcy". *"America's present need"* he proclaimed, *"is not heroics, but healing; not nostrums, but normalcy; not revolution but restoration; not agitation, but adjustment; not surgery, but serenity; not the dramatic, but the dispassionate; not experiment, but equipoise; not submergence in internationality, but sustainment in triumphant nationality."*

Ostensibly with these aims in mind, Harding had set about assembling his administration in the months following his election victory. Aware of his limitations, he had sought reassurance as to his fitness for the post of President by appointing several of his oldest friends to important government posts. Unfortunately, too many of them proved to be less than honest public stewards who dedicated their (mostly and mercifully relatively brief) periods of office to the systematic defrauding of the public finances. Perhaps the most notorious example of these activities (but not the only one) was the Teapot Dome Scandal, masterminded by Albert Fall, Harding's Secretary of the Interior. Essentially, once in office, Fall managed to ensure that Government-owned oil fields held in reserve for use by the US Navy in the event of an emergency were transferred to his jurisdiction, and then arranged for them to be leased to private investors who promised in return to supply to the Navy a proportion of the oil they drilled from the fields. All this happened with President Harding's knowledge. Only later did it emerge that the private investors had bribed Fall and his son-in-law to the tune of several hundred thousand dollars in order to secure the leases. The scandal emerged only after

Harding's death, and Fall was eventually convicted and sentenced to a one-year jail term (the first time an American cabinet officer was sentenced to prison for crimes committed while in office). It remains unclear as to how much Harding knew of Fall's nefarious activities; Harding's wife Florence destroyed many of her husband's papers after his death.

Fall was by no means the only one of Harding's friends appointed to high office who would prove to be unworthy of public trust. To make matters worse, Harding's dishonest cronies had friends of their own who were in turn appointed to lesser government posts, and veins of dishonesty and corruption began to flow deep within the heart of the American Government. The inevitable resulting scandals would eventually tarnish the reputation not only of Harding but also those of the White House and the government generally in a way that would not be seen again until the time of Watergate in 1974.

But not all of Harding's appointees were dishonest. Three at least were talented men who would serve with diligence over the next few years and during that time significantly influence American society and the course of its economic and political development.

The first was Andrew Mellon, one of the richest men in America. Born in 1855, Mellon was an exceptionally skilled but conservative businessman who, together with his father and brother, had built a great financial empire in the last two decades of the nineteenth century and the opening years of the twentieth which extended into such diverse areas as oil, banking, construction, coke and aluminium production. He was a firm believer in the benefits of lowering taxes, which he argued would actually raise tax revenues, and in using the revenues so gained to reduce the level of US Government debt, which had risen sharply as a result of the First World War. He also believed that the Government should support big businesses by interfering with them as little as possible, strictly limit public spending and maintain high tariffs so as to discourage foreign imports while encouraging the development of America's domestic industries. Economic booms and recessions were, in his view, simply part of the natural order of life, and there was little that anyone (least of all a responsible government) could do to regulate them and he believed it was folly even to try. Perhaps unsurprisingly, he had little time for organised labour and little interest in the affairs of ordinary consumers.

These were views that were warmly supported by many in 1920, and there was general approval, at least among the ranks of traditional Republicans, when Harding appointed Mellon as Secretary of the Treasury in March 1921. During his tenure in office (which extended through the later Coolidge and most of the Hoover administrations – in all, he served ten years and eleven months as Secretary of the Treasury, the third longest incumbent in that office), he would vigorously pursue policies which reflected his views, in the process laying much of the groundwork for the 1920s economic boom and (in the eyes of many of his subsequent critics) stoking up the financial cataclysm that would descend on the country in the 1930s.[3]

Another distinguished member of Harding's cabinet was Secretary of State Charles Evans Hughes, a former Governor of New York who had been Woodrow Wilson's Republican opponent in the presidential election of 1916. A lawyer by training, Hughes had been appointed an Associate Justice of the US Supreme Court in 1910, from which post he had resigned in 1916 to contest Wilson for the Presidency.[4] His tenure as Secretary of State during a time of peace and pronounced isolationism (he served until 1925) meant that he could lay claim to relatively few dramatic accomplishments in the field of foreign affairs while in office (something which many of his countrymen considered a worthy achievement in itself); nevertheless, he and Harding succeeded in convening the Washington Naval Conference of 1921-1922, which resulted (for a time) in a lessening of naval rivalries in the Pacific, particularly between the United States, Great Britain and the Empire of Japan.

Notwithstanding popular opinion, Hughes did not endorse the principles of extreme isolationism (nor, incidentally, did President Harding). Instead, he

---

[3] Between 1921 and 1929 he significantly reduced the federal tax burden on earned incomes, not only for the rich, but also for middle and low income tax payers (which was a contributory factor to the general feeling of financial prosperity which permeated much of American life during the last few years before the Great Crash) while at the same time reducing the federal deficit. These successes were reversed in the 1930s as a result of the Depression and President Roosevelt's economic policies.

[4] In February 1930, he was again appointed to the Supreme Court by President Hoover, this time as Chief Justice, replacing former President William Taft who died shortly thereafter.

pursued policies designed to improve relations with the countries of Latin America, which had suffered badly as a result of US interventionist actions over the previous few decades. In all, US troops entered Caribbean or Central American states twenty times between 1898 and 1920, generally for the ostensible reasons of protecting American lives and property, and of securing the repayment of international debts. Some interventions lasted for years (such as the intervention in Haiti in 1915, which lasted for 19 years, until it was brought to an end by Franklin D Roosevelt (FDR) and inevitably, such actions, regardless of the motivations for them, helped to create the legacy of a perception of "Yanqui imperialism" which had a corrosive effect on America's economic and diplomatic interests throughout much of South America.

Relations were, however, particularly poor with Colombia and Mexico. In the case of Colombia, relations had suffered in large part thanks to President Theodore (Teddy) Roosevelt's (illegal) naval blockade of Panama (then part of Colombia) in 1903 in support of Panamanian rebels in their bid for independence. Teddy Roosevelt's actions resulted not only in the creation of the new state of Panama to Colombia's detriment, but also in the United States gaining effective control over the territory that became the Panama Canal Zone. As for Mexico, the US-Mexican relationship, often difficult, worsened significantly as a result of President Wilson's attempts to intervene in Mexico's internal affairs[5] following the outbreak of revolution and civil war in that country in 1911. Bitterly resented by ordinary Mexicans on all sides of the conflict, Wilson's actions helped to set back relations between the two countries for years.

Most Americans were oblivious of the extent to which their country and Government were disliked by many of the people living south of the Rio Grande. Hughes, however, knew that such sentiments were dangerous to American commercial interests, and was determined to try to improve matters. Thus, while he was Secretary of State, the United States recognised Mexico's

---

[5] Which included the dispatch of US marines to occupy the port of Vera Cruz in April 1914, and the crossing of the Rio Grande by US troops under the command of General "Black Jack" Pershing in pursuit of Mexican revolutionary leader Pancho Villa in 1916, following Villa's sacking of the town of Columbus, New Mexico. Villa's attack on Columbus represents the last occasion on which the continental United States was invaded by a hostile force.

revolutionary government led by General Álvaro Obregón in exchange for a Mexican agreement to compensate American citizens whose property had been lost during the Mexican Revolution. Moreover, Congress was persuaded to ratify a treaty with Colombia under which the United States agreed to pay a $25 million indemnity in compensation for Teddy Roosevelt's blockade. Such steps were precursors to the greater efforts that FDR would make to improve US-Latin America relations in the 1930s, efforts that would be invaluable in ensuring broad (if at some times and in some places relatively unenthusiastic) support by the countries of Latin America for the Allies during the Second World War.

Hughes's attentions were also focussed on affairs closer to home; namely the continuing high rate of immigration into the United States. Previously, American businesses had generally welcomed the influx of immigrants, considering them to be a useful source of unskilled (and non-troublesome) labour. However, those days were passing; America's own domestic population was now numerous enough to provide the workforces demanded by her industries, and public sentiment (agitated as it was by fears of the "Red Menace") was swinging in favour of restricting the number of permitted immigrants. Congress responded to such concerns, and during Hughes's term of office introduced new legislation designed to severely restrict mass immigration into the United States and which represented the very firm closing of America's famed Golden Door to the huddled masses who still waited to enter.

The third notable member of Harding's cabinet was Herbert Hoover, a former mining consultant, destined to become the 31st President of the United States and, perhaps more than any other man, for many years rightly or wrongly blamed for the sufferings endured by the American people during the Great Depression. But at the time of his appointment as Harding's Secretary of Commerce[6] in 1921 he was generally well regarded not only by the American public but world-wide for his humanitarian work during and immediately after

---

[6] President Harding offered Hoover the choice of becoming either Secretary of Commerce or Secretary of the Interior. He chose the former because he felt it offered more opportunities to be of service to his country.

the First World War, when he had helped to organise the delivery of food and other relief to war victims throughout Europe. In fact, he was almost too populist in his views for some Republicans; he had supported several of President Wilson's policies (including Wilson's opposition to the imposition of punitive reparations upon Germany under the Versailles Treaty), and had accompanied the President to Paris in 1919. There he had impressed many of the foreign delegates, including John Maynard Keynes, who considered that Hoover *"…was the only man who emerged from the ordeal of Paris with an enhanced reputation"*. At the time of the Versailles peace conference, he had not yet declared himself a Republican, and some senior Democrats (including FDR) openly speculated that he might run for the Presidency on the Democratic ticket. Instead, he declared himself a supporter of Harding, campaigned for him, and the Department of Commerce was Harding's way of rewarding Hoover for his efforts, despite muted objections from some of the more conservative Republicans.

As Commerce Secretary, Hoover pursued policies that promoted "individualism" and voluntary cooperation in business. To Hoover, these were not necessarily contradictory concepts. In particular, he supported what he called "American individualism", which to him was not the selfishly blinkered pursuit of business success regardless of the interests of others, but rather an opportunity for responsible businesses to cooperate voluntarily for the greater good of all[7]. In Hoover's opinion (which he articulated in a book entitled *American Individualism* published in 1922), it was precisely the existence of such "cooperative individualism" in America that negated any need for overbearing state intervention into the affairs of the ordinary American people.

Thus, as Commerce Secretary (a post he held for nearly eight years) he supported initiatives such as the establishment and expansion of trade associations and the exchange of information between competitors with a view to reducing waste and inefficiencies in American industries. He encouraged the standardisation of products and the imposition of industry-wide safety rules, and was a firm believer in the benefits of new technologies such as commercial

---

[7] This did not, however, mean that Hoover promoted or supported actions such as price fixing or cartels or the revocation of the anti-trust legislation.

radio. While opposed to unnecessary interference by the government in business affairs, he nevertheless believed that the government could play a useful role as umpire in certain situations. More than this, he believed that in extreme cases, the government *should* intervene to regulate American industries, but only after industries had been given a reasonable chance to regulate themselves voluntarily. A classic example of this is provided by the radio industry, which grew to a rapid maturity during the 1920s, following the establishment of the first commercial radio stations in 1920. As the number of broadcasters increased[8], some stations with relatively low-powered transmitters found their broadcasts were being overwhelmed due to transmission interference from rivals using more powerful equipment. The Department of Commerce, under Hoover's leadership, originally wanted the broadcasters themselves to find some way of addressing this problem through a form of voluntary agreement, but despite attempts to agree an industry-wide code of practice, many commercial broadcasters continued to experience difficulties until Congress was forced to pass legislation which imposed a federally-mandated broadcast licensing system in order to solve the problem.

Death in California

While Mellon, Hughes and Hoover settled down to run their respective departments, and Fall and other disreputable members of the new administration set about the plundering of the public purse, Warren Harding took up his role as the American President. He was destined to preside over the United States for two years and five months, one of the shortest terms of any President. It is frequently assumed that he achieved little of substance in the field of American politics during his days in the White House, and that most of his time was spent smuggling mistresses into the executive mansion, drinking bootleg whiskey[9] and playing poker with his friends from Ohio. Though he spent much of his time pursuing such activities (particularly in the

---

[8] By way of example of the rapid expansion in the number of radio broadcast stations, by the end of 1921, ten stations had been licensed in the United States for general broadcasting. By the end of 1922, more than 300 stations had been so licensed throughout the country.

[9] For this was of course the era of Prohibition.

last few months before his death), his term as President was not devoid of significance in the domestic arena.

Perhaps his most important acts while President related to the US Supreme Court. In the years preceding Harding's term, the nine justices of the Supreme Court had managed the quite remarkable feat of simultaneously convincing conservatives that the balance of the court's political and social views tended too far to the left in favouring the Federal Government and excessive government regulation at the expense of state rights and those of individuals, and convincing many of a more liberal persuasion that the court, in upholding war-time measures such as conscription, censorship and the jailing of anti-war opponents, was a danger to the freedoms guaranteed under the American Bill of Rights. Consequently, when four vacancies on the Bench arose during Harding's term (including the vacancy for the post of Chief Justice) – an almost unprecedented number of justices for a President to appoint in a single term, especially one cut short as Harding's was[10] – there was intense interest and concern across the political spectrum as to which judges Harding would select to fill the gaps.

Conservative Republicans need not have worried. Harding may have caused concern in some circles by appointing Herbert Hoover to the Department of Commerce, but his choices for the vacancies on the Bench of the Supreme Court – former President William Taft (whom Harding proposed for the role of Chief Justice), George Sutherland, Pierce Butler and Edward Sanford - were scarcely radical and Congress swiftly confirmed their nominations. Thereafter, under Taft, the Supreme Court throughout the remainder of the 1920s tended towards rulings that discouraged excessive economic regulation by the federal or state authorities, while at the same time supporting legal measures aimed at restricting the activities of those who might be thought to threaten the country's political stability. Thus, during the 1920s, the Supreme Court by majority decisions overturned laws that prohibited child labour and mandated a legal minimum wage for women and yet held that the practice of wiretapping suspects did not constitute a breach of the provisions of the Fourth

---

[10] President Taft currently holds the record for appointing more Supreme Court justices (six) than any other one-term President.

Amendment (which prohibits illegal searches and seizures). The Court also upheld state laws that permitted the imprisonment of radicals who spoke in support of revolution, or who simply joined organisations that were deemed to advocate revolution notwithstanding the freedom of speech provisions of the US Constitution.

The legacy of Harding's conservative appointments to the Supreme Court would persist long after his death. Sutherland and Butler continued to serve as Supreme Court justices until the days of FDR, when they would be two of the "Four Horsemen", the four conservative justices who were to form the nucleus of the Court's opposition to many of FDR's New Deal proposals and cause him considerable grief and trouble. Taft, for his part, had always wanted to be Chief Justice, far more than he had ever wanted to be elected President (it had been Taft's wife who had been eager for her husband to run for the Presidency so that she could play First Lady) and he served happily in the role until just before his death in 1930. When he died, as a former President, he was accorded a state funeral, and remains the only Chief Justice to have been so honoured.

Despite successfully securing the appointments of his nominees to the Supreme Court, President Harding rapidly found the pressures of the Presidency almost more than he could bear. Rumours of financial and other improprieties on the part of members of his administration soon began to circulate; Harding tried to ignore them, but in February 1923, Congress decided to investigate allegations of *"waste, extravagance, irregularities and mismanagement"* at the newly created Veterans Bureau, which was tasked with providing medical care, pensions and other benefits for former members of the armed services, and as such, was accorded a special place in the hearts of many Americans. It certainly held a special place in the heart of Florence Harding, the First Lady, who frequently campaigned for the rights of veterans. Ironically, it was she who had initially helped to persuade Harding that Colonel Charles Forbes, a wealthy poker-playing buddy of the President, should be appointed as head of the Bureau, with an annual budget of $450 million. Forbes had no discernible qualifications for the job (although he had helped to supervise the construction of the naval base at Pearl Harbor), but possessed a persuasive and ingratiating style that convinced both of the Hardings that he was just the man to help the veterans. Before long, he was instead helping himself to a substantial proportion of the Bureau's financial assets; it has been estimated that in a period of two years, he defrauded the Bureau of more than $35 million and that his actions eventually cost the Government several times that amount. As the prospect of a Congressional inquiry grew closer, Forbes fled the country, leaving behind a President who was devastated when finally he was convinced of Forbes's guilt. Charles Cramer, a lawyer who had helped Forbes to set up the various legal devices whereby so much of the Bureau's money had been diverted into Forbes' pockets, committed suicide on 14th March 1923 (the suicide note he left behind mysteriously disappeared and opinions still differ as to the extent to which Cramer was a willing accomplice to Forbes's fraudulent actions). Forbes himself was eventually brought to trial, found guilty, fined a (derisory) $10,000 and served two years in a federal penitentiary.

Suspicions also circulated about Harry Daugherty, the Attorney General (and Harding's campaign manager) who, together with his personal secretary, Jess Smith, sold political favours, including the provision of government licenses permitting the sale of "medicinal alcohol", for cash. Their activities involved dealings with a wide range of people within the business, criminal and political arenas, and included the throwing of lurid parties attended on occasions by Warren Harding himself. By May 1923, the investigative spotlight was focussing particularly on Smith; he was suspected of having taken bribes from a German bank in return for securing the release of several billion dollars' worth of securities that had been confiscated during the First World War. On 30th May, he was found dead in the house he shared with Daugherty with a bullet through his head. Officially, the cause of his death was suicide, but there were those who speculated that he had been silenced out of fear of what he knew and may have been persuaded to divulge. As for Daugherty, he remained in office until Harding's death, whereupon Calvin Coolidge unceremoniously sacked him. He subsequently stood trial (twice) but was acquitted (possibly as a result of bribery).

Despite the growing miasma of corruption in Washington, Harding himself still remained popular with the general public, though the 1922 congressional elections saw the Republicans lose seven seats in the Senate and 70 in the

House. In the summer of 1923, he set out on a speaking tour of the western states and Alaska (then, of course, not yet a state – Harding was the first sitting President to visit Alaska) with a view to re-emphasising the Republican message as a prelude to the presidential election campaign due in 1924. He was also eager to seek support from the general public for his proposals that the United States should adhere to the newly re-established Permanent Court of International Justice – otherwise known as the World Court – in The Hague, proposals that had been firmly rejected by the US Senate only a few months before, notwithstanding that the Republicans had managed to retain control of Congress despite the setbacks of the 1922 congressional elections. By now, though, Harding was drinking heavily, beset with concerns about the corruption allegations and worried about his health (he had a weak heart) and that of his wife. To make matters worse, the touring schedule he had set for himself was arduous, with more than 80 planned public speeches. Towards the end of the tour, while travelling from Alaska to California, he suffered a severe attack of food poisoning[11] and upon reaching San Francisco, he was forced to take to his bed in the Palace Hotel, where on the evening 2nd August 1923 he suffered a heart attack (or possibly a cerebral haemorrhage – the doctors who were called to him were unable to agree on a diagnosis) and died. He was 57 years old.

Harding was, in many ways, one of the more tragic figures to occupy the White House. Personally weak in character, easily led, with too great a need to be liked, and too trusting of many of his friends who simply used their influence over him for their own ends, he died before he had an opportunity to demonstrate whether he could have survived the crisis sparked by the scandals within his administration and the challenges posed by his own character flaws. Nevertheless, it must be said that there is little real evidence to suggest that he himself was personally corrupt. One of the most devastating assessments of his character after his death (if only because it would seem to contain more than a grain of truth), was that given by Teddy Roosevelt's daughter Alice Roosevelt Longworth. *"Harding was not a bad man,"* she said, *"he was simply a slob."*

---

[11] For several years after his death, a rumour persisted that he had been poisoned, possibly by his wife. There is no real evidence to support this allegation.

Chapter 2 The Boom Years

"After all, the chief business of the American people is business. They are profoundly concerned with producing, buying, selling, investing and prospering in the world."
President Calvin Coolidge (1872 – 1933)

Keep Cool With Coolidge

Now that Harding was dead, the next man to assume the mantle of the Presidency and who would remain in office throughout most of the rest of the 1920s as America hurtled towards the Crash and the Depression was Harding's Vice President Calvin Coolidge, a man who was, in many ways the antithesis of the President he succeeded.

Calvin Coolidge was born on 4th July 1872 in Plymouth Notch, Vermont. The first, and so far, the only President to have been born on Independence Day, he was the eldest son of John Calvin and Victoria Moor Coolidge, both of whom were descended from solid traditional New England farming stock. Coolidge's mother died young, in 1885; his father, a farmer, school teacher and Justice of the Peace, lived to see his son become the 30th President of the United States before dying in 1926.

Coolidge's character reflected his small town New England upbringing and ancestry, and while President he often seemed strangely at odds with the increasingly hedonistic consumerism that permeated much of the popular culture of the Twenties. A frugal, austere, restrained and laconic man[12] – a "puritan in Babylon" according to his biographer William Allen White – he followed in his father's footsteps by originally training as a lawyer and then spending more than 20 years rising through the ranks of Massachusetts state

---

[12] Such was his taciturnity that he acquired the nickname of "Silent Cal". He was aware of his reputation as a man of few words, and to an extent consciously encouraged it. He once wrote: *"The words of a President have enormous weight and ought not to be used indiscriminately."* On another occasion, he was seated next to a woman at a dinner table who told him that she had bet a friend that Coolidge would say more than two words to her. *"You lose"* was Coolidge's only response. Nevertheless Coolidge gave more formal speeches and held more press conferences than any previous President, and was the first President to allow follow-up questions from reporters.

politics before being elected as Governor of that state in 1919. It was while acting as Governor that he first achieved national fame, during the Boston police strike of September 1919 when three quarters of the policemen in the city went on strike demanding the right to form a trade union. This demand was fiercely resisted by Boston's Police Commissioner (and former mayor of the city) Edwin Curtis and in the absence of an effective police presence, the city soon fell victim to looting and rioting. Initially, Coolidge was disinclined to intervene, suggesting that the disorder was a matter for the local authorities. Not until Boston's mayor Andrew Peters had himself called out several units of the Massachusetts National Guard and begun the process of restoring order to the city did Coolidge act; he called out more Guard units and took personal control of Boston's police force, reinstating Curtis to his post as Police Commissioner from which he had been suspended by Mayor Peters. Coolidge received a telegram of protest from the leader of the American Federation of Labor, Samuel Gompers. Coolidge's public response included the statement: *"There is no right to strike against the public safety by anybody, anywhere, anytime..."*.

Coolidge's reply to Gompers was widely reported by the press and Coolidge found himself hailed as a hero by many ordinary Americans across the country, concerned as they were at this time by the dangers of Bolshevism and anarchy. This in turn led directly to him being nominated and selected as Harding's running mate during the 1920 Republican Convention, and subsequently to his election as the 29th Vice President of the United States.

When President Harding died in his hotel room in California on 2nd August 1923, Coolidge was on vacation at his father's farm in Vermont (which had neither electricity nor a telephone) and could not easily be contacted. Not until the early hours of 3rd August did word reach the farm of the President's death, and when it did (in the form of a messenger who had travelled twelve miles from the nearest telegraph office), Coolidge had already gone to bed and the news was first received by his father. John Coolidge called his son down and broke the news and the two of them decided that no time should be lost in swearing Coolidge into office. Traditionally, Presidents of the United States are sworn in by the Chief Justice, but neither Coolidge nor his father (who was a notary public and thus empowered to administer oaths) could see any reason why Coolidge could not be sworn in then and there by his father. Thus, at 2.47

am, on the morning of 3rd August 1923, in the presence of Coolidge's wife Grace, a stenographer, a congressman and two reporters newly arrived at the farm, John Coolidge administered the oath of office and swore his son in as the 30th President of the United States. Sadly for posterity, the newspaper reporters were not allowed to take photographs of the event.[13]

As President (he had no Vice President during his first term, there being no requirement under the US Constitution at that time for a replacement to be appointed when an incumbent succeeded to the Presidency), Coolidge continued the policies of his predecessor in many respects, and significantly, he retained Mellon, Hughes and Hoover in his cabinet (though Hughes resigned in 1925 at the beginning of President Coolidge's first full term and was replaced as Secretary of State by Franklin B Kellogg). Like Harding, Coolidge was not an extreme isolationist, and under his Presidency, the United States pursued a general policy of cautious engagement with other nations while avoiding long term major overseas commitments. At home, Coolidge continued the policy of supporting businesses by interfering in them as little as possible, firmly believing that it was the responsibility of the government to encourage economic growth by wherever possible avoiding unnecessary regulation, so as to allow businesses the maximum opportunity to realise profits. Fiscally conservative, he agreed with Mellon as regards the desirability of reducing the tax burden, once observing: *"The collection of taxes which are not absolutely required, which do not beyond reasonable doubt contribute to the public welfare, is only a species of legalised larceny. The wise and correct course to follow in taxation is not to destroy those who have already secured success, but to create conditions under which everyone will have a better chance to be successful".* Similarly, Coolidge agreed with his Treasury Secretary as regards the need to rein in federal spending, and to reduce the public deficit. A Republican Congress agreed with them both, but President Coolidge in some respects was even more hawkish in his fiscal views

---

[13] Later, doubts were expressed about whether John Coolidge had the power to administer the Presidential oath of office, and the oath was quietly re-administered by a federal judge just in case, much as occurred in the case of President Chester Arthur in 1881 (another example of a Vice President succeeding to the Presidency as a result of death in office of the previous incumbent) and in the more recent case of President Barack Obama.

than Congress, on occasions vetoing spending plans that Congress had approved. Such views and actions raised the hackles of many on the political left, who before long were openly bemoaning the fact that in many ways, Coolidge was even less progressive in social and business affairs than his predecessor had been. Such criticisms did not, however, prevent Coolidge from winning the 1924 presidential election with ease, gaining 54 percent of the popular vote, and this despite the fact that Coolidge was then grieving for the untimely death of one of his sons.[14]

One major advantage for Coolidge during the presidential election was that while Vice President he had kept his distance from Harding's cronies, and thus there was no suggestion that he was personally tainted by their wrongdoings. To reinforce the point, upon attaining the Presidency, Coolidge had moved swiftly to remove those suspected of irregularities from office, his dismissal of Attorney General Harry Daugherty being a prime example. The American public approved. The Republican Party generally also benefitted, and retained substantial majorities in both houses of Congress following the 1924 congressional elections.

Peace, apparent prosperity at home (the so-called "Coolidge Prosperity") and a candidate whose reputation for personal integrity appeared beyond reproach were not the only reasons for the Republican electoral victories in 1924. The Democrats during the course of their 1924 National Convention held at Madison Square Garden in New York between 24th June and 9th July had seemed divided and in disarray. Supporters of the Ku Klux Klan (then perhaps at the peak of its power) were seen to wield such influence during the course of the Convention's deliberations that it became popularly known as the Klanbake. There were clashes between pro and anti-KKK factions on the floor of the Convention, with KKK supporters supporting the candidacy of William

---

[14] It was during the 1924 presidential election that Coolidge adopted the campaign phrase *"Keep cool with Coolidge"*. His running mate during that election was Charles Dawes, author of the Dawes Plan, designed to assist Germany in rebuilding her economy after the First World War, and a future American Ambassador to the Court of St James. Dawes would go on to win the Nobel Peace Prize in 1925 for his work on the Dawes Plan. Unfortunately, he had a stormy relationship with Coolidge, and the two men did not work well together.

DARK REALITIES

G McAdoo of California and opposing that of popular New York Governor Al Smith, principally on the grounds of his Catholicism, and a record number of 103 ballots had been required for the Convention's delegates to choose a compromise presidential nominee. When they finally did so, they chose John W Davis, a former Congressman, US Solicitor General and Ambassador to the Court of St James, with Charles W Bryan (younger brother of former Democratic presidential contender William Jennings Bryan) as his running mate. Unfortunately for Davis, he was seen as too conservative by many on the more liberal wing of his party, who promptly switched their support to Wisconsin Senator Robert La Follette of the Progressive Party. At the same time, Davis' support of black voting rights lost him votes in the South and elsewhere. With the non-Republican votes so split, and the Democratic Party apparently in chaos, Coolidge's election victory was almost inevitable.

So for the foreseeable future, the Republicans were to retain control of both the White House and Congress and, to many casual observers, it must have seemed that the hopes of liberals and reformers were dashed, perhaps for as long as a generation. And this was a state of affairs of which many Americans approved in late 1924. By and large, times were prosperous, and ordinary people were, to an unprecedented degree, enjoying their share of that prosperity, which was increasingly regarded as simply the entitlement of Americans everywhere. Certainly, life was still hard for some people – most notably farmers, and especially for African-Americans trapped in the increasingly impoverished rural economy and blatantly discriminatory political system of the South, or in the slums of the northern industrial cities – but by and large, many Americans, perhaps even a majority, were satisfied with their lives, and anticipated even better times in the future. With financially prudent men in government, with American industries ever expanding and demonstrating to the world the unequivocal superiority of America's unbridled capitalist system, and with America actively avoiding potentially costly foreign entanglements, what could possibly go wrong?

The Resignation of a President

In August 1927, Calvin Coolidge surprised many observers and most of his supporters (including his wife, with whom he had not previously shared his plans) by announcing during one of his press conferences that he would not run for a second full term as President. Characteristically, the close-mouthed President contented himself with providing the press with the barest outline of his decision not to seek re-election, and then after refusing to answer any questions on the subject, departed to go fishing with a friend. He left behind a host of queries and conjectures about his decision which, in one form or another, have continued to this day.

Why did Coolidge refuse to run for another term? The answer seems, at least in part, to lie in his moral character and personal beliefs. He was no believer in enhancing the power or glamour of the Presidency – or of the Federal Government generally – beyond that absolutely necessary to allow those institutions to operate competently. He believed that regular changes in the occupancy of the White House were conducive to good public service. To a friend, he once commented that had he run and won (as seems likely would have occurred had he decided to seek another term), by the end of his second full term he would have served as President for ten years, which he felt was too long for any President to remain in office. Moreover, unlike many other Presidents (and would-be contenders for that post), he was not particularly enamoured of the trappings and privileges of the Presidency; he did not need them to validate his sense of self-worth, and so he found it easier than other may have done to step down from his office than others may have once he felt his duty to that office had been done. This was particularly so after the death of his son Calvin Coolidge Jr. in 1924 from blood poisoning, after which Coolidge later said, *"the office became more of a burden than anything else".*

Then too, although only 55 years old, he was concerned about his health and that of his wife, and although neither was seriously ill in 1927 (Coolidge may well have been somewhat of a hypochondriac), in fact he only lived another five and a half years, dying on 5th January 1933. Had he been elected for another term, he would have died in office. And so concerns about ill-health may also have prompted his decision.

Inevitably, once the stock market suffered the Great Crash, and the Depression arrived, there were suggestions that Coolidge had foreseen the oncoming financial cataclysm, and had resigned to avoid criticism, leaving his successor Herbert Hoover to shoulder responsibility for the downturn in his place.[15] There is, however, no real evidence to support this contention. In the summer of 1927, the US economy though booming, had yet to show unmistakeable signs of veering out of control although faltering demand for new housing stock, coupled with the collapse of a land boom in Florida the previous year, should have given more careful observers of America's economic miracle cause for concern. Unemployment was lower than it had been for several years and continuing to fall, and while equity prices had been slowly rising for the previous two years, not until December 1927 would the stock market begin its final breathtaking climb into hitherto untested financial heights that ultimately culminated in the Crash in October 1929. Many observers of the time felt that if there had to be a change of President, Coolidge's announcement was perfectly timed so as to cause the least disruption to anyone. Certainly, Coolidge himself felt this, as evidenced by his final State of the Union Address to Congress on 4th December 1928, in which he included in his concluding remarks the observation that *"The country is in the midst of an era of prosperity and of peace more permanent than it has ever before experienced"*. There seems little doubt that he (and just about everyone else) expected these conditions to continue under his successor.

The Joys of Capitalism

The optimistic picture painted by President Coolidge in his 1928 State of the Union Address was borne out at that time by many objective measures – and by the most subjective measure of all – the day-to-day experiences of ordinary Americans. The country over which Calvin Coolidge had presided had prospered economically as never before. It has been estimated that between 1921 and 1929, the income of the average American employee increased by 30 percent, albeit that the discrepancies in income in different parts of the country, and between different sectors of society had not changed much since 1920, with the result that as the 1920s approached their end, 40 percent of American families still lived at or below the poverty line. Poverty of course

---

[15] Much as Britain's former Prime Minister Tony Blair was criticised in some quarters for leaving office mid-term in 2007 and allowing the then Chancellor of the Exchequer Gordon Brown to assume the Premiership just before the full impact of the economic downturn was widely felt by the general public.

remained particularly acute in rural areas where farming communities still were suffering from the effects of the agricultural depression which had followed the end of the First World War. The average urban worker however found his financial circumstances slowly but steadily improving as the 1920s progressed. Even more impressive was the increase in the profits of businesses during that decade, helped by Andrew Mellon's benign taxation regime and the business-friendly policies adopted by the Coolidge administration generally; the profits of the 300,000 largest US corporations rose by more than 60 percent during this period. And more US businesses were being created than ever before, aided by those same policies. This in turn led to the creation of more jobs and a reduction in unemployment levels from 5 million unemployed during the 1920-21 post-war economic slump to approximately 1.5 million unemployed on the eve of the Great Crash. Even inflation was relatively benign; the annual average increase in prices between 1922 and 1929 was less than 1 percent, whilst the nation's gross national product grew by a steady 2 percent each year.

High levels of employment and adequate wages led people to feel more secure about their personal financial circumstances, and optimistic for the future. For the first time in American history, a significant proportion of the population had at least some money that did not have to be earmarked for food, shelter and clothing, and (cautiously at first but then with increasing enthusiasm) people began to look for ways to enjoy themselves. Many of them, especially those living in the cities and larger towns, had ample opportunities to spend their money, and they could do so in ways that their parents and grandparents could not even have imagined. Many Americans in the mid and late 1920s were flirting with the temptations of popular consumerism as never before, helped by all the wonderful new goods and services that modern American capitalism could produce, and the resulting buying spree in turn helped to sustain large factory orders and high business profits.

Perhaps nothing demonstrates America's new-found financial freedoms of the Twenties better than her relationship with the automobile. In 1920, one American family in three possessed a car, most of them, of course, Model T Fords which Henry Ford's factories had been producing in ever-increasing quantities since 1908 (except during the war years when Ford's production facilities had been dedicated to the war effort). By 1929, 80 percent of American families owned a car (although it might be second- or even third-hand), and there were over 26 million cars on America's roads.[16] In less than a decade, America became a true car-owning democracy, and not only did this lead to the paving of the American landscape with tarmac roads and the introduction of gasoline stations, advertising hoardings, motels and hamburger stands alongside those roads, not to mention fundamental changes in social mores and behaviour, but also to the adaption of many of America's industries to satisfy the varied needs of her car manufacturers and their customers. It has been estimated that by 1929, one in eight of American workers were working in industries that were connected in one way or another with the production and operation of automobiles.

Apart from cars, there were other goods and services for Americans to buy during the heady years of the Coolidge Prosperity. The electrification of the country had reached a stage where most urban dwellers now had access to mains electricity in their homes, as well as in public streets and factories. This, in turn allowed them the opportunity to acquire a wide range of electrical labour-saving appliances. Even the simple availability of electrical lighting (both public and in the home) revolutionised life within towns and cities and seemed to symbolise the difference between modern urban America and life only a decade or two before (and, even more strikingly, the difference between contemporary urban and rural life in America, where electricity was still largely unavailable, and would remain so until well into the 1940s). Urban electricity also made possible other forms of popular entertainment, such as movie theatres and floodlit sports stadia, to which audiences flocked in increasing numbers throughout the 1920s in search of recreational diversion. Electricity, and the appliance of electricity in everyday life, rapidly came to be seen throughout the world as something that symbolised modern America, and ever since the 1920s, for most people in the world, it has become impossible to think of America – and the American Dream – without electricity and consumer products powered by electricity.

---

[16] By 1929, however, it was increasingly unlikely that the car would be a Ford, thanks to Henry Ford's stubborn refusal during the mid-1920s to recognise that the day of the Model T was drawing to an end, which allowed rival manufacturers (most notably General Motors) to claim an increasing portion of the popular car market at Ford's expense. In 1923, Ford had controlled over 50 percent of that market; by 1926, Ford's domestic market share had slipped to a little over a third.

Reliable washing machines and refrigerators were not generally available until the 1930s, but there were other appliances that people were eager to buy, such as vacuum cleaners and irons and electric water-heaters and sewing machines, as well as kitchen products such as electric kettles, egg beaters and coffee grinders. The advent of commercial radio meant that the purchase of a radio receiver became a high priority. Only ten years before, most people would have regarded such items as almost unattainable – in some cases (particularly radio) unimaginable – but now they were freely available in department stores and by mail order across the country, and eagerly acquired, particularly by consumers with pretensions to middle class status. Within a few years, they came to be taken for granted, and regarded as everyday necessities, which the average American aspired to own in order to demonstrate his or her worldly success.

A significant factor that encouraged such consumer spending was the development of personal credit, and particularly the willingness of lenders to make personal loans allowing the purchase of goods on an instalment repayment plan. "Instalment buying" had originally emerged in the latter half of the nineteenth century as a method of allowing farmers to acquire the new farm tools that were being invented and produced. Home mortgages swiftly followed, and it became possible to purchase household goods such as sewing machines on the instalment plan, but general consumer credit initially suffered a poor reputation thanks to the prevalence of loan sharks and other forms of unscrupulous lenders. In an attempt to eliminate the more outrageous practices (such as interest rates at several thousand percent, which were not unknown), the Federal Government and various states passed a stream of consumer credit protection laws, and in 1916 the more respectable lenders banded together with a view to raising the profile and the reputation of the personal finance industry generally. Nevertheless, there continued to be a stigma attached to using credit to purchase personal goods until the practice became popular as an accepted method of financing the purchase of automobiles, a practice pioneered by General Motors but also encouraged by the other major automobile manufacturers who soon established consumer credit facilities of their own. Thereafter, as the 1920s progressed, it became more and more acceptable for people to purchase not only cars but a wide range of consumer goods by means of instalment buying, and many did so, with the result that by the end of 1924 (according to some estimates), outstanding instalment credit in the United States had risen to $2 billion, from approximately $19 million in 1920. By the end of 1929, the total value of outstanding credit loans was $3.5 billion, nearly half of which had been borrowed to fund the purchase of automobiles. For the first time, many ordinary Americans were now servicing substantial personal debts, and the practice of living on credit and servicing the debt from one pay-packet to the next had arrived.

The Presidential Election of 1928

Calvin Coolidge's refusal to run for another term meant that the Republicans had to look elsewhere in 1928 for a presidential nominee, and as Republicans gathered in Kansas City, Missouri during the second week of June for their National Convention, it was clear that there was only one credible candidate, namely Herbert Hoover. As Commerce Secretary, not only was he the most visible member of Coolidge's administration after the President himself, but his actions the previous year, when he had organised a successful relief effort in the wake of catastrophic flooding by the Mississippi, had further embellished his reputation as a humanitarian amongst the general public. There were Republican Party elders who still disliked Hoover, who could appear disdainful of political colleagues when he chose to do so, but the inescapable fact was that he was probably the most popular Republican in the country in the summer of 1928, and at the National Convention, he convincingly won the nomination on the first ballot.[17] The Convention chose Kansas Senator Charles Curtis (who had briefly sought the Presidential nomination for himself before Hoover's first ballot victory) as the Republican Vice-Presidential candidate. Two weeks later, the Democrats at their National Convention in Houston selected Al Smith, the Governor of New York, as their Presidential candidate. Al Smith had failed to secure the nomination four years previously;

---

[17] Coolidge himself was somewhat ambivalent in his views about his Commerce Secretary. He recognised Hoover's drive, self-confidence and determination to succeed, and admired his willingness to take responsibility for the various tasks (such as organising the Mississippi flooding relief) that Coolidge, a firm believer in practising the art of delegation whenever possible, loaded upon Hoover's shoulders. At the same time though, the President was wary of Hoover's ambitions and found his taste for dramatic publicity distasteful. He privately referred to Hoover as "Wonder Boy" and did not noticeably exert himself in support of Hoover's candidacy.

this time he claimed it without serious opposition and with Senator Joseph Robinson of Arkansas as Smith's running mate, the election was underway.

In Al Smith, the Democrats had chosen a progressive politician to challenge the Republicans. The first Roman Catholic and Irish-American to run for the Presidency, Smith was born in New York in 1873, and had been raised in relatively humble conditions following the death of his father when Al was 13. He gained his first political post in 1895 as a clerk for the commissioner of jurors. He spent the next two decades working his way up the ladder of local politics, before being elected Governor of New York State in 1918. A supporter of government reform, while Governor he had worked tirelessly to encourage better conditions for working men and women, and had successfully introduced legislation that improved widows' pension rights and the rights of workers to seek compensation for work-related injuries. He believed that government could play an important role in addressing urgent social needs, and in this he differed sharply from Hoover, who believed the role of the government and its ability to intervene in the life of ordinary citizens should be sharply defined and limited lest it undermined people's ability to be self-reliant.

The two men also differed in their attitudes to Prohibition, for Al Smith was a "wet", a supporter of the repeal of Prohibition, while Hoover publicly supported the Volstead Act and the Eighteenth Amendment, describing Prohibition as an experiment *"of noble purpose"*. This gained Hoover support amongst those who still supported the ban on the sale and distribution of alcohol. Smith's Roman Catholicism (and the fact that Irish American city politicians were generally distrusted in the country at large) also helped Hoover. There was widespread reluctance to place a Catholic in the White House, and within a few weeks of his nomination millions of leaflets and posters opposing Al Smith's election had been printed and circulated. Much of this was the work of the Ku Klux Klan, but Smith's presidential bid was also opposed by many Protestant clergy, who far preferred the idea of Hoover (who was a Quaker) as President. The bigotry expressed by some clergymen was extreme, and one Baptist preacher told his congregation that if they voted for Al Smith, they would be voting against Christ and thus be damned for all eternity. Another described Smith as *"the nominee of the worst forces of hell."* It is to

Hoover's discredit that he failed to effectively rebuke those of his supporters who resorted to such tactics.

However, the real deciding factor in the 1928 presidential election was the state of the economy. People were still enjoying the Coolidge Prosperity, and identified Hoover with it. They wanted to believe him when he made statements foretelling the imminent end of poverty in the United States. As had been the case in the 1924 presidential election, for so long as people were enjoying the good times, and as long as they could trust the Republicans (and Hoover in particular) to maintain the Prosperity, there was in reality little or no chance that the Democrats could capture the White House, and this was reflected in the results of the election which was held on 6th November 1928. Hoover gained over 58 percent of the popular vote, and 444 votes of the Electoral College, as compared to Smith's 41 percent and 87 electoral votes. It was a landslide in favour of Hoover, but even more impressive from the standpoint of the Republicans (who had also done well in the Congressional elections) was the fact that Hoover succeeded in carrying several of the southern states, including Texas, Florida, Tennessee, North Carolina and Virginia. He was the first Republican Presidential candidate to capture these ex-Confederate states since the end of the Civil War. And now he was going to the White House on a tide of popular support and goodwill from virtually all parts of the country. How he must have looked forward to his term of office.

DARK REALITIES

Chapter 3 The Storm Clouds Gather

"The primary cause of the Great Depression was the war of 1914-1918"
President Herbert Hoover (1874 – 1964)

The Florida Land Boom

Although it was little appreciated at the time, the factors and forces that would destroy the Coolidge Prosperity and plunge the country into the Great Depression were already gathering strength as Hoover took the Presidential oath of office on 4th March 1929. They had been doing so for some time, and one of the earliest signs that things were not quite as they should be, and that (neither for the first time in American history nor the last) ordinary Americans by the thousands were increasingly willing to be tempted into foolish speculation by the promise of easy money manifested itself in the early 1920s in the form of a classic land boom in Florida.

Before the 1920s, Florida was mostly a land of excessive humidity, alligators, orange groves and stifling mangrove swamps, little changed in substance from the days when it had formed part of New Spain. There were few towns of significance, the state was still relatively sparsely populated. This was despite efforts by men such of Henry Flagler, who made a fortune in the oil industry at the side of John D Rockefeller of Standard Oil, and then subsequently spent a substantial portion of it building railroads and hotels and other amenities in an attempt to encourage America's wealthy elite to move there during the winter months.

This all changed in the years following the end of the First World War, when wealthy businessmen spotted the possibility of marketing Florida to America's newly prosperous middle classes as the ideal location for a winter or retirement home and set about developing resorts and suburbs and generally improving the state's infrastructure. Before long, an influx of real estate speculators and salesmen, some honest, some not (including Charles Ponzi, one of the worst swindlers in America's history) had succeeded in portraying Florida as a land of idyllic beaches with a welcoming climate. Thanks to the now ubiquitous automobile and improved railroad links, thousands of people flocked there in search of their ideal retirement or vacation spots, boosting not only the state's economy but also its population which rose by more than 20 percent between 1920 and 1925. Still more were attracted by the sharp rise in land prices that the new developments, the influx of newcomers and the blandishments of the real estate salesmen generated, and throughout the country, people beguiled by the thought of quick and easy riches were persuaded that an investment or two in Florida land was an opportunity not to be missed.

By early 1925, all the hallmarks of an unsustainable land boom were obvious for all to see. Florida land prices were soaring higher and higher, demand for new property investments was outstripping the ability of developers to complete sites already under construction, with the result that more and more deals involved people investing in projects that had not even left the draughtsmen's desks. By now though, this was a matter of minor concern for many of the investors flooding into the state. And the salesmen made it easy for the newcomers to invest. In some parts of Florida, a ten percent deposit would suffice to acquire a building lot, with the balance being funded by a variety of financial sleights of hand. Almost anyone could join in the game. Many would-be investors did not even bother to inspect the land they were acquiring, convinced as they were that they could sell their new acquisitions within months for substantial profits. If they had investigated the land they were buying, many would have found that much of it was scrub land or swamp, far from the nearest human habitation and amongst the last places where anyone would wish to build a house. In some cases, the land being feverishly acquired and then sold on was actually under water. In others, salesmen cheerfully invented towns and villages with a view to boosting the attractions of the available lots. Perhaps the most blatant example of this was the infamous case of the city of "Nettie", which could not be found on any map of Florida of the 1920s (or indeed, today) but was invented to help to sell the charms of a new development called Manhattan Estates, supposedly only three quarters of a mile away from Nettie's city centre. Nettie was actually the location of an abandoned turpentine dump. Nevertheless, interests in Manhattan Estates sold swiftly and expensively and investors remained unconcerned as long as they could be sure of finding someone willing to buy the plots they acquired from them for a handsome profit; it was the money they wanted, not the land.

It should have been obvious that this land boom, like all speculative booms before and since, was sustainable only for so long as new investors could be found willing to pay ever higher prices that would allow those who had already invested to escape with a profit. For a while, though, there was no shortage of new investors; so many had flocked to the State that they were frequently forced to sleep in their cars for want of sufficient accommodation and anyway, rental prices were extortionate. In Miami (where, by the middle of 1925, there were estimated to be over 2,000 real estate offices), the city authorities were obliged to pass bye-laws preventing people from buying and selling property in the streets in an attempt to reduce traffic congestion.

And the reality was that many people were making money, which in turn encouraged others to try their hand, exacerbating the general frenzy even more. The occasional raised dissenting voice protesting that the boom was ultimately unsustainable and could not continue forever was drowned out by the shrieks of those who had made small, and sometimes not so small, fortunes, some actual but more often simply on paper. Even today, some of the stories of the profits that could be made seem impressive: one woman who had acquired a piece of Florida land in 1896 for $25 sold it in 1925 for $150,000. A substantial plot of land in Palm Beach had been valued at $240,000 during the years of the First World War; in 1923, as the boom was really just commencing, it sold for $800,000; one year later it was split into building lots with an aggregate value of $1.5 million. By 1925, the land was valued at $4 million. Another lot in Miami Beach valued at $800 at the start of the 1920s was sold for $150,000 in 1924. In one celebrated case, a soldier traded an overcoat for ten "worthless" acres near Miami, and found it valued during the Florida Boom at $25,000. And there were many other examples. With tales such as these abounding, it is not surprising that so many people succumbed to temptation and plunged into land speculation.

Inevitably, the boom did not last. By October 1925, so many people had moved into the state that the railroad companies were obliged to refuse to transport all but essential food and medical supplies; building materials became scarce meaning that developers were unable to meet their construction deadlines, and throughout the autumn and winter months of 1925 major investors began to back away from projects and opportunities which only a few months before they would have eagerly sought out. The influx of new would-be purchasers into the state began at last to ease, and by the spring of 1926, increasingly desperate sellers were finding it harder to sell the property lots they had acquired. The upward spiral of land prices slowed sharply, and showed signs of reversing, panicking those who had bought near the top of the market, and deterring new investors even more. Then, in the autumn of 1926, nature decided to deliver the *coup de grâce* to the Florida land boom in the form of a major hurricane that struck the Miami area in the early hours of 18th September. With wind speeds in excess of 120 miles per hour, the (unnamed) hurricane tore through Miami's streets and partially completed developments, tearing up trees, smashing cars and obliterating buildings by the lot. Thanks to confused weather warnings, and the inexperience of many of Florida's new residents of the dangers posed by hurricanes, the city had not been evacuated. There were 400 casualties and 50,000 people were rendered homeless. Adding to the disaster, the hurricane caused a storm surge in the waters of Lake Okeechobee, northwest of Miami, flooding the nearby town of Moore Have and adding more names to the casualty lists.[18]

In the wake of such disaster, land prices fell even faster than they had risen over the previous two or three years, leaving Florida encumbered with unfinished developments of all sorts, and completed developments now worth only fractions of the prices for which they had been acquired and developed. Some investors who managed to survive the financial carnage and retain their properties would eventually find they made a respectable profit after all, when Florida land prices finally recovered in the 1950s, and the dreams of the original promoters of Florida as a popular vacation wonderland finally began to be realised. Most though found themselves trapped in negative equity, obliged to pay more in annual taxes and mortgage payments than their properties were now worth, and for many, bankruptcy was the only viable option. For such unfortunates, the Great Depression arrived three years early.

---

[18] The 1926 hurricane was just a prelude to the Okeechobee hurricane of September 1928, one of the worst hurricanes in American history, which struck southern Florida with even greater ferocity, causing more than 2,500 casualties and widespread devastation.

Post-war Europe

While Americans were pursuing dreams of near instant and effortless riches in the new developments of Florida, other events were unfolding on the far side of the Atlantic. There, during the 1920s, the nations of Europe were seeking to adjust to the end of four years of fighting. Some of them had only been nations for a handful of years, having emerged from the collapsing empires of central Europe at the end of the war; nevertheless they and older European countries such as Britain and France faced the difficulties of seeking to rebuild and stabilise their economies while meeting the social and economic costs of the war. Individual nations enjoyed differing circumstances and attempted to meet these goals in differing ways (and with differing degrees of success); in the end however, the economic policies they pursued all contributed one way or another to the events that would lead to the Great Crash. In particular, those nations which had acquired large American loans, either during the course of the war or in the years that immediately followed, found that the need to repay those loans locked their economies more closely into that of the United States than had been the case before 1914, which inevitably meant that when America suffered the Crash, the nations of Europe to a greater or lesser extent all suffered too.

Of those European nations, the most significant in terms of economic power was Great Britain[19], which despite the emergence of the United States as the world's new industrial superpower remained one of the greatest industrialised nations on the face of the globe. However, Britain had emerged from the fighting victorious but with her people exhausted and her society psychologically scarred by the loss of nearly a million men dead or wounded in four years of war. Although not bankrupt, her treasury was drained by the cost of the conflict, her national debt (much of it owed to the United States) had increased from £625 million to nearly £8 billion and despite claims by her politicians that they would use the new era of peace "to build a land fit for heroes", the years immediately following the Armistice of 1918 were for many in Britain years of unsettling social change and economic hardship in the form

---

[19] Germany may well have successfully contested this title had she not borne the burden of having lost the war.

of increased taxation, stagnant wages, high unemployment and depression. Britain remained the heart of a great empire; indeed, in terms of territorial extent, the British Empire was at its peak, but the loss of earnings from the overseas investments that she had sold during the war made her more dependent upon exports,[20] and more vulnerable to downturns in world markets than she had been before the war. At the same time, the dominance she had once enjoyed in world trade, particularly in areas such as steel and textiles, could no longer be taken for granted as more trading competitors emerged onto the world stage. As a consequence of these difficulties, British economic output declined by about 25 percent between 1918 and 1921, before showing signs of a mild recovery. Unemployment remained a perpetual problem.

Inevitably, such economic difficulties and uncertainties affected the British currency, the pound sterling. For nearly a hundred years prior to the outbreak of the First World War, ever since May 1816 when the British Government had declared that the value of the pound sterling was fixed at 123.25 grains of gold, Britain had been on the gold standard, allowing British bank notes to be freely convertible into gold. This freedom was suspended in the opening days of the First World War in order to protect Britain's gold reserves (the other major belligerent nations, most notably Germany, France and Austro-Hungary did likewise) and the suspension remained in force in the years immediately following the Armistice in 1918. In the hearts and minds of many Britons in those early post-war years, the gold standard represented a symbol of the days

---

[20] At the end of the nineteenth century, Britain's overseas investments amounted to £4 billion. This was nearly twice the combined overseas investments of the United States, Germany and France at the time, and generated revenue of the order of £750 million; indeed, revenue on such a scale was one of the major reasons why Britain was the world's dominant economic and industrial power for most of the nineteenth century. The growth of Britain's overseas investments had continued during the first years of the twentieth century, and by 1914, Britain's overseas investments equated to 186 percent of her GNP. It has been estimated that Britain was forced to sell approximately one quarter of those investments during the First World War in order to meet the costs of the conflict. Still more were sold during the course of the Second World War in order to fund Britain's contribution to the Allied fight against Hitler's forces and for Britain's own survival.

of national strength and power to which so many yearned to return. Unsurprisingly therefore, there were insistent calls for the gold standard to be restored, and in April 1925, Winston Churchill, the Chancellor of the Exchequer, announced Britain's return to the gold standard to widespread (but not universal) acclaim.

With the usual advantages that hindsight offers, many political and economic commentators have since declared the restoration of the gold standard to be a major mistake on the part of Churchill, and there is no doubt that the move was ultimately to have severe repercussions for both Britain and the world. Churchill himself (who by his own admission, was far better suited to roles requiring political or military expertise than those demanding financial acumen) had initially been uneasy about the decision to return to the gold standard, a decision which had already been taken by the British Treasury and Churchill's predecessor (and indeed eventual successor) as Chancellor, Labour politician Philip Snowden, several months before Churchill's appointment to that office in November 1924. Churchill had sought the views of John Maynard Keynes (a trenchant opponent of the policy), but had been persuaded by the Prime Minister, Stanley Baldwin, and by his own lifelong passion for maintaining and if possible enhancing British imperial strength and prestige, that the plans for the restoration of the gold standard were now too advanced to be easily cast aside and that in any event the move would benefit both the country and the Empire.[21] Moreover, Churchill allowed himself to be persuaded that Britain

---

[21] More than two decades later, Labour Prime Minister Clement Attlee would severely criticise Churchill in the House of Commons for the return to the gold standard, calling him *"the most disastrous Chancellor of the century"* (a claim which is open to challenge, particularly having regard to more recent incumbents in that post). Attlee went so far as to observe that: *"... much of our troubles today can be traced back to that error of ignorance and his simple trust of others in a field where he had little knowledge."* Churchill, no doubt with relish, pointed out that he had acted on advice, *"... on the advice of a Committee appointed by Lord Snowden, the Chancellor in the Socialist government in 1924, of which Mr Attlee was himself a member."* Snowden would be reappointed Chancellor of the Exchequer as part of the minority Labour government that returned to office following the June 1929 general election (which incidentally saw Churchill consigned to the backbenches of the House of Commons where he would remain for more than ten years until the advent of the Second World War). Snowden himself took no steps to abandon the

should return to the gold standard at the old, pre-war rate which equated to a dollar-pound exchange rate of $4.87 to one pound.

Unfortunately, this ignored the effects of wartime and post-war inflation upon economically weakened Britain, and overvalued the pound as compared to the dollar. The immediate consequence was that overseas buyers found British goods more expensive than those of Britain's foreign competitors. Bearing in mind Britain's enforced dependency on maintaining a healthy export trade, this was a disaster for the British who were forced to lower prices of export goods in an attempt to remain competitive. Moreover, British purchasers found they could profit by exchanging pounds for dollars or other currencies (or gold) at the favourable (Churchillian) exchange rate and then using that currency or gold to buy goods abroad, thus lessening demand for British goods and raw materials even more and causing gold to drain out of the country (principally in the direction of the United States) at an alarming rate.

Before long, the effects of the new policy were obvious for all to see: higher interest rates, idle factories, high unemployment and lower wages, which inevitably led to social stresses which manifested themselves most dramatically in the form of the General Strike of 1926[22] and a relatively weak economy for much of the rest of the 1920s.

---

gold standard until September 1931, by which time the Labour government had collapsed in economic and political confusion and been replaced by a coalition known as the National Government to which Snowden transferred his allegiance. But by then, the damage caused by Britain's return to the gold standard had been done and the Great Depression had fallen upon the world.

[22] A general strike organised by the British trade union movement in May 1926, largely comprised of workers from the railways, iron and steel works, printers and dockyards, principally in support of miners who were being forced by mine owners to accept drastic cuts in wages and a general worsening of working conditions. At its peak, more than 1.5 million workers were on strike. The strength of feeling demonstrated by the strikers and their supporters initially surprised and frightened the British Government, who feared a breakdown of law and order and possibly even a revolution; within days however, it became apparent that while many sympathised with the plight of the miners, the Government and its supporters were in effective control of the situation, and the General Strike itself petered out after only ten days. The miners themselves

Nevertheless, despite the difficulties posed by the re-introduction of the gold standard, industrial militancy at home and increased overseas competition not only in "new industries" such as chemicals, radios and automobiles but also in the more traditional fields such as iron and steel production, shipbuilding and engineering, where the British had for decades enjoyed an easy – almost effortless – superiority, the economic horizon at the end of 1926 from Britain's perspective was not entirely dark. She remained one of the world's greatest trading and industrial nations. She may have sold off a great quantity of her overseas investments, but much still remained, and as long as the budget could be kept balanced without imposing an unacceptable strain on the pound, there was always the hope that the overseas investments could be rebuilt. Despite increased competition from the United States and (once she had recovered from the war) Germany, Britain remained the world's greatest exporter of manufactured goods, which was absolutely crucial to Britain's post-war economic strategy. She still had (at least on paper) the benefit of a globe-straddling empire which offered not only valuable raw materials but also ready markets for British goods. Unemployment remained a problem, as did low wages, but prices for manufactured goods at least remained relatively low as well, and this helped to generate feelings of recovery and even to a degree, a perception of prosperity, albeit such prosperity was at best a pale reflection of the Coolidge Prosperity now well underway across the Atlantic.

Britain was not the only European nation to face economic difficulties in the 1920s. The war had left central Europe littered with small new countries carved out of the old empires of Austro-Hungary, Tsarist Russia and the Kaiser's Germany, all of whom faced the difficulties of economic reconstruction and political reorganisation. However, the economics of most of these new countries were largely dominated by agriculture rather than

---

largely remained on strike until November 1926 when hunger and poverty forced them back to work. The strike left a legacy of mistrust and hatred between industrial workers and employers that helped to poison relationships between them for decades and was in part responsible for the long decline during the 1950s, 1960s and 1970s in the power of Britain as an industrial nation, and even today manifests itself on occasion.

industry, and thus it tended to be agricultural difficulties[23] which demanded the attentions of their politicians and financiers at this time rather than the issues of financial stability, currency strengths, war debts and the need to re-establish peacetime industries and trade that so pre-occupied the leaders of western Europe. The economic difficulties of central Europe thus made little impact on the world at large, save where they seemed likely to lead to small-scale wars between rival powers, and even then, the major nations tended to regard such matters in political and military terms rather than economic.

Of the other major powers, Russia struggled not only with the need to repair the war damage she had suffered but also with the self-inflicted economic and political wounds caused by her embrace of communism and the loss of considerable territory occasioned by her retreat from Tsarist empire. Between November 1917, when Lenin's Bolsheviks seized power from the provisional liberal government that six months earlier had ousted the Tsar, until March 1921, when the Soviet Union finally made peace with the invading armies of Poland who had been eager to expand the territories of their fledgling state at Russia's expense, Russia had been wracked not only by civil war between supporters of the Bolsheviks and adherents to the old Tsarist regime but also by the "intervention" of foreign troops on the extremities of her territories, troops whose governments did not look upon the Bolsheviks with affection, and which added further to the carnage and the economic chaos. Desperate to maintain the Red Army as a fighting force, Lenin implemented economic policies of "War Communism" – effectively the confiscation by force not only of the goods and properties of the adherents of the old Tsarist regime but also those of the ordinary peasants and workers who had never had very much of anything but now found they had even less. Such policies were the cause of yet more economic misery. Agricultural production plummeted as peasants found their crops and livestock commandeered by government forces and they responded by refusing to work the land. Famine in the years following the Bolshevik seizure of power was widespread, particularly in the cities, and with little or no food being transported to urban areas, factories and businesses

---

[23] And associated issues such as the re-distribution of land to smallholders and hitherto landless peasants.

ground swiftly to a halt and Russia's overseas trade almost completely collapsed.

By 1920, the lot of the average Russian after three years of communist rule was far worse than it had been under the Tsars and even Lenin could see that his policies were not working. Peace with Poland in 1921 and the final victories of the Red Army over the last supporters of the Tsarist regime allowed him to improvise a new economic policy, which amounted to a repudiation of War Communism. Peasant farmers were now allowed to keep a proportion of the crops they grew and to sell those crops in local markets for personal profit. Similar commercial incentives were offered to industrial workers. It was little enough bearing in mind the devastation Russia had suffered but it was enough – just – to stabilise the situation, and by the time Lenin died in 1924, it was clear that the Soviet authorities had succeeded in stamping their control on the country and that the collapse in material living conditions had been halted, even if not substantially reversed. However, the Soviet Union was still faced with a world that was largely hostile to the supposed benefits of communism. Fearful that the western powers might yet find some way of eradicating the communist state, the Soviet government responded by strictly limiting Russia's interactions with other countries, militarily, economically and politically, with the result that within a few years, Winston Churchill could truthfully describe Russia as *"a riddle, wrapped in a mystery, inside an enigma"*. Such isolation would in due course offer Russia a degree of protection (though not complete immunity) from the economic effects of the 1929 Crash and the Great Depression that followed, while the Russian government under the firm grasp of Lenin's successor Joseph Stalin implemented a succession of five year plans intended to reorganise and expand Russia's industries on a massive scale.

France provides yet another example of the ways in which European countries sought to recover from the First World War, one which differs from both the British model (dependent as it was from the outset on extensive international trade) and the Russian (which stressed rigorous central planning of all sectors of the economy and strictly limited international interactions). Before 1914, foreign trade had been far less important to France than it had been to Britain, and moreover, France at that time had not travelled as far down the road of industrialisation as her neighbour across the Channel. Nevertheless, the necessities of war-time production (exacerbated by the temporary loss of important industrial and mining areas as a result of German occupation) led to a dramatic expansion in France's industrial capabilities during the war years, and this trend continued after the arrival of peace. As it did so, exports became increasingly important to the French economy, while at home France suffered a shortage of workers able to work in her new factories. Unlike the case of Britain, unemployment was not a problem in France during the 1920s.

Despite the undoubted advantages conferred by her rapid industrialisation, France too faced serious problems in recovering from victory. Those problems were principally of a fiscal nature, compounded by the very real material damage inflicted by the Germans on the French territories they had captured during the war.[24] The war had left France with 1.4 million casualties (which exacerbated France's post-war labour shortage) and a national debt of ff219 billion (approximately £8.5 billion at the time of the Armistice). In 1913, French national debt had amounted to ff33.5 billion. In order to pay for the war, France had unleashed her printing presses and issued vast quantities of paper currency; the inevitable result was a collapse in the value of the French franc, which by Armistice Day had lost almost two-thirds of its pre-war value. The franc continued to fall in value in the months and years that immediately followed the end of the war.

The French had blithely assumed that Germany would pay substantial reparations which not only would discourage her from future military aggressions but also would allow an easy French economic recovery, permitting France to stabilise her currency and to pay down her war debts. This delusion received its first setback during the Versailles Treaty negotiations, when President Wilson made it clear that he would refuse to support the more rapacious demands for reparations. There was also only limited support for the French from the British, who not only were becoming vaguely aware that imposing too stringent reparations on Germany would simply create future problems, but also were increasingly inclined to see

---

[24] This was also true of the Belgians, who had seen nearly the whole of their country overrun by the Germans. Belgium's difficulties in the post-war years, and the economic policies she adopted as a result largely reflected those of France.

Germany as an important future trading partner. In any event, although Germany's liability for war reparations was eventually fixed at 132,000 million gold marks ($33 billion or £6.6 billion), Germany paid only a fraction of the reparations due (and indeed, some economic historians argue that after taking into account international loans that were made to Germany in the post-war years but never repaid, Germany on balance paid no reparations at all other than those paid in kind immediately following the end of the fighting). France therefore was unable to rely on German reparations as the solution to her economic problems and her citizens soon became accustomed to regular budget deficits.

The inability of the French to extract all the reparations they considered their due from Germany added further to the pressure on the French franc. By the middle of 1926 (when the French Government under the leadership of Raymond Poincare managed at last to introduce a degree of stability to the French currency), 226 francs were required to purchase one pound sterling. On Armistice Day, the exchange rate had been 26 francs to the pound.

Such currency weakening naturally led to inflation which restricted the ability of French workers to buy goods (although it also helped to reduce the burden of France's national debt). Inflated prices in turn led to repeated workers' demands for higher wages, industrial militancy being encouraged by left wing politicians and unions, many of whom pointed openly to revolutionary Russia as an example – indeed, according to socialist and communist agitators, the only example – to follow. These urgings were vigorously opposed by those on the right and ultimately the political enmity shown between the extremes of the French political spectrum would play an important part in France's inability to resist the German invasion of 1940. Before then, however, throughout the 1920s and 1930s, strikes and general industrial discord severely tested the French political and economic systems which were further strained by the urgent need to provide pensions and other forms of social support in respect of those killed or injured during the war.

Reparations and War Debts

If Great Britain and France, victors of the Great War, had their economic difficulties in the years of peace that followed the Armistice, it is not surprising that Germany suffered too. In some ways, she had been lucky, for allied troops had not reached Germany's borders by the time of the Armistice and her lands had not suffered from foreign occupation during the war as had those of France and Belgium. Nor (other than in a few specific instances such as the Rhineland and the Saar) was she occupied by the Allies after the fighting ceased.[25]

Nevertheless, as a consequence of the Versailles Treaty, in addition to being obliged to pay reparations of 132,000 million gold marks (this amount only being finally settled in April 1921), she had seen great swathes of her eastern territory stripped from her and awarded to the nascent state of Poland, other more minor border adjustments, the confiscation of her overseas colonies and (perhaps most important of all) the return of Alsace-Lorraine to France, which deprived Germany of important industrial and mineral resources. She had also been obliged to accept strict limits on the size and capability of her military forces. These terms were bitterly resented by the Germans, the bitterness exacerbated by the inclusion of the "War-Guilt Clause" in the Treaty whereby Germany was forced to admit that responsibility for the war rested solely with Germany and her allies.

Unquestionably, compared to the terms imposed on France by Germany following the Franco-Prussian War of 1870, many of those imposed on Germany after the First World War now appear harsh, and (given that they ultimately helped to secure support for the Nazi Party) unwise. They did so to

---

[25] Unlike the situation following the end of the Franco-Prussian War of 1870, when Germany installed substantial numbers of troops in northern France pending payment by France of reparations of 5 billion francs. It has been suggested by some historians that the Allies generally made a tactical error in not insisting on a greater occupation of Germany; one of the reasons why the French made a great effort to pay off the reparations forced upon her by the Germans following the end of the Franco-Prussian War was the desire to see the departure of the occupying German troops. The Germans had no such incentive to pay the reparations levied upon them following the end of the First World War and moreover, the fact that allied troops largely failed to set foot upon German soil during the First World War encouraged the view (widely propagated by the Nazis) that Germany had not been defeated militarily but rather betrayed by her politicians.

many observers at the time; in 1919 John Maynard Keynes savagely criticised them in his book entitled *The Economic Consequences of the Peace*, which helped to foster the view (in Great Britain at least) that the Versailles Peace Treaty asked too much of Germany. Even Winston Churchill, a member of the British Government which signed the Treaty subsequently commented that he believed the reparation obligations imposed on Germany to be *"...malignant and silly to an extent that made them obviously futile"*. On the other hand, the world had seen (in the shape of the Brest-Litovsk Treaty) the terms that Germany had forced upon Russia in early March 1918 as the price of Russian withdrawal from the war, and that the Germans themselves had no hesitation in imposing harsh reparation obligations upon the vanquished when they were in the victor's seat.

The first instalment of reparations (1,000 million marks) was due to be paid in May 1921; the deadline was missed, and it was only after the Allies had threatened to occupy the Ruhr and a loan from London had been hastily arranged that it was finally paid in August. Thereafter the Weimar Government (which replaced the German imperial government in 1919) contrived over the next few years to make payments in kind but made no further payments in cash. At the same time, Germany (which, unlike Britain and France, had not incurred large war loans during the conflict itself) began to accumulate debts at an alarming rate, not only to shore up her now distinctly shaky economy but also to meet the cost of those reparations she did pay and the costs of reconstruction.

The political and economic uncertainties of the immediate post-war years, and the general realisation of the extent of the burdens imposed on Germany at Versailles, all contrived to cause the German financial situation to deteriorate sharply after 1921. Inflation began to run out of control as the German Treasury began to print ever greater quantities of increasingly worthless paper currency, and the value of the mark began to depreciate with increasing rapidity. In January 1921, a dollar was worth about 60 (paper) marks; a year later nearly 200 marks were required to buy a dollar, and by January 1923, nearly 18,000 marks were required.

But worse was to come. In January 1923, the Weimar Government announced that it was unable to meet its next reparations payment and unilaterally sought to suspend the payments schedule. France and Belgium (without British or American support) promptly sent troops to occupy the Ruhr with a view to seizing the amounts that were owed; the local inhabitants, with the tacit support of the German Government (supported heartily by popular opinion throughout the rest of Germany[26]) carried out a programme of passive resistance, including strikes and occasional acts of sabotage. The Ruhr region was paralysed, many of Germany's industries ground to a halt, and Germany's inflation problem turned into one of hyperinflation as the German currency simply collapsed. By September 1923, a dollar was worth perhaps 100 million marks and by November, 200,000 million. By this stage the mark was effectively worthless.

Naturally, the effect of hyperinflation on ordinary Germans was catastrophic. Those rich enough to own substantial amounts of land or factories or goods, or lucky enough to have reasonable quantities of cash in the form of foreign currency, could benefit from the spectacular rise in prices and prospered accordingly. But for ordinary Germans, dependent on their pay packets, poverty arrived swiftly and painfully. Salaries could not even begin to keep pace with rising prices, even when they were increased on a daily basis (as happened in the autumn and winter months of 1923 in some cases). Savings, pensions and paper investments were wiped out[27], and people were reduced to bartering for the essentials they needed to survive. The middle classes were pauperised almost overnight, and the psychological effects of the currency collapse were at least as severe as those that Americans were to suffer in the Crash of 1929. Distrust of the democratically elected Weimar Government became axiomatic for many of those who suffered, and would help to bring the Nazis to power a decade later.

Faced with a worthless currency, the German financial authorities were forced to try to bring stability to their financial systems by introducing a new one. This first took the form of the rentenmark, backed (thanks to a lack of gold in

---

[26] So much so that one American political observer remarked, only half-jokingly, that *"Only two people have been able to bring about German unity: Bismark and Poincare"*.

[27] On the other hand, so were debts, provided they were payable in marks, whether owed by individuals or public bodies.

Germany) by land and industrial bonds, and was introduced in November 1923 at the rate of one rentenmark to one trillion old marks (or to put it another way, one US dollar would buy 4.2 rentenmarks). It was only ever intended to be a temporary currency and technically had no legal status, but it was accepted as valid tender by the German population and played a major role in allowing the hyperinflation to be brought under control.[28] The rentenmark itself was replaced on 30 August 1924 by the reichsmark, but rentenmarks in circulation remained valid until 1948.

Another factor which assisted the German authorities in stabilising the currency was the Dawes Plan. This was a plan proposed by an international committee of experts chaired by Charles Dawes (who as previously noted would later go on to be Vice-President during Calvin Coolidge's term as President). The Dawes Committee had been established (principally at the urgings of Great Britain and the United States) by the Allied Reparations Commission following Germany's failure to honour its reparations obligations with instructions to find some way to enable Germany to meet its debts without collapsing into economic and political chaos. The Dawes Plan called for a temporary halt of two years on Germany's reparation payments schedule, the evacuation of French and other foreign troops from the Ruhr, the re-organisation of the German Reichsbank under Allied supervision and (crucially) the making of an American loan to Germany of 800 million marks. The Allies and Germany accepted the terms of the Plan in August 1924. For a time, the Plan brought distinct economic benefits to Germany, enabling her to balance her budget and return to the gold standard and improving her creditworthiness in the eyes of foreign lenders. Consequently, Germany was once again able to borrow lavishly abroad which in turn allowed her to invest heavily in public works and to renew and expand her industrial plants, so much so that by 1929, it seemed that prosperity had once more returned to Germany

---

[28] In fact, so rapidly was the hyperinflation eliminated that some foreign observers speculated seriously as to whether the entire episode had been a ruse by Germany to allow her to inflate her debts away. If this were so, then a lot of people, not only in Germany but also (thanks to the Nazis whose passage to power was aided by memories of the hyperinflation and supposed economic incompetence of the Weimar government) throughout the world paid a very high price for its success.

(though as in Britain, unemployment remained a serious problem).[29] The Dawes Plan, and Germany's increasing international indebtedness did however make Germany more dependent upon foreign nations, and particularly the United States, not only as sources of capital loans but also as markets to which the products of the new German factories could be sold. Thus when the Great Depression struck America, drastically reducing not only the availability of funds for loans but also the demand for imported goods, Germany would suffer as much as her European neighbours.

Dependence upon the economic health of the United States was the case for nearly every nation of western Europe; America's emergence during the Great War as the world's greatest creditor nation effectively meant that it was essential to the economic well-being of Europe that America should continue to prosper. In 1926, however, few in Europe were thinking in terms of Europe's vulnerability to a downturn in the American economy, or the possibility that such a downturn could lead to a world depression. For the first time since the First World War, it seemed that economic stability and prosperity had either returned, or at least was on the horizon. Nevertheless, regardless of whether economic recovery followed the British, French or German patterns, it remained far more fragile in many European nations than many economic experts of the time cared to contemplate.

---

[29] In the longer term, however, it remained obvious that Germany would still be unable to meet its reparation obligations in full, and the Dawes Plan was eventually superseded (in 1929) by the Young Plan (also produced at the behest of the Allied Reparations Commission) which sought to lessen the reparations burden on Germany by extending the payment timetable to a period of 59 years. Before the Young Plan could be fully implemented, however, the world fell into the Great Depression, and in 1932 at an international conference held at Lausanne, it was effectively agreed that payments of war reparations by Germany should cease indefinitely.

Chapter 4 Meanwhile on Wall Street....

"I see no reason for the end-of-the-year slump which some people are predicting."
Charles E. Mitchell, President of the National City Bank and Director of the Federal Reserve Bank of New York (1877 – 1955)

The Great Boom

Back in America, the effects of Florida's land boom and bust were felt in communities all across the country, and yet remarkably in the country at large, the collapse did little to shake general confidence in the robustness of the Coolidge Prosperity, or the then widely-held belief that all Americans could become rich, and that there were quick and easy ways of achieving this goal. As 1926 rolled into 1927, and 1927 into 1928, Americans dissatisfied with traditional savings vehicles such as bank deposit accounts or postal savings began to look towards securities offered by America's major corporations as a sure route to wealth and like moths to a flame, began to invest in the offerings of Wall Street. And they did so as the stock market began to rise, modestly at first in the years preceding 1927, but then with an ever-increasing speed (but also increasing volatility) through 1927 and 1928 and the first nine months of 1929. The relentless rise in the market was reflected by the Dow Jones industrial average, which stood at 121.25 on 2nd January 1925 (having risen from 63.9 on 24th August 1921, when the market had bottomed out following the 1920-1921 slump). By 31st December 1925, it had climbed to 156.66. During 1926, price movements were erratic, and the stock market ended the year at 157.20, little higher than at the start of the year. During 1927, however, prices generally followed a sharp upward trend, and the Dow Jones industrial average closed the year at 202.40. The upward trend became a boom in 1928, with the Dow Jones standing at 307.01 on 2nd January 1929. And on 3rd September 1929, weeks before the Crash the Dow Jones industrial average reached 381.17. It would not achieve this peak again until 1954.[30]

---

[30] It is worth remembering, of course, the New York Stock Exchange was not the only exchange in the United States at which the public could buy shares. Exchanges also flourished in other cities as far apart as Boston and San Francisco, while share dealing

There were valid reasons why the market should have risen in 1925 and (to the extent that it did) in 1926 and (possibly) 1927, not least the continued steady growth in GDP, increasing corporate profits and improvements in productivity. By 1928 however it had become difficult to find any rational justification for the continued rise in prices, which now appeared to bear no relation at all to any reasonable assessments of the values of the underlying companies. Yet the volume of trading on Wall Street continued to increase dramatically and people and institutions continued to invest.

The purchase of securities was made easier by the application of instalment purchase plans to the field of investing. By now, consumers had become familiar with the concept as a means of buying consumer goods on credit; the extension of such plans to brokers' loans seemed to many not only logical but also highly attractive. Just as a new Ford or General Motors automobile could be acquired with a modest down payment, effectively borrowing the balance and paying it off over a number of years, so too could investors buy shares "on margin" from a broker, paying perhaps only 10 percent (but more typically 40 to 50 percent) of the purchase price as an upfront payment, while borrowing the balance of the purchase price in the form of a loan from the broker which was secured by the value of the shares purchased. Moreover, although an automobile would depreciate while the balance of the loan was being paid off, the continuing upswing in stock prices seemed to suggest that repayment of the broker's loan was almost an irrelevance and that once it had been paid off, the investor would almost inevitably own an asset worth more than he or she had originally paid for it. Few individuals bought shares with the intention of holding them for significant periods of time, and buying on margin during a time of rising share prices allowed investors to take advantage of the effect of leveraging (whereby upon the eventual sale of the shares bought on margin, once the loan had been repaid, any further realised profits belonged to the investor), significantly multiplying potential profits. And for as long as prices continued to rise, this argument had considerable merit – during 1928 and early 1929, it was by no means impossible for a lucky buyer to realise a 1000

---

also flourished on the curb (that is, outside recognised exchanges, and sometimes literally on the curb of the street).

percent profit on share purchases and subsequent disposals thanks to the leveraging effect, which in turn encouraged others to join in the buying spree. As in the case of the Florida land boom of only a few years before, not many people seem to have considered the consequences of a reversal of share prices, or the fact that investors would still be liable for outstanding margin loans even if the price of the shares upon which the loans were secured were to fall.

The investments of individual American investors alone, however, would never have fuelled the rise in stock prices during the second half of the 1920s. To begin with, there were too few of them, perhaps only 3 million individual investors in all, and some estimates put this figure as low as 1.5 million. Despite popular myth, although many Americans did indeed invest in securities for the first time in their lives during the years immediately preceding the Crash, the vast majority – 97.5 percent of the population according to one estimate, 99 percent according to another – owned no shares or corporate bonds at all on the eve of the Great Crash. Furthermore, individual investors tended to invest hundreds or thousands or at most tens of thousands of dollars – they simply did not have the financial resource to fuel the surge in share prices of the late 1920s.

Many corporations did have the resources however. Thanks to Treasury Secretary Mellon's policy of reducing corporate tax rates, American companies reported rapidly increasing net incomes between 1922 and 1929, and many began to invest their surplus funds in the market, often on margin. Banks too were investing, partly because the rising profits of the large corporations meant that they had less need for the banks' traditional services than had been the case a decade or so before and the banks needed to find alternative sources of profit. Banks were also providing funds for brokers' margin loans, for which demand was rising rapidly, a task in which they were joined by other non-banking lenders such as the larger corporations, who by 1929 were providing a significant proportion (more than 70 percent according to some estimates) of the funds provided to the brokers' loan market, generating substantial profits in the process. The sums involved were immense; by October 1929, funds for brokers' loans from non-banking lenders amounted to $6.6 billion, with Bethlehem Steel and The Electric Bond and Share Company (a subsidiary of General Electric) each having contributed more than $150 million, Chrysler

Corporation having provided a further $60 million, and Standard Oil of New Jersey having provided $97 million. This increase in the funds available for leverage borrowing by individuals and institutions for investment purposes in turn helped to nourish the appetite for stock market speculation. And the more individuals and institutions who bought shares on the expectation of rising prices, the more the stock market rose.

Complicating matters still further was the emergence into popular investment culture of investment trusts. Similar in many ways to modern day mutual funds and unit trusts (though far less regulated), such trusts had originated in Great Britain in the second half of the nineteenth century as a means whereby small investors could pool their resources by buying stock in an investment trust which would in turn invest the trust monies in the chosen investment field. Such an approach was presumed to have the advantage of not only spreading (and as a result, reducing) the investment risk of each of the individual investors, but also by hiring suitably qualified managers, the trust allowed small investors to benefit from specialised investment knowledge and techniques not widely available to the general public. By and large, with some exceptions, investment trusts were successful in the British context and the monies so raised were invested widely not only in Great Britain but also throughout the British Empire and the wider world.

Before the 1920s, however, they had not proved to be very popular in the United States, with only (according to one estimate) 40 being established in the years before 1921. In the years immediately following 1921, that changed, as American financial institutions realised the potential of investment trusts and set about sponsoring them to the general public with enthusiasm. Sometimes investment trusts themselves set up other investment trusts. By the end of 1927, an estimated 300 had been created, and 1928 saw the creation of a further 186. By September 1929, they were being created at the rate of nearly one a day, and some were massive in scale. The Founders Group, for example, was an agglomeration of investment trusts, the first of which had been established in 1921. Over the years it had grown, frequently by means of leveraged investments, acquiring companies, cross-investing and selling securities to the public so that by 1929, the group as a whole had assets valued in excess of a billion dollars. Another famous example is that of the

Shenandoah Corporation. Formed by a subsidiary of Goldman Sachs on 26th July 1929, its initial share offering to the public was intended to raise $102.5 million. It sold so well that as Time magazine pointed out on 5th August 1929, *"by mid-afternoon of the first day's sale, there was no [more] Shenandoah stock available."* Twenty five days later, the Shenandoah Corporation itself launched another trust, Blue Ridge Corporation, with a share capital of $142 million which was also heavily oversubscribed. And there were many more.[31]

The scope and activities of the trusts changed as more were created. The earliest had specialised in respectable conservative stock offerings, and tended to operate within the parameters of self-imposed but strict rules stipulating which shares could and could not be bought and on what basis. This meant that their portfolios, once established, changed little over years, and investors had a (reasonably) clear idea as to how their money was being invested. The later trusts, however, tended to stress active management of their investment portfolios by the trusts' promoters, and their investment rules were more lax, with the result that the trusts' investments were made and organised and sold at the whims of their promoters and managers, greatly increasing the volume of stocks being traded. Many trusts sought to maximise their investment returns by means of leveraged investments and often invested in other companies that themselves were making leveraged investments (with the obligation of servicing the debts associated with those investments). Rickety chains of leveraged investments in leveraged investments in leveraged investments began to appear, with the businesses actually creating real wealth at the very bottom. Those businesses were thus called upon to produce profits large enough not only to support themselves and their business activities but also to cover the financial burdens of the parties higher up the chains, who needed to realise sufficient money to enable loans and bonds and preference share obligations to be met, not to mention the commission and other professional charges levied by the investment professionals (which were substantial). A lot of money would therefore be leached out of the system

---

[31] One Goldman Sachs partner at the time was asked why his firm formed so many investment trusts. He replied *"Well, people want them."* And so they did. For a while, anyway.

before any return could be made to the private investors who had acquired interests in the trusts at the top of the chain. And of course, the whole edifice could only continue to function as long as the wealth-creating businesses continued to create wealth, and the price of the leveraged shares continued to rise. Little of this was understood by the general public, and one wonders how much was understood by some of the professional investment firms involved in organising and sponsoring investments.[32] Some promoters, it was generally agreed, were of a dubious character, and were unlikely to care as long as they made money and didn't themselves get caught, but others (such as the House of Morgan) had respectable names and places in the investment world and notwithstanding the substantial profits they were making should have understood the risks involved. Yet, they were caught up in the folly of the leveraged trusts. In any event, the trusts proved popular with the public to whom they were marketed (even though the New York Stock Exchange only permitted the listing of investment trusts in 1929, and then only with some reluctance). By 1929, an estimated $3 billion worth of securities in investment trusts was being marketed to the public, and enthusiastic investors were frequently willing to pay substantial premiums for those securities over the ostensible offer prices.[33]

The 1920s also saw a rapid growth in the number of holding companies in the United States. Unlike investment trusts, holding companies had a long (and sometimes controversial) history, with the first being established in the latter years of the nineteenth century as a means of combining different businesses

---

[32] To make matters worse, most investment trusts were extremely reluctant to disclose their asset holdings to the public (even to their own investors), almost as if their investment portfolios were trade secrets to be closely guarded. (This attitude changed sharply following the Crash when investment trusts (at least those that survived) became eager to demonstrate they were still solvent).

[33] The initial Shenandoah Corporation share offering, for example, sold at a premium of 103 percent. Blue Ridge sold at a premium of 46 percent. Such premiums were by no means unusual during the last few months before the Crash. It has been estimated that the median investment trust premium during the third quarter of 1929 was 47 percent. By the summer of the following year, the median investment trust was selling at a 25 percent discount.

within the same corporate group. One early example was Standard Oil, which allowed John D Rockefeller and his associates to gain effective control over most of the country's oil refining and distribution businesses by the start of the twentieth century.

Holding companies were distinct from the operating companies which they owned and which actually provided the goods and services that created wealth in that they generally acted as little more than a central point of financial control over their subsidiaries. They were widely used in the 1920s as a means of implementing business mergers, of which there were thousands between 1919 and 1929, particularly in the public utilities, mining, manufacturing, railroad and banking sectors. Thus, as the holding companies expanded their industrial and financial empires, more and more formerly independent businesses were assembled together within the confines of a common ownership. The corporate structures of the holding companies and their subsidiaries were frequently complex, sometimes to the point of opaqueness; nevertheless, canny promoters soon found that holding companies could generate funds by issuing bonds and (typically preferred) stock to the public, which in turn allowed them to buy and hold stock in operating companies which in turn provided the wealth (in the form of dividend payments) which could be used to service the interest and dividend payment obligations of the holding companies. Again, leveraged investments were frequently made. So successful was this approach that by 1928, a majority of the active corporations listed on the New York Stock Exchange were either pure holding companies or holding and operating companies; only 86 (out of 573) were operating companies.

As in the case of the investment trusts, the financial stability of holding companies and subsidiaries depended upon the ability of the operating companies to generate sufficient funds to service the needs of the companies higher up the corporate chain. Anything that threatened the upward flow of funds threatened the existence of the group as a whole. However, the need to service the interest and debt obligations of the group as a whole meant that fewer funds were available for re-investment in the operating companies' businesses, which over time began to affect their earnings. Thus there was a fundamental flaw in the business structure of many of the companies listed on the stock exchange that would become all too apparent after October 1929. For the time being however, apparently oblivious to the risks, investors scrambled for the securities offered by the holding companies.

Enter the Federal Reserve

Rising business profits resulting from benign tax rates and a booming consumer economy were not the only sources of the funds which fuelled the relentless rise in stock prices in 1927, 1928 and 1929; there was also the Federal Reserve. The Federal Reserve system had come into being in 1914 following a long (and frequently turbulent) battle dating back to the earliest days of the United States between those who supported the creation of a US central bank and those who opposed it. The system finally came into being as a response to a series of financial panics, most notably the Panic of 1907 which had triggered a series of bank runs and the collapse of a worryingly large number of banks, leading to calls for financial and currency reform. The Federal Reserve system was a response to these problems, and was intended to introduce a measure of financial stability to the United States by ensuring (amongst other matters) liquidity within the US banking system. However, rather than following the approach adopted in several European countries (including Great Britain and France) of having a single central bank, which raised the ire of those Americans who feared that a central bank would be dominated by "Eastern money interests" (and run for their benefit at the expense of the country as a whole), the Federal Reserve was to be a system established on the basis of three tiers. First, there would be twelve regional Federal Reserve Banks, one in New York and the others in major cities throughout the United States. Secondly, there would be a Board of Governors in Washington DC. Thirdly, there would be "member banks" (not to be confused with the Federal Reserve Banks who effectively acted as depositaries for the member banks). All national banks were obliged to join the system; state-chartered banks (perhaps three-quarters of all the country's banks) were permitted (but not obliged) to join if they could satisfy various requirements, including rules as regards the value of financial reserves held against customers' deposits. Unfortunately, many of the smaller state-chartered banks were unable to meet the membership requirements and remained outside the system. So, the stronger banks benefitted from the Federal Reserve system while the weaker banks (perhaps 65 percent of the total) remained unprotected even though they were potentially most in need of the support the system offered,.

One of the advantages of membership of the Federal Reserve system was the ability of member banks to be able to borrow from the Reserve Banks. When doing so, the member banks effectively paid interest for the privilege at "rediscount rate" (sometimes called simply the "discount rate"), which was set by the Federal Reserve and which it sought to use as a tool to control the money supply. Although the rediscount rate varied somewhat throughout the 1920s, it was generally substantially less than the rates paid on loans to brokers, which for much of this period typically ranged from 6 to 12 percent. Member banks found it profitable indeed to borrow from the Federal Reserve at the rediscount rate and then relend that money into the brokers' loan market and of course did not hesitate to do so. Thus the Federal Reserve system itself was indirectly providing much of the funding that was fuelling the Great Boom.

No one was more aware of these issues than Benjamin Strong, a respected New York banker who in 1914 had been appointed Governor of the New York Federal Reserve Bank, a post he held until his death in 1928 from tuberculosis. Ironically, although he had opposed several aspects of the Federal Reserve system[34], he became perhaps its most powerful member, working closely with Treasury Secretary Andrew Mellon, with whom he saw eye to eye over the need to maintain low interest rates at home and the necessity of restoring the gold standard as the basis for international financial transactions. Thus it had largely been under his tutelage that the rediscount rate had been maintained at low levels during most of the Coolidge years, which had been a major factor in maintaining the Coolidge Prosperity. However, notwithstanding the relatively low rediscount rate in the United States, gold had continued to flow into the country, not least as a result of the troubled conditions in Europe and Britain's ill-judged return to the gold standard in 1926. A keen advocate of global solutions to monetary problems, Strong had

---

[34] Most notably, he was critical of the Federal Reserve Board in Washington, fearing that many of its members would be political appointees lacking the requisite knowledge of banking and economics to enable them to carry out their responsibilities, which indeed proved to be the case.

lent a sympathetic ear to pleas in 1927 from Britain and Germany (and the French who, although themselves a net recipient of gold, were anxious to stabilise international currency rates in order to provide some much needed respite for the French franc) for lower American interest rates, in the hope that this would help to staunch the westward flow of gold. Largely as a result of Strong's urgings, the Federal Reserve in the autumn of 1927 cut the rediscount rate from 4 to 3.5 percent. The flow of gold was not noticeably reduced, but the cost of borrowing was markedly lowered, making commercial lending to brokers look even more attractive. According to many (but not all) commentators, this act, more perhaps than any other, was responsible for the loosening of the financial restraint that led directly to the Great Crash. Certainly, the timing of the cut was unfortunate, coming just as the stock market was beginning to break free from reality and commencing its final ascent into the financial heavens. On the other hand, a tightening of the money supply at this time may not have helped either; had the Federal Reserve raised the rediscount rate substantially at this time, banks may have cut back on their more conventional (and potentially riskier and almost certainly less profitable) "normal" commercial lending rather than walk away from the money machine that was the provision of money for brokers' loans. This was a risk that the Federal Reserve was keen to avoid in the autumn of 1927.

Within a few months, however, increasing concern about the level of market speculation and the growth in the volume of commercial lending to the brokers' loan market prompted a change in policy. Partly at the urgings of Strong (who, for all that he was a supporter of low interest rates and the need to maintain global financial stability was no fan of speculation), the Federal Reserve acted three times in 1928 to raise the rediscount rate from 3.5 percent to 5 percent. While the effects of these increases were rapidly felt in the world beyond Wall Street, where there was a noticeable slowdown in commercial activity, the increase had little effect on the stock market itself. Banks and other commercial lenders still found it profitable to fund brokers' loans, and continued to do so. Then, crucially, after a failed operation for tuberculosis,

Strong died on 16th October 1928; without his leadership, the Federal Reserve seemed to give up any attempt to actively control the situation.[35]

In truth, the Board of Governors and the directors of the regional Reserve Banks were aware of the delicacy of the situation, but were split as to the best way to deal with it. Broadly speaking, the Board of Governors favoured applying pressure to those member banks who were borrowing funds from the Federal Reserve to lend to the stock market; many of the Reserve Banks, and particularly the Federal Reserve Bank of New York, argued there were no legal grounds upon which member banks' requests for loans could be refused, and favoured instead following the example of Strong and raising the rediscount rate. In the meantime, critics in the press and elsewhere pointed out that the Federal Reserve had produced no evidence to show that "speculative loans" were detrimental to business which added further confusion as to the appropriate course to take. For the moment, with no effective leadership, the Federal Reserve was paralysed. Fatally, it refrained for the time being from making further increases to the rediscount rate, allowing it to remain at 5 percent; it remained so until August 1929, only two months before the Great Crash, when at last the rate was raised to 6 percent. By then, it was far too late to dampen the speculation fuelling the Great Boom.

Concerns about the now roaring bull market were to be heard in other quarters too. Early in 1929, Moody's Investment Service and the Harvard Economic Society[36] both warned that stock prices had reached levels that could not be objectively justified and Paul Warburg, a former member of the Federal Reserve Board, warned a few months later that if excessive share speculation continued, the country would be plunged into a depression. In February 1929, Roy Young, a Minneapolis banker and Chairman of the Federal Reserve Board also criticised the speculation, and hinted that action might have to be taken by

---

[35] Some economic historians consider that had Strong lived, the Crash might have been avoided, or at the very least, its effects mitigated.

[36] Though by mid-summer, when the fall in prices it had predicted had not materialised, the Society recanted of its pessimism, and declared that a stock market fall and subsequent depression was not on the cards, a view it persisted in holding even after the Crash had occurred and the Depression had arrived.

the Federal Reserve against banks who continued to fund brokers' loans. By and large, the warnings were ignored by Wall Street, the speculation continued and the banks and other commercial lenders poured scorn upon the heads of the doom-sayers. Critics were particularly savage about Warburg, accusing him of *"sandbagging American prosperity"*, and implying that he was anxious to drive down share prices for his own nefarious purposes.

Then, in mid-March 1929 (within days of President Hoover's inauguration), the market took a tumble, principally in response to rumours that the Federal Reserve might, after all, be considering taking action to restrict the amount of credit available to those banks which were lending to the stock market. The interest rate for brokers' loans began to rise in anticipation of action by the Federal Reserve, and by 25th March it had reached 14 percent. The worst day was 26th March, with the market falling rapidly in early trading (it fell so fast that the ticker was unable to cope with the trading volume and fell rapidly behind the market) and many small investors who had bought on margin suffered substantial losses as brokers exercised their rights to sell the investors' shares in order to recover their loans. At that moment, when the Federal Reserve was conspicuously silent (as was President Hoover), the spotlight fell on Charles E. Mitchell, president of the National City Bank, one of the largest of the New York banks, and one which had been heavily involved in lending to the stock market. At the beginning of 1929, he had also been made a director of the Federal Reserve Bank of New York, which placed him in a position of a potential conflict of interest, although this seems to have bothered neither him nor anyone else at the time. Although the Federal Reserve, drifting as it was in the wake of Strong's death, had no realistic plans to raise the rediscount rate in March 1929, Mitchell was concerned that a market collapse might result if it did so. He therefore publicly announced on 26th March that if it became harder to borrow money as a result of increases to the rediscount rate, National City would make $25 million available to the brokers' loan market. He also indicated that National City intended to continue to borrow funds from the Federal Reserve come what may. The effect of this announcement was dramatic; by the end of that day's trading, the market had largely recovered, and the rate for brokers' loans had stabilised at 15 percent, having peaked a few hours earlier at 20 percent.

Voices were raised in Congress questioning the propriety of Mitchell's actions, and there were threats of a public inquiry, but these soon petered out as it became clear that investors generally did not care so long as the market had recovered. The Board of the Federal Reserve, as was by now to be expected, said nothing of substance publicly (privately, several of its members agreed with Mitchell's stance), and this despite the fact that Mitchell's announcement was generally perceived as a slap in the face for the Board. President Hoover too said little, though he broadly favoured direct action by the Federal Reserve to limit the banks' access to credit rather than a hiking of the rediscount rate, and was by no means a supporter of Mitchell (he hadn't been a great admirer of Benjamin Strong either). There were those who openly supported Mitchell, however, including the New York Times, which criticised scolding Senators for failing to realise that Mitchell had acted to defuse a serious crisis in the money market, while some well-known businessmen (most notably William Durant, the former President of General Motors who in recent years had become a major speculator on Wall Street) openly attacked the Federal Reserve system as being inimical to US business interests. Mitchell himself refused to enter into a public argument with his critics, announcing that he considered the incident to be closed, while at the same time issuing a half-hearted warning about the dangers of "unbridled speculation". In April, he seemed to gain credibility when the National City Bank recommended increasing the rediscount rate to 6 percent (a call that was for the time being ignored). The furore over Mitchell died down; it seemed to be – for a while –"American business as usual".

The Last Days

Mitchell's actions had essentially bought the speculators a few more months of time – one last "summer of fun" as one commentator subsequently described it. The speculation continued, the borrowing of Federal Reserve funds continued, the loans to the brokers' market continued. But now some sensed that the situation had changed, or at least was changing, that the credit controversy signified a break with the past and that Wall Street was standing on the brink of a new era, where new rules would apply and the old certainties vanish. A strange *fin de siècle* sensation now seemed to permeate the air. Brokers and investors alike kept a wary eye on the Federal Reserve, fearing a sudden increase in the rediscount rate, while the stock market itself seemed unsettled, rises in the Dow Jones industrial average in April 1929 being followed by a series of short but sharp falls from mid-May onwards. By the end of the month, the Dow Jones stood a few points lower than it had at the beginning of January. Brokers' loan rates fluctuated, rising and falling between 6 and 16 percent, and share volatility increased markedly as measured by the daily swings of the Dow Jones industrial average. In June, trading volumes suddenly decreased markedly, and for a time, the market seemed to have stalled, before prices started to lurch upwards once more. By the end of the month, the Dow Jones industrial average recorded a month-on-month increase of 34.67 points. The bull market, it seemed, was back, and trading volumes exploded once more in July as prices thundered upwards. At the beginning of July, the Dow Jones stood at 335.22 (then a record high); by the end of the month, it reached 347.70.

Bullish commentators tried to justify the continuing rise in prices by arguing that it was underpinned by (and was a reflection of) the continuing prosperity of American business, but this explanation failed to satisfy more cautious observers. American businesses generally were experiencing a slowdown in demand, some were failing and factory warehouses were rapidly filling with unsold goods. Despite, or perhaps because of the continuing massive flow of cash into the stock market, money remained strangely tight in the real business world. Automobile manufacturers were reporting a falling demand for new cars. The Federal Reserve had already noted that the number of building contracts being awarded was declining rapidly, frequently a precursor of an economic slowdown. The depression in agricultural prices remained a problem, while overseas, there was talk of faltering economies and concerns that the continued flow of gold to the United States[37] would prompt countries such as Britain, Italy and Germany to raise their base interest rates, despite the

---

[37] During the first half of 1929, the United States gained $210 million of gold. France, another net recipient, gained $182 million. Such was the flow of gold out of Great Britain that by the end of September 1929, the Bank of England's gold stock had been reduced to $640 million, having declined by nearly 20 percent in just four months. From the point of view of maintaining Britain's gold reserves, the Great Crash came just in time.

danger that such rises would pose for their own businesses. Interest rate increases eventually manifested themselves in the spring and summer of 1929, and the increased cost of borrowing reduced economic demand in many European countries, reducing the ability of consumers in those nations to buy American goods. There was therefore little justification for the continued bull market so far as the business world was concerned, particularly one showing the exuberance that the market manifested in July, and more cautious (or discerning) commentators – such as the New York Times – observed that there seemed to be two markets in operation at once, one a bull market and the other a bear market. The rise in the stock market was now being powered by a select (and relatively small) class of apparently favoured stocks which continued to rise in price, and upon which the attentions of the speculators were focussed; brokers found it hard to interest clients in other lower-priced stocks (which made up the bulk of the stocks listed on the New York Stock Exchange) whose prices showed little signs of vaulting upwards. Many indeed were drifting down.

By now popular attention was firmly fixed on Wall Street. Even those who had not a cent invested in the market were following the rise in share prices with fascination. Newspapers across the country printed detailed daily reports on the state of the markets, popular magazines covered financial matters in depth, and books were published by the score promising would-be investors the "inside track" of Wall Street success. Talk of stocks and shares, and tales of who had just made a killing (or who was about to make a killing) abounded. Less well reported were details of the darker side of Wall Street – such as the extent to which deals on the Street relied on inside information, and the ways in which stock prices could be manipulated by investment pools set up by the sophisticated few at the expense of more innocent investors.[38] Astrologers and

---

[38] Legal at the time, investment pools essentially involved small syndicates of collaborators selecting a stock and agreeing to sell it back and forth between themselves, thus forcing an artificial rise in the share price that would tempt more innocent investors into the fray. Once the price had risen to an agreed level, the syndicate members would quietly offload their shares and take their profits, leaving the shares in the hands of the gullible who would watch bemused and out of pocket as the share price promptly fell back again. Far from such activities being widely reported,

sooth-sayers too got in on the act, as speculators sought any hint they could glean as to the latest hot stock. Perhaps the most famous of all was Evangeline Adams, who was probably the best known American astrologer of her day. Born in New Jersey in 1868, and the subject of a famous court trial in New York in 1914 in which she was charged with fortune telling,[39] by the 1920s, she was providing advice as to future share movements to a select group of clients including Charlie Chaplin, Mary Pickford, Tallulah Bankhead and J P Morgan, as well as issuing a newsletter dispensing investment tips to less august followers (at $20 an issue). In February 1929, she predicted that a dramatic upswing in stock prices, and then repeated that advice on 2nd September, when she claimed *"the Dow could climb to Heaven"*. The next day, the Dow reached its peak of 381.17 and ever since her supporters have held this out as proof of the efficacy of financial astrology. Unfortunately for her many followers, Evangeline Adams failed to predict the Crash or the Great Depression that followed only a few weeks later.

But you didn't have to go to Evangeline Adams, or read the newspapers or even talk to your broker to get investment advice. It seemed everyone was dispensing it – cab drivers, barbers, elevator boys, even shoeshine boys. For some shrewd investors that summer, this was a warning sign. Bernard Baruch, famed Wall Street investor, and an optimist as to the prospects for the stock market as recently as June 1929, is credited with observing: *"When beggars and shoeshine boys, barbers and beauticians can tell you how to get rich, it is time to remind yourself that there is no more dangerous illusion than the belief that one can get something for*

---

some newspaper reporters actually collaborated with pool organisers, touting stock favoured by the organisers in exchange for substantial rewards of their own. Pools were big business – it has been estimated that in 1927, they sold $400 million of shares to the public, while 1928 saw that figure nearly double to $790 million. Unsurprisingly, successful pools were capable of generating substantial profits for their organisers. Men such as Mike Meehan, Jesse Livermore and Arthur Cutten, made millions from investment pools during the last few heady years before the Crash when Wall Street was still largely unregulated. Their principal concern was to make money from investment pools before someone made it illegal.

[39] She was acquitted.

nothing". He began to sell his holdings, and advised his friends (including the actor Will Rogers, who heeded his advice) to do likewise.

Another who heeded the warning signs was Joseph P (Joe) Kennedy, father of future President Jack Kennedy. Kennedy, who had made his initial fortune on the Wall Street of the early 1920s (and according to persistent rumour, out of clandestine bootlegging), had moved to Hollywood in 1927 where he had flung himself into a number of highly profitable transactions in the movie business, including one that led to the creation of RKO. He had also indulged himself in an affair with Gloria Swanson, one of the most glamorous movie actresses of her day. The affair with Swanson had petered out after a film project that he had promised to produce for her (Queen Kelly) came to nothing and so, exhausted, but considerably richer than he had been a few years before, Kennedy had returned to his family (who had been left safely ensconced in New York during Kennedy's Hollywood years) in the spring of 1929. Stressed and suffering badly from ulcers, on his return Kennedy was forced to check into a hospital for several weeks, but on his emergence, he took a closer look at the stock market and didn't like what he saw.

"Only a fool holds out for top dollar" he told one friend, and disregarding advice to reinvest his Hollywood profits in the stock market, he began quietly and systematically to liquidate the shareholdings that he did own into cash.

Three days after Evangeline Adams made her prediction that the Dow was destined to ascend heaven-ward, and two days after the Dow reached its pre-World War Two peak of 381.17, Roger Babson, an economist and financial statistician, and one who had grown increasingly alarmed at the state of the markets during the course of 1929, was scheduled to give a speech at the National Business Conference in Wellesley, Massachusetts. During that speech, he commented: *"Sooner or later a crash is coming which will take the leading stocks and cause a decline of from 60 to 80 points in the Dow Jones Barometer. Fair weather cannot always continue. The Federal Reserve system has put the banks in a strong position, but it has not changed human nature. More people are borrowing and speculating today than ever in our history. Sooner or later there is a crash coming and it may be a terrific one."* Advising that people should reduce their debt levels and avoid margin speculation, he went on to predict that if a crash occurred, factories would shut down, unemployment would rise and the result would be a serious business depression.

Two things immediately happened following Babson's predictions. First, when news reached Wall Street, the market fell sharply by 3 percent, a fall now known as the Babson Break, and this notwithstanding that Babson's views were fairly well known on the Street. The New York Times, for one, was surprised at the market's reaction: *"It seems incongruous that Wall Street...should have taken fright at the remarks of a statistician for whose judgment it has shown little respect in the past"* it opined.

Secondly, scorn was poured down on the head of poor Babson. Irving Fisher, one of America's most noted economists contradicted Babson's views a few hours after his speech: *"There may be a recession in stock prices"* Fisher admitted, *"but not anything in the nature of a crash."* Wall Street wanted to listen to Fisher and not to Babson. Scorn throughout much of Wall Street became outright derision the next day as the market staged an abrupt turnaround, recouping much of the losses of the previous day. Financial editorials were published suggesting that no one acquainted with the notorious inaccuracy of Babson's previous statements should take him seriously.

Once again, the markets seemed to have stood at the edge of the abyss and then turned away at the last moment. But as in the case of the falls in March, when Mitchell had intervened, the entire episode left Wall Street feeling distinctly nervous and the markets unsettled. The next few weeks saw a series of sharp falls followed by minor rallies, though trading volumes remained high; by the middle of September, many observers were conceding that there was now no precedent for current market conditions. The last week of September saw further sharp falls and minor rallies, and the month ended with the Dow Jones having lost 36.88 points. Yet at the same time, brokers' loans had increased to a record level of $6.76 billion. Private investors and institutions were still buying on margin.

Chapter 5 Like a Bolt out of Hell

"Stock prices have reached what looks like a permanently high plateau. I do not feel that there will soon, if ever, be a fifty or sixty point break below present levels, such as Mr. Babson has predicted. I expect to see the stock market a good deal higher than it is today within a few months."

Professor Irving Fisher (1867 – 1947) – Statement on 15th October 1929, quoted in the New York Times

Black Thursday

The beginning of the end came on 24th October 1929 – Black Thursday as it became known. For the previous few weeks, the decline in the stock market that had manifested itself in September as a series of sharp falls followed by rallies had continued. As the market staggered downwards, many small investors who had bought on margin earlier in the year were now finding their margins evaporating, and were facing demands for more money from their brokers; those unable to find additional funds were already in the process of being wiped out. Then, on Friday 18th October, the fall accelerated, with heavy volumes of selling being reported on exchanges across the country, a trend that continued into the short trading session held on Saturday, with the ticker once more lagging well behind actual trading. By the end of that session, the Dow Jones had fallen to 323.87 (28.82 points down from the previous week) and all but the most extremely bullish traders were now openly referring to the existence of a bear market.

Many spent the rest of that weekend in fear, hoping against hope that the markets would recover on the Monday; they were doomed to disappointment, for prices continued to fall when the markets opened on Monday morning, as investors tried to escape while they could. More than 6 million shares were traded, the third highest trading volume recorded up to that time. Again, as the day progressed, the ticker fell behind, adding to the confusion. Then Professor Fisher commented that the falls represented only *"the shaking out of the lunatic fringe"*. Perhaps people believed him because towards the end of the day, prices recovered a little, but not enough to offset more than a small fraction of the losses of the day; the rally, such as it was, continued into Tuesday, 22nd October. That was the day on which Charlie Mitchell returned to New York from a vacation in Europe and told the press that he thought *"the decline had gone too far"*. Babson, on the other hand, urged investors to sell their stocks and buy gold.

Wednesday, 23rd October started quietly and ended horribly. Initial trading was light, but as the session progressed, sales of shares increased dramatically, led by a sharp sell-off of automobile stocks. Brokers and their clients were unable to keep track of price movements as the ticker fell more than two hours behind; bad snowstorms disrupting communications in the Midwest made matters worse. The last hour of trading was little more than carnage, with more than 2.5 million shares traded in that hour alone. The day as a whole once again saw more than 6 million shares sold, the Dow Jones falling by more than 20 points (the greatest daily fall seen up to that time) and $4 billion wiped off share prices. The Times industrial average fell 18.24. Writer and historian Frederick Lewis Allen subsequently called the events of the day *"a perfect Niagara of liquidation"*.

The big question that evening was how the markets would react on the following morning. Brokers throughout the country were awash with shares that they had already seized by way of foreclosure from investors who had been unable to honour their margin commitments, and inundated with unexecuted sell orders from other clients now desperate to escape – all those shares would have to be sold into the market the next day. Even as people speculated as to what would happen when all those shares hit the market, further margin calls were flooding out from brokerage offices to frightened clients, calls which would, one way or another, generate yet more sell orders in the morning. Then there were those investors in the Midwest who had been unable to contact their brokers thanks to the snowstorms – how would they react when they heard the news of the market falls? And what was the position of the principal Wall Street players – the major banks and other institutions? Many were seen as remaining eager to purchase securities. They also had substantial reserves of free cash and the powerful incentive of not wanting to see their existing share portfolios fall any further. How would they react?

The magnitude of the collapse in share prices that Wednesday had, to some extent, caught Wall Street by surprise and there had been no sign of, or indeed an opportunity for, any form of coordinated response to the market falls.

Now, on Wednesday evening, rumours abounded as to whether the rich and powerful were prepared and able to provide organised support for the market in the morning so as to stabilise prices. Older denizens of Wall Street were in demand as they recalled J P Morgan Sr.'s personal intervention during the Panic of 1907. Then, Morgan had organised a response by the banking community to a falling market which was credited with halting the Panic in its tracks. But by October 1929, J P Morgan Sr. had been dead for more than 16 years, and the days in which a private individual or even a group of private individuals, no matter how wealthy or influential, could dictate the market's behaviour had passed into financial folklore, never to return. Desperation caused many to overlook this fact, and their collective gaze fell on Charlie Mitchell and other leading Wall Street men as potential saviours. Nevertheless, that evening, there was no sign of a coordinated response from any of the leaders of Wall Street. Meanwhile, the Federal Reserve, the body that should have been taking measures to restore financial stability (or at least have been giving an impression of doing so) true to recent form did little but watch and wait.

Inevitably, in the absence of any kind of official statement or apparent coordinated plan of action, people feared the worst. Early on Thursday morning, before the trading session opened, small groups of people began to gather in Wall Street and the surrounding financial district, anxious to witness the events of the day for themselves. They were later joined by police officers, posted at regular intervals along the streets by the city authorities who were concerned that further market falls could lead to civil unrest, and by newspaper reporters and motion picture cameras eager to record the anticipated turmoil of the day. Investors, great and small, thronged brokers' and investment managers' offices waiting for the stock tickers to begin churning out their messages of hope or despair. The atmosphere was tense and apprehensive, the trading floor of the New York Stock Exchange crowded; NYSE Supervisor William R Crawford remembered afterwards that it was as though *"there was electricity in the air so thick you could cut it"*. Other observers recalled a silence that descended upon the waiting crowds as the clocks ticked steadily towards the hour of 10.00 am, when Crawford would ring the gong signifying that the floor of the New York Stock Exchange was open for trading.

At 10.00 am precisely, Crawford struck the gong and the market opened, a broker subsequently claimed, *"like a bolt out of hell"*. A cacophony of sell orders poured forth, and the day's trading was underway. For the first few minutes, it seemed to more optimistic observers that prices were holding up surprisingly well, despite the heavy volume of trading, which saw more than 1.5 million shares sold in the first half hour. Gradually though, prices began to sag as wave after wave of sell orders from all over the country buffeted the market. Many of those orders were to sell "at the market", that is, for the best price that could be found. But now traders were finding there were too few buyers, and large blocks of shares that would have been snapped up only a few months ago now failed to find buyers at any price, depressing the market further. This in turn generated yet more unmet margin calls which led to yet more sell orders. And so a cycle of sell orders triggering price falls which in turn triggered yet more sell orders was quickly established. Meanwhile, bearish speculators were selling the market short, intent on extracting what value they could from the collapsing stocks, which caused prices to fall even further.

By 11.30 am, carnage had again returned to the floor of the New York Stock Exchange. The ticker, falling further and further behind actual trading, was now running 48 minutes late; brokers throughout the country were finding it impossible to get accurate quotes or to appraise prices. They only knew that prices were lower than the ticker was depicting, and were continuing to fall. The mood on the trading floor had now moved beyond fear; amongst the screaming bedlam there was actual panic on the part of many, hysteria on the part of some. News of the collapse had by now spread to the general public and the early onlookers in the streets outside the Exchange were joined by many more, milling about and exchanging frightening rumours of suicides and failures. So many tried to enter the Exchange's spectators' gallery to see events for themselves that officials were obliged to close it,[40] fuelling rumours that the Exchange itself had been forced to suspend trading.

By noon, more than $9.5 billion had been wiped off share prices and prices were still falling, both in New York and on other exchanges throughout the

---

[40] Amongst those who had managed to cram himself inside the gallery before it closed was Winston Churchill, then on a lecture tour of the United States.

country. At that time, however, a group of the country's leading bankers were gathering at the offices of J P Morgan & Co, namely Thomas Lamont, Morgan's senior partner (J P Morgan Jr. then being in Europe), Albert Wiggin, (Chairman of the Chase National Bank), Seward Prosser, (Chairman of the Bankers' Trust), William Potter (President of the Guaranty Trust) and (inevitably) Charlie Mitchell. They spoke privately for twenty minutes (no written record of the meeting was kept), and then the four visitors departed, leaving their host Lamont to face a press conference. Utilising a gift for understatement that ensured his comments to the waiting reporters would forever be remembered within the financial annals of America, Lamont conceded *"There has been a little distress selling on the Stock Exchange..."* but insisted it was the consensus of the bankers who had gathered *"that many of the quotations on the Stock Exchange do not fairly represent the situation..."* He assured the reporters that the group of bankers had decided to act to improve matters. When news of this reached the trading floor, stock prices slowed, and in some cases halted their downward plunges as brokers, traders and investors alike waited to see what would happen next.

They did not have to wait long. At 1.30 pm, Richard Whitney, vice president of the Exchange, acting on instructions from the bankers who had met at Morgan's, walked onto the trading floor and up to the trading post for US Steel. Coolly, conspicuously, he bid 205 for 10,000 shares in the company, though the price had already slipped below 200. He then made the rounds of other trading posts, placing bids for shares of other major blue chip companies, until he had placed more than $20 million-worth of orders.

The result was dramatic; traders and brokers concluded that here was the organised support that they had been awaiting. Anticipating a re-run of the events during the Panic of 1907 following Morgan's intervention, they immediately initiated a burst of buying. Prices rallied, and though sell orders continued to pour in from across the country, by the time trading had ended at 3pm, the market had clawed back nearly all the losses of the day, with the Dow Jones closing a mere 6.38 points down on the day. The Times average was down 12 points. Some major stocks (including US Steel) actually showed small gains on the day. It was a day that had seen 12.9 million shares change hands (a new record), and the ticker kept running until 7.08 pm, more than 4 hours after trading had ended.

The rally had come too late to save thousands of investors – the minnows – who had already been broken by the financial demands of unmet margin calls; nevertheless, for many on Wall Street, and in financial centres across the country, there was on the evening of Black Thursday widespread, in some cases perhaps even incredulous relief that the intervention seemed to have succeeded. There was praise for Lamont and his fellow bankers for organising their intervention, and encouragement was drawn from their announcement that they and other bankers were organising a new pool of funds and were ready to intervene again if necessary.[41]

There was even hope on the part of some that a corner had been turned, and that better times for the market lay ahead. Certainly this was the general tenor of the various public pronouncements issued that evening and the next day by a host of notables, many of whom stressed that they considered that the "fundamentals" underpinning the stock market, and the American economy generally, were sound. Amongst those who expressed such views was President Hoover, who declared *"The fundamental business of the country, that is the production and distribution of commodities, is on a sound and prosperous basis"*. He declined to comment on the specifics of the stock market however.

The market's behaviour the next day, and during the short session on Saturday appeared to justify such a positive outlook. It seemed the relentless price falls were over, for the markets opened firmly on Friday and at the end of the day's trading, the Dow Jones closed up 1.75 points and the Times industrial average up 0.79 points. Admittedly, during Saturday's trading session, the Dow Jones fell back 2.25 points, (and the Times industrial average fell 2.63 points) but compared to the events of the previous few days, this was widely accepted as a most acceptable example of price stability. True too, trading volumes remained relatively high, with nearly 6 million shares traded on the Friday, and more than 2 million on the Saturday. It seemed that there were still sellers anxious to

---

[41] Such praise did not extend to the Federal Reserve, which again had been silent during the events of the day, notwithstanding widespread hopes that it would support the market by reducing the rediscount rate. It took no such step.

escape the market while they could, but for now at least, there were buyers willing to take their stocks. Perhaps the crisis was over after all, and calmer times lay ahead?

That weekend saw the financial press indulge itself in a frenzy of opinion and speculation. Praise continued to be lavished on the bankers who had sponsored Whitney's buying spree (which the bankers gravely accepted as being only their due), while explanations were sought as to the market's behaviour. It was generally accepted that speculation was to blame, and that speculation had led to excessive price rises - the "price corrections" of the previous few weeks had therefore been necessary and even desirable as a means of eliminating "the gambling type of speculator". Alfred Sloan of General Motors spoke for many when he declared the market turmoil as being "a healthy thing", before going on to say that he hoped that people would now get back to work rather than continue to cherish the idea that it was possible to get rich overnight. Nobody expected a return of the full-blown bull market, but the consensus of the expert commentators on the weekend following Black Thursday was that calmer times lay ahead. Some that weekend even predicted a buying bonanza when the markets opened on Monday – after all, shares were now cheaper than they had been for months or even years, and wouldn't investors be bound to be keen to snap them up at their new bargain basement prices? But the suspension of trading that weekend also gave surviving investors a chance to pull themselves together after the nightmare of the past week, and the opportunity to assess their positions in the light of changed circumstances and to plan their next steps. Investors that weekend had to choose between following the optimistic notes sounding in the popular press, or to heed the unease and pessimism that was now lurking in many of their hearts. And many, given the opportunity of a brief respite, decided (if they had not already decided before) that enough was enough. It was time to leave the party.

Black Tuesday

One of the notable features of the Wall Street Crash, and the immediate months that followed it, was that whenever a key event in the saga occurred (such as Black Thursday), most people would persuade themselves that the worst had now arrived, that a turning point had been reached, that affairs simply couldn't get any worse and that thereafter (perhaps not rapidly, but inevitably) matters would begin to improve. Time and time again in the months and years that followed, such hopeful optimism was to prove to be misplaced, for as J K Galbraith subsequently observed, a singular feature of the Crash was that *"the worst continued to worsen"*. That this was so was demonstrated by the events of Monday, 28th October. Before the day's trading started, many brokers and traders had been quietly optimistic that prices would remain firm, and that the day would essentially be a repeat of the previous Friday; after all, little or nothing of substance appeared to have changed. That something had changed became apparent from the start of trading, for as the gong sounded, sell orders began to sound out. Once more, few buyers were to be found, and by mid-morning, as prices plummeted, the scenes on the floor and other exchanges throughout the country were reminiscent of those of the morning of Black Thursday. They were, perhaps, worse. And this time, the falls in prices were far steeper – one observer described them as falling *"almost perpendicularly"*.

Again brokers, traders and investors looked for signs of organised support for the market, and there was a brief flurry of hope at 1.10 pm when Charles Mitchell was seen to enter Morgan's office. But this time no one stepped forward to proffer support, and share prices continued to tumble, even those of the most conservative blue chip companies which hitherto had been the least affected by the recent turmoil in the market. Again, a flood of unmet margin calls helped to depress prices even further.[42] In the last hour of trading alone, nearly 3 million shares changed hands (and it almost goes without saying that the ticker once again fell well behind events); the day as a whole saw nearly 9.25 million shares traded. That was fewer than on Black Thursday, but with no last minute rally, the losses that Monday were far worse: by the end of the day's trading, the Dow Jones had fallen 38.33 points (a new record, representing a 12.82 percent fall) , closing at 260.64. Likewise, the Times average fell 29.22 points closing at 224.33. More than $14 billion of share values had been lost. This time, noticeably, it was the blue chips which had

---

[42] So many margin calls were issued by telegraph that Western Union was obliged to hire a fleet of taxis to help with their delivery.

particularly suffered: General Electric was down 47½ points, Westinghouse 34½, US Steel 17½, Union Carbide 20, and Eastman Kodak 41. Nearly all the minnow investors had long since departed the scene, many of them bankrupted, and it was the investors with the deepest pockets, the major Wall Street operators, the wealthy magnates and the financial institutions (who so far by and large had managed to ride out the storm) who now suffered.

At 4.30 pm that afternoon, after the day's trading had ended but while the ticker was still scrambling to catch up, the bankers who had led the intervention on Black Thursday assembled once more at Morgan's offices, and again, after a meeting of nearly two hours, Thomas Lamont faced the awaiting reporters. On this occasion, he stressed the group's desire to maintain an "orderly market" rather than maintain prices. The market, he argued, had continued to function as it should, albeit with sharp price falls; there had therefore been no need for the group to intervene that day. Other than making a generalised observation that there would no doubt be some people interested in buying shares at the right price, he declined to speculate as to what would happen the next day.

The truth was that the bankers had accepted that they could not prevent the market from falling further if a sufficient number of shareholders decided to sell. Nobody could. All they could do was to try to avoid unsettling the markets any more than they had to, while trying to protect their own investment positions as best they could. That evening, though some newspapers hopefully suggested that some form of organised support might manifest itself the next day, no realistic newspaper reader who read an account of Lamont's statement to the press could doubt that the bankers had decided to step aside and allow prices to fall as they would.

The following day, 29th October 1929 – Black Tuesday – saw a continuation of the falling market. It would indeed be remembered as one of the very worst in Wall Street history, and saw the Dow Jones tumble by a further 30.57 points, to close at 230.07 representing a 11.73 percent fall.[43] The falls would have been

---

[43] The Times industrial average fell 24.66 points to 199.67, a figure not seen since August 1928. For many years, history books recorded 29th October 1929 as the worst day in Wall Street history (notwithstanding that the price falls of Monday, 28th October

even worse but for a short rally fifteen minutes before trading ended. The trading volume was far greater than had ever been seen before: more than 16.4 million shares changed hands that day on the New York Stock Exchange alone (and a further 7 million on the curb) and America's stock tickers issued more than 15,000 miles of paper tape. Once again, large losses were also recorded on other exchanges throughout the country, and in Canada and (once the news had crossed the Atlantic, which didn't take long) in London.

Another $14 billion dollars of stock value had been lost while chaos and hysteria once more held sway on America's trading floors. And this time, it wasn't merely the volume of trading that was noticeable, but also the size of the sale orders that had been generated: blocks of 1,000, 5,000, 25,000 and even 50,000 shares were dumped into the market for sale at market price. It was clear that the large institutions and big Wall Street players had decided they had suffered enough and were now trying to escape the market literally at any price. In the process fortunes were lost in minutes.

The collapse in share prices was exacerbated by the reappearance of a phenomenon that had first been noted on Black Thursday and which the bankers who had gathered at Morgan's had been pledged to fight: "air holes", where traders offering stock for sale could literally find no willing buyer. This was something that was not supposed to happen in an orderly market but it happened on Black Tuesday and Lamont and his colleagues were powerless to stop it. The result was almost perpendicular price falls.[44]

Lamont, Mitchell and their fellow bankers met twice during Black Tuesday, at noon and in the late afternoon following the end of the trading session at 3

1929 had been even worse), until the events of Black Monday, 19th October 1987 which saw the stock market lose over $500 billion of value, with the Dow Jones falling 22.6 percent. However, unlike the case in 1929, the market soon rebounded from the 1987 fall, so perhaps Black Tuesday still deserves to retain its title.

[44] The extent of the collapse in prices, and the chaos in the market can be gauged by the tale of the enterprising messenger boy at the Exchange, who for a joke, called out a bid of $1 a share for a block of 100 shares of White Sewing Machine; he got it, for no other buyer could be found. A few weeks before, the company had been valued at $48 a share, and even on the Monday before Black Tuesday, its shares had been selling at more than $11 a share.

pm, but their meetings produced little of substance. This time, when Lamont faced the press after the end of the second meeting, he found himself having to defend not only the non-intervention of the group in the market, but also accusations that they had been short-selling stock. Lamont denied the accusations of short selling (although it later transpired that Albert Wiggin of the Chase National Bank had been quietly selling the stock of his own bank short since early September); the prestige which the group had garnished for their actions on the previous Thursday disappeared overnight.

It is not, however, true to say that no bankers stepped up to the mark on that fateful day. The collapse in share prices on Monday 28th October and Black Tuesday was bad enough, but unbeknownst to many, falling share prices were not the only danger facing the market at that time. Ever since the events of Black Thursday, many of the financial institutions and corporations that had been lending funds to the brokers' loans market had been developing cold feet about the practice, and had been steadily pulling out. As they had been providing nearly 60 percent of the funding for margin loans before Black Thursday, this withdrawal of financial support led to the threat of a dangerous credit vacuum developing, even though demand for margin loans fell dramatically after 23rd October. This danger had been recognised by George Harrison, who had succeeded Benjamin Strong as the President of the New York Federal Reserve Bank the previous year. Harrison (with the support of his fellow directors but without the prior approval of the Federal Reserve Board itself) unilaterally announced that the New York Federal Reserve Bank would purchase $100 million worth of US Government securities and use these assets to fill any vacuum which might threaten to develop. In doing so, Harrison (and some of the New York commercial banks who also made credit available) fended off what could have been a sharp credit crunch, which almost certainly would have made the events of Black Tuesday far worse than they actually were. Harrison received little or no public recognition for his actions that day.

On the evening of Black Tuesday, the newspapers again published reports suggesting that the worst had been seen, that the bottom of the market had now been reached, and that the stock market falls now represented a marvellous buying opportunity. Many newspapers emphasised the fact that the underlying economy was still functioning, as indeed were the institutions on Wall Street itself. That latter point in particular was true and was, rightly, a source of pride for workers on Wall Street (albeit the financial machinery of Wall Street and the country's other exchanges had been strained to their utmost by the market falls of the past few days). By now, however, anyone and everyone connected with the stock market was showing signs of extreme exhaustion. It seemed clear that the human elements of Wall Street could not continue to work at the pace demanded of them over the past few weeks without some respite. Some of the telegraph operators employed by various brokerage operations had been working without sleep for more than thirty hours. Clerks and secretaries were collapsing at their desks, their work unfinished, and had to be sent home. Traders and brokers were making mistakes as they tried to function amidst the chaos; sell and buy orders were becoming lost or misquoted with increasing frequency.

It was not, however, bad for all: local restaurants abandoned their normal working hours, and stayed open for business (with packed tables) until the early hours of the morning. Local hotels found themselves fully occupied as Wall Street firms block-booked their rooms so that at least some of their staff could sleep without having to waste time commuting home. And local speakeasies found there was great demand for their services; if ever there was a night when a man needed a drink, it was the evening of Tuesday, 29th October 1929.

Then, almost miraculously, Wednesday brought some much needed relief to the exhausted denizens of Wall Street. The start of the day saw a flurry of buy orders, and buy orders continued to appear during much of the rest of the day. This was followed at 2 pm by news reaching the floor of the Exchange that John D Rockefeller Sr., one of the principal founders of the Standard Oil empire and a tycoon who had been increasingly reclusive for a number of years, had been persuaded to make a public statement intended to promote public confidence in the stock market. "*These are days when many are discouraged*" Rockefeller declared. "*In the ninety years of my life, depressions have come and gone. Prosperity has always returned, and will again. Believing that the fundamental conditions of the country are sound and that there is nothing in the business situation to warrant the destruction of values that has taken place on the exchanges during the past week, my son*[45] *and I have for some days been purchasing sound common stocks.*" Comedian Eddie Cantor (who himself lost a small fortune during the Crash) later responded to this with the jibe: "*Sure – who else has got any money left?*" Rockefeller's statement seemed in accord with the mood on Wall Street and the buying spree continued, encouraged perhaps by the news that the Exchange's governing committee, who had been weighing up the merits of shutting down the Exchange for a few days, had decided that the floor should only open for three hours on Thursday and be closed on the following Friday and Saturday to allow everyone a chance to recover from the events of the last few days and to put their affairs in order (for many brokerage houses and other financial institutions were now desperately behind in their paperwork and records keeping). The news was greeted with cheers on Wall Street, and other exchanges throughout the country hurried to make similar announcements.

The day's trading closed with the Dow Jones showing a rise of 28.40 and the Times average 17.66, with 10.7 million shares traded. Thursday brought more good news: the Federal Reserve Board published figures to show (unsurprisingly) that the demand for brokers' loans had fallen by more than $1 billion over the previous week, and that it judged it safe to reduce the rediscount rate from 6 percent to 5 percent. Many thought that was too little, too late, but share prices continued to rise on the back of brisk trading; the volume for the day was more than 7 million though the trading floor had only been open for three hours. Remarkably, by the time trading ended that day and for the month of October 1929, the Dow Jones was showing a rise of 15.04 points on the day, closing at 273.51 while the Times average rose 12.67 points, closing at 230. This represented a recovery by the Dow Jones of more than 63 percent of the losses sustained on the previous Monday and Tuesday. Similarly, the Times average had recovered 56 percent of the losses of the first two days of the week.

But this was cold comfort to those who had lost fortunes in the Crash and the partial recovery in prices during the last two days of the month could not hide

---

[45] John D Rockefeller Jr., to whom his father had by now passed the bulk of his fortune and philanthropic commitments.

the gaping wounds torn in the stock market that signified, unequivocally, the end of the bull market of the 1920s. Trading that month had exceeded a volume of 142 million shares, a record, and one that would not be broken until the mid-1960s. For the month of October 1929 as a whole, the Dow Jones had lost 69.06 points and the Times average 57.70, and all the gains in share prices recorded in 1929 had been lost. Yet both indices still stood higher than they had in the autumn of 1928. The question now facing Wall Street was whether the gains of 1928 and before were also about to be lost.[46]

No Respite

Predictably, the newspapers that first weekend of November 1929 were once more filled with analyses and reports suggesting that the worst was now over, that prices were stabilising, that the future was brighter. The Ford Motor Company chose that weekend to announce a reduction in the prices of several of its models, describing this as a contribution to the *"...continuation of good business..."* Messages of hope and encouragement were also heard from other quarters, and some talked hopefully of stacks of buy orders waiting to be issued on Monday morning. But the newspapers were also reporting the collapse of the Foshay business consortium of Minneapolis, valued at $20 million, and when the markets opened on Monday morning for another day of restricted trading it rapidly became clear that prices once more were on a downwards slide, fuelled at least in part by brokerage houses who had spent the weekend updating their records and issuing yet more margin calls. Unmet margin calls in turn led to another flood of sell orders hitting the market, overwhelming such buy orders as there were, and by the end of the day, the Dow Jones stood at 257.68 having lost a further 25.55 points. The Times average had similarly shed 22.96 points to close at 217.59. The New York

---

[46] By now, the newspapers (both domestic and foreign) were reporting with relish stories about the suicides of ruined speculators, creating a myth that has lasted to this day. While there were some suicides, they were by no means as widespread as is generally believed, and as J K Galbraith has pointed out, the suicide rates in the summer months preceding the Crash were actually higher than in the months of October and November. Suicides rates did rise markedly in 1930, 1931 and 1932, and can be linked to the effects of the Depression.

Stock Exchange was closed on Tuesday, 5th November 1929 due to the city's Mayoral elections (in which incumbent Democratic Mayor Jimmy Walker convincingly beat Republican challenger Fiorello La Guardia), but when the markets reopened on Wednesday, the downwards plunge in prices continued, with the Dow Jones falling another 25.55 points and the Times average 22.96. A brief rally on Thursday 7th November was followed by further minor falls on Friday, and much more serious falls on the Monday, Tuesday and Wednesday of the following week. The market closed that Wednesday with the Dow Jones at 198.69 and the Times average at 166.15. Nearly all the gains recorded in 1928 had indeed been lost, and lost within the space of a few days.

Finally, Thursday 14th November 1929 saw a halt to the downward slide in prices that had dominated the previous three weeks, and an end to the 1929 Crash (though no one knew it at the time) attributable in part, according to some commentators, to several pieces of good news. The Rockefeller family, horrified at the collapse in the price of Standard Oil stock, had intervened the previous day to support the stock by placing an order for a million shares at 50 cents a share.[47] At almost the same time, the Federal Reserve Board announced a further reduction in the rediscount rate to 4.5 percent. General Motors announced it was paying a special dividend of 30 cents a share. And in Washington, Treasury Secretary Mellon announced proposals to reduce personal income and corporate tax rates by 1 percent, subject to the ratification of Congress. The market responded by rising over the following few weeks in a series of staggered jerks, punctuated with sickening if relatively shortlived falls, with the Dow Jones closing at the end of the year at 248.88 (58.53 points below its position at the start of the year). The Times average showed a fall of 28.4 points over the year, closing at 206.4. At these levels, both indices were still higher than they had been at the beginning of 1928.[48]

---

[47] Before the Crash, the stock had been selling at 83 cents a share. By April 1932, it was being valued at 19⅞.

[48] The Crash may have ended on 14th November 1929, but this did not prevent a further decline in stock prices over the next few years as the Great Depression took its toll on America. The Dow Jones would finally reach a low of 41.22 on 8th July 1932, representing the loss of 32 years of share price gains.

Some observers tried to take comfort from this. Alexander Noyes of the New York Times predicted the return of *"quiet and normal markets"*; others pointed to the absence of major bank failures which had accompanied previous stock market panics. Although it was anticipated that demand for luxury goods might falter, at first it seemed as though the Crash would have little impact on unemployment levels. But the Crash had wreaked its damage nonetheless. Over the few weeks of the Crash, exuberance and confidence seemed to have been banished from Wall Street, to be replaced with fear and uncertainty, and this was soon replicated in the country at large. And in the wake of such fear and uncertainty came the first indications of an economic slowdown.

Chapter 6 The Onset of the Depression

"Once upon a time my political opponents honored me as possessing the fabulous intellectual and economic power by which I created a worldwide depression all by myself."
President Herbert Hoover (1874 –1964)

"No one in his place could have done more"

President Hoover is often pictured as a man content to play a supine role in the months immediately following the Great Crash, firm in his belief that there was little that could be done to avoid the consequences of the stock market collapse, and at best indifferent to the business failures and rising unemployment in the world beyond the gates of the White House. This picture is inaccurate; Hoover was well aware in November and December 1929 that America stood on the brink of a financial apocalypse, and was determined to do all he could to ensure that the country avoided such a disaster. Such determination was fully in accord with the principles he had been expounding for years, and his belief that while there was a role for the Federal Government to play in assisting businesses, business problems were usually best solved by businesses themselves adopting sensible measures and working together in a spirit of cooperation. Thus, while he anticipated the probable need for some government support and guidance following the Crash (subject always to maintaining a balanced federal budget), he believed that in the final analysis, recovery could only be achieved by the efforts of American businesses and the American people themselves. *"...Mr Hoover"* declared one journalist writing for the New Republic magazine in December 1929 *"is apparently to try the experiment of seeing what business can do when given the steering wheel. Mr Hoover insists that there should be a steering wheel but he will let business do the driving..."*

President Hoover wasn't alone in his views in the winter of 1929, but many other political leaders and influential businessmen at that time held more orthodox opinions, believing that they faced a typical business downturn and that the situation simply required the usual response to such downturns, namely cautious retrenchment in the form of cutting orders, slowing production, reducing wages and laying off workers. Treasury Secretary Andrew Mellon, true to form, was an outspoken and extreme proponent of this approach and advised the President to *"liquidate labor, liquidate stocks, liquidate farmers, liquidate real estate."* This would he argued *"purge the rottenness out of the system. High costs of living and high living will come down. People will work harder, live a more moral life. Values will be adjusted, and enterprising people will pick up from less competent people."* Adopting any other course of action, Mellon believed, would simply interfere with the natural business cycle and delay the onset of any recovery.

Hoover wasn't prepared to go as far as his Treasury Secretary advocated (and in his memoirs, he stated that he rejected Mellon's advice), and argued that the Federal Government should use its powers to "cushion" the nation from the economic shock of the Crash. He was particularly worried that the new mood of pessimism and fear that had seemingly and almost overnight replaced the boundless confidence and hope of the boom years would lead to businessmen adopting too cautious and timid an approach. Laying off too many workers, shutting down too many plants and factories, inhibiting their abilities to respond positively to the downturn, and would possibly trigger the very state of affairs – a severe depression – that they most feared. As Christmas approached, he had, he believed, ample evidence that this process had started; steel production was falling rapidly, as were exports, and automobile manufacturers were already reporting a sharp decline in the sales of new and second-hand cars as unemployment started to rise and ordinary people and businesses alike began to restrain their spending. Demand for luxury goods had (as predicted) evaporated almost overnight. Although there were aspects of the economy that still seemed relatively healthy – the banking sector for instance continued to perform well, interest rates were still relatively low, credit was freely available and the basic production facilities of the country remained intact – Hoover knew that fear of the unknown could pose a greater threat to the American economy than the losses sustained in the Crash. Then it had been investors who chiefly suffered; a loss of confidence in the essential economic well-being of America could threaten everyone.

It was the job of the Federal Government, Hoover concluded, and thus pre-eminently his job, to lead the nation (and to be seen to lead the nation) in such a way as to restore confidence in the economy. As a first step to achieving this goal, he announced that he was summoning business and government leaders to a series of conferences to be held during a two-week period starting on 19th

November 1929 to discuss the economic situation and the prospects for the country, and to agree a plan of action. *"Any lack of confidence in the economic future or the basic strength of business in the United States is foolish"* he declared. *"Our national capacity for hard work and intelligent cooperation is ample guarantee for the future."* However, he went on to emphasise that *"words are not of any great importance in times of economic disturbance. It is action that counts."*

President Hoover's conferences appeared to be successful. Railroad companies agreed to spend in aggregate $1 billion in 1930 on capital improvement projects. This was matched, indeed surpassed by a similar pledge by the spokesmen for the utility companies who pledged to spend $1.8 billion during the following year. Adamant that the burden of the downturn should fall primarily on profits rather than jobs and wages, the President persuaded the gathered industrialists to agree not to sack workers; as a *quid pro quo*, union representatives agreed not to strike or to agitate for higher wages. State governors too promised to maintain public spending levels in their states so as to sustain local employment. It was Hoover's hope that by supporting normal levels of expenditure both by businesses and by the state and Federal Governments, the effects of the downturn could be countered by maintaining the purchasing power within the economy.

Other measures were also announced. At the Treasury, the Federal Government's finances were anticipated to show a surplus and Mellon proposed a reduction in both corporate and individual income tax rates of 1 percent, a measure Hoover had first mooted on 21st October 1929 and which Mellon insisted should be pursued despite the Crash. Hoover agreed with him, on the basis that lower taxes would allow greater spending on the part of both businesses and individuals alike. The Federal Farm Board (a body created before the Crash by Hoover himself with a mandate to attempt to support American agriculture and a budget of $500 million) promised to introduce measures intended to stabilise agricultural prices, particularly those of wheat and cotton which had been falling steadily since the early 1920s. And the Federal Reserve, having recently announced a cut to the rediscount rate, announced plans to ensure that credit remained available for legitimate business needs.

In his State of the Union Address to Congress given on 3rd December 1929, President Hoover surprised some observers by referring to the Crash and the subsequent downturn in restrained terms. He wrote afterwards that he did this so as not to *"add alarms to already rising fears."* Instead, after noting the dangers to the economy posed by unwarranted pessimism and fear, he announced a projected government surplus of $225 million by the end of 1930, and recommended Mellon's proposed tax cuts to Congress. He went on to summarise the results of his conferences, stating that he had already undertaken *"systematic, voluntary measures of cooperation with the business institutions and with State and municipal authorities to make certain that fundamental businesses of the country shall continue as usual, that wages and therefore consuming power shall not be reduced, and that a special effort shall be made to expand construction work in order to assist in equalizing other deficits in employment."*

President Hoover was breaking new ground in advocating that the Federal Government had a duty to use its powers to cushion the nation from the effects of the downturn. Previous Presidents in times of economic difficulty had tended to follow the orthodox view that downturns were part of the natural business cycle and (like Mellon) they had generally believed that interference on the part of the government in the business cycle would only make matters worse. Hoover, clearly, was not of this breed. However, in 1929 Hoover faced the significant difficulty that the powers of the Federal Government were circumscribed, as were its financial and administrative resources. Federal spending in 1929 accounted for less than 3 percent of the country's gross national product.[49] The instigation of construction programmes had long been regarded as a potentially powerful way of applying a stimulus to the economy, and yet federal spending on construction projects in 1929 amounted to a mere $200 million, while the individual states spent in aggregate a sum closer to $2 billion. In contrast, private industry spent $9 billion. During the 1920s, the Federal Government employed approximately 553,000 civilian employees[50] and there were no federal social welfare programmes (other than those provided to veterans and such assistance as could be provided by the

---

[49] By 1999, federal spending would amount to more than 20 percent of GNP.
[50] By 2010 the number of civilian federal employees had grown to more than 2 million.

Children's Bureau). There was no reliable unemployment data, and would not be any for several years. Even the ability of the Federal Government to control the Federal Reserve was (deliberately) limited, which in turn restricted the government's ability to influence the markets. Hoover and the Federal Government in December 1929 simply did not have the resources or the administrative machinery with which to launch major programmes of public spending designed to minimise the effects of the downturn. Furthermore, he was determined if at all possible to keep the federal budget in surplus, thus limiting even more his scope for action. Therefore, Hoover had little option but to seek the cooperation of the private sector. In practice, his ideological stance on the comparative roles of the government and private businesses would have impelled him to pursue such an approach in any event.

Congress responded positively to President Hoover's Address (indeed the House passed Mellon's tax reduction proposals without quibble within a few days); the press and the general public initially took a favourable view of his active leadership too. *"Too much praise cannot be given the President for the prompt and resolute and skilful way in which he set about reassuring the country after the financial collapse"* declared the New York Times. *"No one in his place could have done more; very few of his predecessors could have done as much."*

However, while Hoover was trying, with the scarce resources at his disposal, to coordinate a positive response by government and business to the downturn, a measure was passing through Congress that would make the financial landscape much bleaker, and help to transform the downturn into a full scale depression. This was the Hawley-Smoot tariff bill of 1929, introduced (originally with Hoover's blessing) by Oregon Congressman Willis C Hawley and Utah Senator Reed Smoot. The bill had been passed by the House in May 1929, and by December 1929, it was subject to debate in the Senate.

Despite vociferous complaints from her international trading partners, the United States had already in 1922 imposed formidably high tariffs on various imported goods under the terms of the Fordney-McCumber Tariff Act, the intention being to protect American agriculture as the post-First World War agricultural depression started to bite[51] and America slipped into isolationism. Inevitably, many of America's trading partners began to retaliate by imposing high duties of their own on imported American goods (France for example slapped a 100 percent tariff on American automobiles – much to the fury of Henry Ford who was firmly opposed to the Fordney-McCumber tariffs and had much to gain from being able to trade freely with France). Despite this, many Republicans (and some Democrats) deep in their isolationist dreams believed the Fordney-McCumber Act did not go far enough, and there were calls for still higher import duties. The result was the Hawley-Smoot bill. At the time of the 1929 presidential election, Hoover had publicly supported the proposals, not from any deeply-held belief in the value of high import duties as such, but mainly because he wanted to aid farmers by raising tariffs on some imported agricultural products (he was less convinced of the need for imposing higher duties on imported manufactured goods). He also saw the bill as a means of giving the Tariff Commission wider power to vary import duties without having to fight endless battles through Congress and hoped that once the bill was enacted, he would be able to use the Tariff Commission's new powers to lessen the effects of some of the more excessive tariff hikes.

Unfortunately, once President, Hoover was unable to control the passage of the bill through Congress as he had hoped. In May 1930, the Senate passed the bill in a form which would raise import duties to their highest levels in American history and sent it to Hoover for signature or veto.

By now, there was no shortage of people who could see that the effects of the bill would be catastrophic for both the United States and for the world. Republican Senator George Norris called it *"protectionism gone mad"*. Over a thousand economists sent a petition to Hoover begging him to veto *"the asinine Hawley-Smoot Tariff"*, as Thomas Lamont of J P Morgan & Co dubbed it. (Lamont later blamed the new tariffs for being at least partly responsible for the rise of extreme nationalism throughout the world in the 1930s). Henry Ford, by now incandescent with rage as to its potential effects travelled to the White House to make his opposition known, pointing out that the US

---

[51] Though many farmers opposed the tariffs, and blamed them for causing the agricultural depression in the first place.

automobile industry was the most powerful in the world and therefore needed no protection.[52]

President Hoover was by now no supporter of the bill, calling it *"vicious, extortionate and obnoxious"*; he feared its effects on international relations and he warned that other nations would be bound to retaliate. But he was unable to resist the pressure brought to bear on him by the Republican Party and isolationist business leaders and he eventually signed the bill into law as the US Tariff Act of 1930 on 17th June 1930.

The effects of the new tariffs were immediate and long-lasting. As well as France,, some of America's other trading partners had imposed retaliatory duties of their own on American products before Hoover signed the bill. Canada for example raised duties on more than one hundred classes of American products, accounting for approximately 30 percent of America's trade with her northern neighbour. Italy and Switzerland raised tariffs on American automobiles. Over the next few months other countries took similar steps, including Great Britain who, together with the other nations of the British Empire and Commonwealth, instituted the Imperial Preference System in 1932 effectively erecting a trading wall between the Empire and the rest of the world. As time went by, it became apparent that the new tariff barriers, both American and foreign, were having a devastating effect on international trade, which by some estimates dropped in value from approximately $36 billion in 1929 to $12 billion in 1932,[53] a decline of approximately 66 percent.

---

[52] Ironically, the tariffs raised by the French on American automobiles in response to the American actions probably did allow the French motor industry time to consolidate itself in the 1920s and 1930s by delaying the post-war penetration of the French market by Ford and the other major American car manufacturers. By the time the world had seen sense and began trying to dismantle barriers to international trade, the French had a thriving motor industry of their own which was quite capable at least in its domestic markets of giving the American car companies a good run for their money. Thus the American tariffs operated in this instance at least to protect overseas industries at the expense of their American counterparts.

[53] In which year incidentally both Hawley and Smoot ran for re-election but lost in the Democratic landslide, one of the reasons cited for their personal failures to gain re-election being their sponsorship of their tariffs bill.

According to the US Department of State, US imports from Europe declined from a high of approximately $1.3 billion in 1929 to $390 million in 1932; US exports to Europe fell from over $2.3 billion to $784 million over the same period. As trade began to stagnate, international relations began to worsen and the collapse in international trade represented yet another burden to be borne by the struggling economies of the world's trading nations. For Hoover, signing the Hawley-Smoot tariff bill into law represented the first of a series of major mistakes which would help to create the Great Depression.

Dark Times Approach

In the meantime Wall Street, rather to the surprise of some observers, had enjoyed something of a muted recovery in the first three months of 1930, though trading volumes were low in January and February (so low that during one day's trading in January, the ticker, far from falling behind trading actually paused because there were no new orders to report). Nevertheless, prices gradually edged upwards. It was a professionals' market, however, and one in which pessimism and fear continued to hold sway; the speculators had for the moment at least deserted the field. In March and April (perhaps encouraged by the New York Federal Reserve cutting the rediscount rate in February and then again in March so that it now stood at 3½ percent), trading volumes began to recover and on 13th April, the Times average reached a high for the year of 242.66. Two days later on 15th April the Dow Jones followed suit reaching 294.07 points.

This was encouraging news, but the overall economic picture continued to give cause for concern notwithstanding all of President Hoover's efforts. In January, Irving Fisher indicated that he had recanted his bullish optimism by predicting the onset of a major business depression within two years. In February, the American Federation of Labor estimated that there were more than 2.7 million unemployed men in the country, the unemployment total having risen from approximately 1.3 million in October 1929. As more and more people lost their jobs, breadlines began to appear in the major cities and despite the efforts of Hoover's Federal Farm Board, the agricultural depression deepened. In response to the rising gloom, the stock market began to fall back during the second half of April, with the Dow Jones closing at the end of the month at 279.23. The Times average closed at 232.18.

The beginning of May saw yet another reduction in the rediscount rate to 3 percent (accompanied by interest rate cuts in both London and Paris); the markets paid little attention and continued to fall, responding to the poor first quarter results that were now beginning to be reported. Sharp reported falls in exports (24 percent year on year) and imports (28 percent year on year) and a major decline in steel production added further cause for gloom. For the remainder of May, the stock market was depressed and the signing of the Hawley-Smoot tariff bill into law in June (something which Wall Street had long been dreading) prompted further falls. Even though the Federal Reserve cut the rediscount rate again to an unprecedented 2½ percent, the Dow Jones ended the month at 226.34. The Times average closed at 193. Most of the gains that had been made since the end of the Crash had now been lost once more. Also worrying was the continuing collapse in the prices of commodities such as zinc, tin, copper, rubber and lead due to a lack of industrial demand and many commodities were now trading at prices that had not been seen for at least a decade. It seemed as though every month brought further bad economic news and if Wall Street had been tempted to feel even the slightest degree of cautious optimism during the first few months of year, it had abandoned it by the end of June.

The Trials of President Hoover

President Hoover was right in identifying pessimism and fear as two of the forces driving the American economy down. For a brief moment following the State of the Union in December 1929, there had been a spark of hope on the part of many that the Government and businesses working together could save the economy, but before long, the limitations of the government became all too apparent. Hoover could talk and promise that matters would improve, even announce that they were improving (as he did on 1st May 1930 when he visited the American Chamber of Commerce and declared: *"I am convinced we have passed the worst and with continued effort we shall rapidly recover."*), but he was increasingly seen as delivering remarkably little. This view was bolstered by his determination to maintain a budget surplus; close observers noted that during the spring months of 1930, President Hoover began to talk less of federal spending on new projects and instead started to emphasise the need to reduce public expenditure, apparently oblivious to the effect this might have on the unemployment figures. An increasing lack of trust in the President only encouraged further pessimism and fear for the future, and Hoover's failure to veto the Hawley-Smoot tariff bill did little to help his reputation. By the end of June, his credibility in the eyes of the general public was falling fast.

To make matters worse, his relationship with the press, which for a long time had been generally positive, was also deteriorating. At the beginning of his administration, there had been a widespread expectation that his White House would be more open and transparent than that of Calvin Coolidge (indeed, during his very first press conference as President, Hoover had cheerfully announced new rules for the press room that had been widely welcomed by reporters). However as the weeks and months passed, many reporters began to believe that the Hoover administration was trying to manipulate them by interpreting the new rules in such a way as to restrict the amount of useful information being released. Some reporters claimed that the administration had reduced White House press conferences to little more than an arena in which were distributed presidential hand-outs, *"palpably propagandist in character"*. At the same time, there were accusations that Hoover favoured reporters who were willing to write stories that presented the facts as Hoover wished, granting them special access and private briefings in exchange for their cooperation.

Having a press that did not automatically hail him as a public saviour and a great leader was a new experience for Hoover and a disagreeable one. Unable by his nature to shrug off the criticisms as Coolidge would almost certainly have done, or essentially ignore them (as Harding would have done), convinced that he was right to operate within the strict parameters that he had set for himself (parameters which reflected values in which he had believed for many years), he reacted by withdrawing still further from the press. Such behaviour simply exacerbated the perception that the President was not keen on having his actions reported or questioned and was out of touch with the increasingly desperate situation beyond the gates of the White House. By the late spring of 1930, stories were beginning to appear challenging his leadership and the efficacy of the steps he was taking.

The downward slide in President Hoover's reputation, and increasing public doubts as to the ability of the Republican Party generally, were clearly seen in the results of the Congressional elections of November 1930, which saw the Republicans lose their absolute majorities in both the Senate and the House of Representatives. They fared worse in the House than the Senate, where with 48 Republicans to 47 Democrats (and one Farmer-Labor member) they could still claim nominal control over the Chamber. Nevertheless, even in the Senate, President Hoover could not rely on every Republican vote; by his estimate only 40 Senators were "reliable" – the remaining seven were "too left-wing" for his tastes, meaning that he judged them to be sympathetic to calls for increased federal spending to help the unemployed regardless of the effect that this was likely to have on the federal budget, an approach that continued to be anathema to him.

As for the House of Representatives, the results on election night showed that the Republicans had lost 52 seats. Notwithstanding such losses, they should still have retained sufficient seats to allow them a majority of one over their opponents in the House (218 Republicans to 216 Democrats, and one Farmer-Labor member). In fact, several representatives and representative-elects died before the 72nd Congress could be assembled. By the time it was assembled in December 1931 following several special elections for various vacant seats, the Democrats had gained control (by a slender margin) of the House of Representatives. The Democrats promptly elected as speaker Democratic Representative John Nance Garner of Texas, who was later to be President Franklin Roosevelt's Vice-President for two terms. As speaker for a Democratically-controlled House of Representatives, Garner was in a position to influence President Hoover's relations with Congress to a significant extent. Unsurprisingly, one of Garner's primary objectives once installed as speaker was to use all his powers to gain the White House for the Democrats, and notwithstanding that he agreed with President Hoover on the need to maintain a balanced federal budget (and indeed on several issues he seemed more right-wing than the President), he was soon to prove himself a major thorn in Hoover's side. *"I fought President Hoover with everything I had"* he later boasted.

By the beginning of December 1930, it was obvious that President Hoover was failing in his efforts to reverse the effects of the economic slump. While the continued absence of reliable data made it difficult to assess employment levels with certainty, by the measures then available, it seemed clear that unemployment rates were continuing to rise. Partly as a consequence of this, and partly because those Americans lucky enough still to be in work were choosing to save their money rather than spend it, consumer spending was sharply down. Corporate investment in plant and equipment was also falling, as were corporate profits, while federal and state spending levels were insufficient to make any noticeable difference to the economic outlook. Indeed, the need to provide basic relief to the growing ranks of the unemployed was increasingly swallowing up such public funds as were available, at the expense of public spending projects across the nation.

Nevertheless, even during the last months of 1930, it was still possible for people to conclude that what they were suffering was an ordinary economic downturn, albeit a severe one. And then, in the weeks of December 1930, a series of bank failures suddenly made it clear that America and the world was facing something far more serious than a traditional downturn, namely a worldwide economic slump of unprecedented scale.

Bank failures were, unfortunately, not uncommon in American life and even during the boom years of the 1920s, American banks had failed at a rate of approximately 650 a year, typically because of bad investments and unwise lending which led to liquidity problems and ultimately to the loss of customers' funds. The banks which failed were usually small rural banks with inadequate capital reserves operating outside of the scope of the regulations laid down by the Federal Reserve and the national banking system. Consequently, when they ran into difficulty, they were unable to take advantage of the protections offered by the Federal Reserve system. Nevertheless, while the collapse of these banks usually meant economic hardship for their customers and their local economies, such failures had relatively little effect on the wider banking system or the country at large.

In 1929, 659 American banks failed, a figure that was well within the range experienced over the previous ten years. The rate of bank failures continued to hold approximately steady for the first ten months of 1930, and then suddenly, the failure rate increased, with 600 banks failing in the last two months of the year. By the end of December 1930, 1,352 banks had closed their doors to business. The next year saw no relief: by the end of 1931, a further 2,294 banks had failed, spreading economic hardship in their wake.

The contagion of bank failures seemed to follow a broad general pattern. Many banks had been weakened as a consequence of the Crash. Any hint that a particular bank might be in trouble would instantly be spread as rumour (even if the bank in question was in no immediate difficulty at all), crowds of anxious depositors would appear seeking to withdraw their money and a bank run would be underway. Inevitably, the bank would not have sufficient liquid assets on hand to honour all the demands being made on it, and so it would seek to call in its outstanding loans and sell such assets as it had. This added to the financial burdens of its borrowers (typically farmers and local businessmen, but also home owners who had borrowed from the bank by way of mortgage) who might well be unable to repay their loans at that particular time. As a result, they went bankrupt and the banks would seek to seize as much of their property as they could. Mortgage foreclosures would depress the local property market and the local economy. This in turn would weaken the position of other local banks, and so the contagion would spread. In the meantime, the bank suffering the run would often find that even with the mortgage foreclosures and forced asset sales it could not meet the withdrawal demand and would have no choice but to shut its doors. When this happened, depositors would be lucky to recover even a small fraction of their deposits, causing yet more damage to the local economy and community. Unsurprisingly, as the rate of bank failures accelerated in the winter months of 1930, the public's faith in the American banking system dwindled rapidly.

At first, the burst of bank failures in November 1930 seemed largely to affect only rural banks in mid-western states such as Indiana, Illinois, Missouri and Iowa, and a few of the southern states such as Kentucky and Arkansas. Then, in early December, the perception of bank failures being principally a problem of the rural banking system was shattered when a rumour spread that the Bank of the United States in New York City, a bank which had been established in 1913 and had grown to be the third largest in New York, was in financial difficulty. The rumour was false – with deposits in excess of $280 million and over 60 branches, the Bank of the United States was in no more parlous a state than many other New York banks – nevertheless the result was a run on the bank on 10th December 1930, with thousands of people gathering at the bank's branches seeking to withdraw their deposits. On 11th December 1930, the bank's directors concluded that they had no choice but to shut the doors and call in the Superintendant of Banks to supervise the bank's assets. Wall Street reacted at once and negatively to the closure, with the bank's stock price dropping from $11.50 a share to $3.00 a share.

Half-hearted attempts were made to save the Bank of the United States through proposed rescue mergers with other banks, but none succeeded, partly it was alleged through anti-Semitism and class snobbery on the part of the traditional Wall Street houses. The Bank of the United States (which, despite its name had no connection with the US Government) had been established and was operated principally by Jews and had largely catered to the Jewish immigrant population, and according to some commentators was regarded by some of the more upper-crust banking institutions as an unfortunate intruder into New York's banking system, one perhaps less worthy of assistance than others. Whether this view was widespread is debateable; nevertheless, a general agreement seemed to be reached amongst would-be rescuers that the Bank of the United States should be abandoned to its fate, and so it was – the largest commercial bank failure in the United States up to that time. The result for the bank's 400,000 depositors was that many of them lost their lifetime savings. As for the banking system itself, the Federal Reserve's inability or unwillingness to organise a rescue of the Bank of the United States lessened public confidence in the Federal Reserve itself. Henceforth, banks would be more inclined to protect themselves whatever the cost might be to other banks, and the US banking system would be weaker as a result.[54]

Terrible though the bank failures of late 1930 were, there were again those who now hoped that this represented a final outbreak of economic malignity from the Crash of more than twelve months before. Again, for a brief moment, it appeared that the hopes of the optimists might be justified; the rate

---

[54] Adding to the sense of outrage on the part of those who criticised the failure of the traditional New York banking houses to rescue the Bank of the United States was the fact that other banks running into difficulties at this time did receive substantial support from their fellow banks.

of bank failures noticeably slowed during the first quarter of 1931, and economic activity seemed to be stabilising. But those hopes were rapidly dashed as the economy began once more to slump, and it became clear that the "economic downturn" was rapidly turning into a depression. Matters were made worse because it was now becoming apparent that the economic difficulties faced by America were not solely the result of home-grown "American" problems such as falling domestic demand for consumer goods, a failing banking system and a ten year agricultural depression – just as America's woes were affecting overseas countries, so too could events overseas have dire consequences for the United States. This had already been demonstrated by the overseas backlash against the Hawley-Smoot tariffs, which was crippling demand for American exports.

By the summer of 1931, it was apparent that Britain's return to the gold standard in 1926 had been a mistake. Gold was continuing to flow out of the country (largely in the direction of the United States) threatening Britain's economic stability. As a consequence (not for the first time, and certainly not for the last) the pound sterling was seen as being increasingly vulnerable on the world's currency exchanges, a state of affairs which posed its own set of economic dangers. Other countries, faced with similar difficulties, had already raised interest rates and imposed restrictions on the ability of investors to export gold but Britain, at the heart of a great empire and one of the mainstays of the world's financial network, had been reluctant to go too far down this road, not least because of the dangers that such actions could pose to the British economy in the wake of the downturn in world trade. Nevertheless, by the late summer of 1931, even British politicians could see that matters could not be allowed to continue as they were, and on 21st September, Britain abandoned the gold standard. She was rapidly followed by a number of other countries, including Japan and Sweden.

Britain's decision sent shockwaves through the world's already battered financial systems. World trade, already declining as a result of the hiking of tariff barriers, slowed still further. For the United States, this was serious but not in itself disastrous, as the country was not as dependent on foreign trade as some other countries; however, one effect of Britain's decision which did have serious repercussions in the United States was that foreign investors now began to withdraw their gold deposits from the United States. US depositors, seeing what was happening, hastened to do likewise. Capital thus began to drain out of the American economy. The Federal Reserve, observing the flow of gold out of the country, responded in the traditional way and raised the rediscount rate by one percent. This was a time when the American economy desperately needed cheap money; thanks to the actions of the Federal Reserve, America instead experienced a tightening of its money supply. The consequence was not only that America's businesses now found it harder to borrow money but also there was another burst of bank runs, far worse than that which had struck in November and December 1930. Over 500 American banks failed in October 1931; by the end of the year, 2,293 banks had closed their doors. America plunged deeper into depression.

Britain's escape from the straitjacket of the gold standard paved the way for it to enjoy a (modest) economic recovery in 1932; President Hoover, faced with calls that America should follow Britain's example and also abandon the gold standard, chose to ignore them. For Hoover (and indeed most of his contemporaries), adherence to the gold standard represented the recognition of an absolute standard against which the fundamental worth of a currency could be measured. Abandoning that standard was for him a sign of national weakness and the suggestion that America might follow in Britain's footsteps was almost unthinkable for him. As a result, for the remainder of Hoover's term, the American economy had to struggle on under the burden of the gold standard, and America had to wait for the Presidency of Franklin D. Roosevelt before throwing off its shackles.

In the meantime, the economic crisis threatened Hoover's attempts to maintain a balanced federal budget. By the end of June 1931, the federal budget was in deficit to the tune of $900 million, and with the financial demands of the Depression now falling on the state and Federal Governments, there was little hope that this could be remedied without drastic action.[55] Even larger deficits were being forecast for 1932 and 1933. Hoover, who for so long had supported a policy of taxation reduction, but also a policy of balanced

---

[55] At the same time, government receipts from income tax were falling, from $87.8 billion in 1929 to $42.5 billion in 1932.

budgets, effectively found himself between the proverbial rock and a hard place. He could have a policy of (relatively) low taxation, but would be forced to watch the deficit balloon, or he could seek to raise taxes in the hope that this would enable him to balance the government's books. What he could not do, in 1931, was pursue both policies simultaneously.

Key to the decision that Hoover had to make was the answer to the question of whether, in certain circumstances, a deficit in the federal budget could ever be justified. Then as now there was a debate as to whether the best way to nurse an economy through a sharp downturn of the business cycle was to launch large spending programmes (such as construction and other projects) with the aim of creating employment which would (it was hoped) increase consumer and industrial demand. To an extent, Hoover was sympathetic to this idea, but he still clung to the notion that this was best achieved by businesses themselves, with the government standing on the sidelines encouraging industry and seeking to tackle problems such as high interest rates and an excessively tight money supply. His critics, then and later, charged that the correct response would be to introduce large spending programmes at the public expense, if necessary accepting that the immediate price for doing so was a deficit in the federal budget, and remedying that deficit later when the economic situation had improved. One of the most important advocates of this approach was economist John Maynard Keynes, who had been advancing arguments in favour of a counter cyclical public spending policy for a number of years, though he would only marshal all his thoughts and theories on the topic in 1936 when he published his great work *"The General Theory of Employment, Interest and Money"*. His views were, however, largely ignored by most mainstream financial experts (with a few exceptions), and the majority of economists of the time adhered to the orthodox view that the maintenance of a balanced budget was essential. A balanced budget, it was believed, was vital if the value of the nation's currency was to be sustained. So, Hoover was not without his supporters when he argued in favour of a balanced budget. Indeed, this was one area where he saw eye to eye with Speaker Garner, and much of the Democratic leadership generally.

However, also preying on Hoover's mind as he pondered which policy should take priority – lower taxes or a balanced budget – was the need to maintain a sound banking system which could provide easy credit to American businesses. The bank runs of 1930 and 1931 had demonstrated that America's banking system was not as robust as it should have been; money continued to be in short supply and the situation was exacerbated by the interest rate hike administered by the Federal Reserve following Britain's abandonment of the gold standard.

The banks themselves were now loudly demanding federal action be taken to strengthen the banking system. Ogden Mills, Undersecretary of the Treasury (and destined to become Treasury Secretary following the resignation of Andrew Mellon in February 1932), joined in the cacophony demanding that the Federal Government take real, substantive action to protect the banks and other major financial institutions before economic chaos overtook the country. For President Hoover, government intervention on the scale now being demanded was tantamount to a repudiation of much that he had believed in and advocated as an active politician, but the crisis facing the American banking system left him little room for manoeuvre. Finally, tacitly conceding that voluntary cooperation within the banking sector was by itself inadequate to the task of supporting the banking system, President Hoover agreed to the creation in January 1932 of the Reconstruction Finance Corporation (RFC), which Congress agreed to fund to the tune of $500 million (and authorised to borrow up to £1.5 billion). The RFC was essentially intended to function as a conduit whereby public funds could be lent directly to banks, credit unions and other saving institutions, railroads and various agricultural organisations, though Hoover himself, aware of the potential criticism that his administration chose to provide federal aid for banks and corporations but not for the unemployed, declared that the RFC was not *"created for the aid of big industries or big banks."* Rather, he announced, the RFC was *"an insurance measure more than anything else..."*, one which it was hoped would bring a measure of stability to the banks, the banking system and the country.

In many ways the creation of the RFC was a pivotal moment – President Hoover was effectively conceding (though he never admitted it) that the Federal Government had an obligation to become actively involved in the business affairs of the nation – rather than passively legislating from the sidelines – and it was recognised as such by some of Hoover's contemporaries.

Perhaps the most notable of these was Rexford Tugwell, who would go on to be a key player in President Roosevelt's "brains trust" and ultimately be appointed the Governor of Puerto Rico. He commented sardonically that the creation of the RFC was governmental interference of a type that could be expected to horrify a president who was fundamentally opposed to governmental intervention in the business affairs of the nation. Yet he approved of the RFC (more so, once its funding and its scope of operations was expanded under President Roosevelt as part of the New Deal.)

Other contemporaries were more openly generous in their praise for President Hoover's actions. The journal Business Week for instance declared it *"the most powerful offensive force… that governmental and business imagination has, so far, been able to command."* But it was not long before the RFC was being criticised as Hoover had feared it would be, namely that while it offered (some) support to institutions it offered none to the individuals standing in the lines of the unemployed. Important though the work of the RFC was, it is not surprising that within a few weeks of its creation it was being dubbed *"the millionaires' dole"* by critics such as Fiorello La Guardia.

The RFC during what remained of Hoover's administration did some valuable work – according to some estimates, 90 percent of the loans (in terms of the number of loans) it authorised went to small and medium-sized banks and businesses who might well have found it difficult to continue to operate without the assistance that the RFC provided. But according to other assessments (based on the amount of the monies actually loaned) nearly two-thirds of the funds lent by the RFC during its first two years of operation were lent to just three institutions (one of them connected with former Vice President Dawes). Hoover's RFC was simply proof in the eyes of the public, (if proof were needed) that the Hoover administration had now had nothing to offer ordinary Americans. [56]

---

[56] By the summer of 1932, the demands for at least some form of federal assistance for the unemployed had reached such a pitch that President Hoover was forced to agree to a proposal that the RFC be authorised to lend up to $1.5 billion to encourage more public works on a local basis. President Hoover and his advisers however continued to deny that this constituted a federal aid programme.

Be that as it may, the creation of the RFC, and other calls on the public purse, constituted yet another demand on public funds and unsurprisingly gave rise to further concerns about the growth of the federal deficit. Hoover worried that running a federal deficit would lead (inevitably) to a sharp rise in government borrowing and weaken the dollar, which in turn could lead to higher interest rates, and an even tighter money supply. Forced to abandon another of his guiding policies, that of low taxation, he reluctantly concluded that by raising taxes, not only could he (hopefully) balance the deficit but also by avoiding any further increases in government borrowing, he would help keep interest rates low and this in turn would help to maintain liquidity within the money markets. It would also help to protect the dollar in the international currency markets. The decision to raise taxes having been taken, he dismissed fears expressed by some Democrats (and some liberal Republicans) that increasing taxes would simply reduce consumer spending even more, making it yet harder for American businesses to survive.

President Hoover's tax-raising bill was passed by Congress with little trouble (though plans for a national sales tax had to be dropped as a result of strong Democratic opposition) and it became the Revenue Act of 1932, being signed into law by the President on 6th June 1932. As a consequence of that Act, which it was hoped would raise in excess of $1.1 billion, all taxes were increased – it was the largest peacetime rise in tax rates in the country's history. The top rate of income tax rose from 25 percent to 63 percent, estates taxes were doubled and the corporation tax rate increased by approximately 15 percent. There were dramatic increases to America's excise duties. Low income tax exemptions were sharply reduced, and as a result nearly half a million people found themselves liable for federal taxes for the first time.[57]

The Revenue Act of 1932 was Hoover's last major piece of tax legislation before the presidential election of 1932. As an instrument to secure a balanced budget, it failed. Despite the new taxes, government receipts continued to fall throughout the year, and the 1932 federal budget ended the year in deficit to

---

[57] To put this figure into context, before the tax hikes created by the Revenue Act of 1932, approximately 1.9 million people out of a population of approximately 122 million had paid federal taxes.

DARK REALITIES

the tune of more than $2.7 billion (equal to 4 percent of the nation's GDP). Moreover, as feared by some critics, the new taxes constituted yet another burden to borne by the long-suffering American people now entering the fourth year of the Depression. Unemployment continued to rise; by December 1932, the nadir of the Depression years, nearly 24 percent of the American workforce (12.8 million people) was unemployed. Hoover and the Republicans generally were seen to have failed to pull the country out of the economic morass into which it had fallen. More and more ordinary voters were concluding that a change was needed. And increasingly, the eyes of Hoover's critics were turning in hope to the man sitting in the Executive Mansion of New York State: Governor Franklin Delano Roosevelt.

Chapter 7 America October 1929 – December 1932

"Our streets are filled with beggars, with men new to the art of begging"
Sherwood Anderson, author (1876 – 1941)

Hunger, Hoovervilles and Hoboes

The cold statistics of the early years of the Great Depression make for sober reading. For example:

- America's gross national product fell from $104 billion in 1929 to $41 billion by the end of 1932.

- 26,355 businesses (including 1,372 banks) collapsed in the United States in 1930. The following year saw a further 28,285 business failures, and the failure rate continued to increase throughout 1932, when another 31,822 businesses closed as a result of bankruptcy. In 1929, prior to the Crash, there had been an estimated 2.2 million businesses in the country; by the spring of 1933, there were 1.9 million.

- According to some estimates, the value of agricultural property fell by approximately 40 percent between 1929 and 1933 as farmers struggled to survive but too often fell victim to the burdens of an agricultural depression which by the beginning of 1933 was already more than a decade old. Aggregate farm incomes fell from $6 billion in 1929 to $2 billion in 1932.

- Gross domestic investment by American industries fell from $35 billion in 1929 to $3.9 billion by the end of 1932.

- Unemployment levels, estimated at 1.3 million at the time of the Crash, rose to an estimated 4.5 million by December 1930.[58] That figure nearly doubled during 1931 to 8 million, rose again in 1932 to 12 million and again to 12.8 million in 1933, when approximately one quarter of America's workforce was unemployed.

- Wages for those lucky enough to cling to employment plummeted throughout this period. This partly reflected the fact than many workers

---

[58] Given the unreliability of unemployment data for this period, this figure may be an underestimate.

were working reduced shifts, or had part-time jobs, but wages also fell in real terms. It has been estimated that the average per capita annual income for America's workers (allowing for inflation) fell from $681 in 1929 to only $495 by the end of 1932. At one point, 28 per cent of the American public (34 million people) had no income at all.

- 150,000 people lost their homes as a result of mortgage foreclosures in 1930. That figure rose to 200,000 in 1931 and to 250,000 in 1932.

- Perhaps unsurprisingly, the suicide rate in America rose from 13.9 per 100,000 of the population in 1929 to 17.4 per 100,000 by the end of 1932.

But national average figures, such as these quoted here, do not tell the whole story – there were some areas of the country where matters grew far worse much more quickly than the average figures suggest. Unemployment was generally particularly bad in industrial urban areas. In Detroit for example, the collapse in the demand for new cars following the Crash had a catastrophic effect on the local economy almost overnight. Despite promises to do all they could to maintain their workforces, automobile manufacturers had no compunction about laying off workers in an attempt to maintain their profit margins[59] (the average number of workers employed by the Ford Motor Company fell from 101,069 in 1929 to 56,277 in early 1933, for example), and this inevitably had a knock-on effect on other areas of the automobile industry. By the end of 1931, 30 percent of Detroit's workforce – more than 220,000 people – was without work. Michigan as a whole had nearly three quarters of a million unemployed.

Similar situations were to be found elsewhere. By October 1931, 40 percent of the workforce of Chicago, more than 600,000 people, was unemployed. In Cleveland, Ohio, the unemployment rate reached 50 percent. In the coal regions of West Virginia, demand for coal by industry had fallen so much that

---

[59] Not that they succeeded in doing so. 34 motor companies reported average falls in earnings in 1930 of approximately 40 percent as compared to the year before. These included the Ford Motor Company which achieved profits of approximately $40 million in 1930, less than half the figure achieved in 1929 (and by the end of 1931, Ford would be recording a loss of $37 million) and General Motors, which saw its earnings fall from approximately $62 million in 1929 to $44.9 million in 1930.

half the coal mines in the state were closed, leaving (according to some reports) more than 135,000 families in destitution by the end of 1932. Similarly, a collapse in the demand for industrial minerals saw local unemployment levels in Colorado soar in the three years following the Crash, so that by December 1932, local union officials were estimating the unemployment rate to be 50 percent of the workforce. Even wealthy Boston saw local unemployment levels in the early 1930s of approximately 30 percent.

Unemployment did not strike all sectors of the national labour force equally; the young, the old and members of minority and other disadvantaged groups were particularly vulnerable. In 1931, when the national unemployment rate was believed to be in the region of 15 percent, a survey suggested that the aggregate unemployment rate for workers aged between 16 and 25 and over 60 was 35 percent. For African Americans, particularly those in urban areas, the situation was even worse. In 1931, for example, African Americans made up 38 percent of the population of Memphis, but 75 percent of them were unemployed. In the steel regions of Pittsburgh, they were 8 percent of the population but made up 38 percent of the city's unemployed, whilst in Chicago, the figures were 4 percent and 16 percent respectively. In Philadelphia, only 7 percent of the city's population were African American, but again 75 percent of those were without work. Female African Americans fared even worse than the men; in Chicago, 58 percent were unemployed by the end of 1932. In Detroit, the figure was 75 percent.[60]

---

[60] Unemployment amongst minority and other disadvantaged groups generally was exacerbated by a tendency by such businesses as had job vacancies to hire whites, and particularly white males when they could – and there was no shortage of white males willing to fill the vacancies that did arise. Having said that, census figures suggest that the percentage of employed women actually rose during the Depression from 24.3 percent in 1930 to 25.4 percent in 1940, representing a gain of 2 million new jobs. This can be at least partly attributed to employers becoming eager as the Depression went on to hire female workers for lower wages than their male counterparts. On the other hand, in the early years of the Depression at least, there was a general feeling that working married women were somehow depriving married men of the chance to support their families, and as a consequence married women workers were often particularly vulnerable to redundancy.

Taken as a whole, although such statistics can be helpful in demonstrating the scale of the economic calamity that descended upon America in the early 1930s, they can also in some ways be strangely misleading or at least they do not tell the whole tale. In themselves, they convey little of the human cost of the Great Depression, of the misery suffered by millions of ordinary men, women and children who, through no fault of their own, found themselves thrown out of work, in many cases into the streets, forced to live lives of poverty, hunger and hopelessness. Nor do they show the fear of unemployment and destitution that pervaded the lives of those fortunate Americans who were still in work (the majority of the labour force, it must be remembered) and which coloured every aspect of their existence. Such misery did not descend on everyone overnight following the Great Crash; for many Christmas of 1929 was still a relatively jolly time. But as the American economy began to falter, as business expansion ceased and worker lay-offs began to increase, more and more people knew of a family member, a friend, an acquaintance who had lost their job, and they read in the newspapers, heard on the radio and saw on the movie newsreel reports of rising unemployment, and they began to fear that the same fate awaited them. For too many people it often did. And as President Hoover rightly feared, that widely-felt pessimism itself helped to exacerbate the conditions that allowed the Depression to continue and grow.

As the months of 1930 slid by, more and more people found themselves unable to pay their rents, their mortgages, their grocery bills. Many sought to pawn their possessions in an attempt to stave off financial crisis, but this was not enough. Forced to look to others for help and support, they sometimes found it provided by family members and friends, and sometimes by local churches, mutual aid societies, unions and other organisations established to help the new unemployed. Many states in the earliest months of the Depression provided some form of relief for their local unemployed. But as the Depression ground on, local institutions providing such relief found themselves overwhelmed with the rising demand for assistance. By the end of 1932, many private charities were being forced to limit their assistance to the provision of simple food relief. Photographs of the unemployed queuing at soup kitchens established in America's greatest cities would become one of the defining images of the Great Depression. State-funded organisations were also forced to reduce their support as tax receipts dried up. In many cases, even the relief that was provided was often limited to the provision of the most basic (and frequently nutritionally inadequate) of foods. Inevitably, the lack of a balanced diet began to affect the health of those dependent on food relief for survival, and doctors grimly began to record increases in the rates of tuberculosis, rickets and anaemia.

Questioned over the adequacy of food relief, President Hoover defended the ramshackle relief system by declaring *"Nobody is actually starving"*. But some people were – by the end of 1931, social workers were recording the sights of adults and children digging through the garbage dumps of cities such as Seattle, Chicago, St Louis and New York in the hope of finding something to eat. In 1932, New York school officials reported that 20,000 children were malnourished while some reports estimated that in the mining counties of West Virginia, Illinois, Kentucky and Pennsylvania, the proportion of malnourished children was as high as 90 percent. Social workers reported that in the Appalachians, people were being forced to eat dandelions, wild onions and blackberries, and in many places some families were recorded as eating only every other day. For too many, starvation was a very real possibility. Nationally, the death rate due to starvation went unmeasured, but in some places official records did specify starvation as a cause of death. In New York City, for example, official records listed 29 people as dying from starvation in 1933. What is unclear from the records is the number of deaths that were ascribed to other causes but were really caused by starvation, or the number of cases where malnutrition had hastened the end, but there must have been many.

Nationally, overall food sales declined during the Depression (though cigarette sales rose), but food was still freely available in grocery shops for those who could afford to buy it. In the countryside, acres of agricultural produce on America's farms went unharvested for want of demand; farmers found it cheaper to slaughter their livestock than to keep them alive. Unsurprisingly, there were times and places where the sight of food sitting on shop shelves proved too much for starving families to bear, and food riots broke out, in Minneapolis in January 1930, for example, and again in February 1931. Similar riots broke out in San Francisco and Oklahoma City that same year and there were protest demonstrations (which sometimes degenerated into riots) elsewhere, some such as those organised by America's Communist Party, more political than others. What is surprising is that there weren't more riots and protests – most unemployed people seem to have restrained themselves, accepted such relief as they could obtain and tried their best to survive.

Hand in hand with hunger went homelessness. People unable to feed their children properly were unlikely to be able to find money for the rent collector or for mortgage payments, and eviction rates soared. In New York City alone in 1931, there were an estimated 200,000 evictions. Many people, faced with eviction, contrived to find some way of putting a roof over their heads (or at least over the heads of their families) by sharing apartments, moving in with friends or family, seeking beds in cheap boarding houses or even cheaper flophouses but some could not find any such refuge. Again, New York provides an example: in the spring of 1931, the city had an estimated 15,000 homeless and the situation was similar in other cities and towns across the country. Regardless of where they were, the homeless spent much of the day wandering the streets in a fruitless search for work, many begging for nickels or dimes, often without success. At night, some just slept on park benches or shop doorways (when they weren't being moved on by policemen or park wardens or other officials), but thousands clustered into hastily constructed shantytowns which rapidly became known as "hoovervilles" in an acerbic reference to the President. Hoovervilles sprang up on the outskirts of urban areas where free land could be appropriated by desperate squatters (though one of the most famous of the shantytowns was constructed in the middle of New York's Central Park), the shacks of their inhabitants made from whatever materials were on hand, or could be scrounged or stolen. Usually lacking electricity and fresh water supplies, and with only the most primitive of sanitation arrangements (whenever thought was given to sanitation arrangements at all), occupied by desperate displaced people, hoovervilles were more often than not dirty, unhealthy and dangerous places to live. Moreover, they were often fiercely resisted by city and town authorities and "normal" members of the community, who periodically made strenuous efforts to force the squatters to move on, sometimes by ordering the destruction of the shantytowns. Such orders seldom had the desired effect for long, as the inhabitants of the hoovervilles often had nowhere else to go, and could rebuild their tarpaper and cardboard shacks faster than the authorities could arrange their destruction. Like the queues at community soup kitchens, images of America's hoovervilles rapidly became symbolic icons of the darkest days of the Depression, and they continued to exist throughout the 1930s, until a shack elimination programme was finally organised in 1941 which at last led to them being systematically demolished and their inhabitants rehoused.

At the same time as the new shantytowns were springing up, many of the new unemployed were taking to the roads and the railroads. Migrant workers were not a new phenomenon of course; millions of temporary farm workers had been moving back and forth across the country for decades, from the cotton fields of the South to the wheat fields of the Midwest, and from the potato farms of New England to the citrus farms of the Pacific coast, as and when the opportunities for seasonal crop work arose. Now the traditional migrant workers were joined by a great flood of newcomers, often known as "hoboes"[61], some genuinely seeking out the truth of rumours of jobs and opportunities elsewhere, others just wandering the nation and carrying out such casual and temporary work as they could find in the hope of survival. Nobody knows the exact number of people (they were mostly men, but there were women too and sometimes whole families) who became itinerant wanderers, though some estimates place the total as high as two million. Often travelling illegally in the boxcars of freight trains, they faced hard and frequently dangerous lives and were often the prey not only of some of their fellow travellers but also of local police officers and the railroads' own security officials (commonly known as "bulls"), many of whom delighted in persecuting hoboes in the guise of seeking to deter trespassing. Many died every year at the hands of the bulls or as the result of accidents while trying to gain access to guarded stockyards and moving freight trains. Even when they reached their destinations, their troubles were not over, for many towns

---

[61] Not to be confused with the term "bum", which signified those who travelled but had no wish to work, and who contrived to survive by begging.

refused to shelter transients for more than a day at most. And they seldom succeeded in finding long-term employment at the end of their journeys.[62]

Unsurprisingly, the stress of the Depression and unemployment had a detrimental effect on ordinary family life and the nation's mental health. Men who had become used to fulfilling the traditional male role of provider for their families found their self-respect evaporating with their job prospects. Women found themselves being called upon to raise their families under increasingly difficult circumstances. Children grew accustomed to seeing their parents' anguish as they struggled to survive, and they themselves often went out to work at such jobs as they could find in order to bring a few urgently needed dollars into the home. For many unemployed men, being forced to survive on the efforts of their wives and children exacerbated their feelings of hopelessness and inadequacy.

The longer a person was unemployed, the more difficult it became for them to take advantage of the job opportunities that did exist. Their clothes grew shabby, their shoes wore out and it became harder (especially for the homeless) to keep themselves clean. For many, long-term unemployment blunted their work skills. Inadequate food damaged their health and sapped their energies. Psychiatrists noted that many began to succumb to psychological depression, which sometimes manifested itself as a form of fatigue, which caused some sufferers to lose interest in the world around them, resigning themselves to

---

[62] Some chose to leave the country entirely and seek opportunities elsewhere, and this was particularly tempting to those whose families had only relatively recently emigrated to the United States and who still retained close links with their "old countries". Exact numbers are not available but it is believed that thousands may have left the country in this way, often returning to a Europe their fathers or grandfathers had left only a few decades before. In addition, at least half a million Mexican Americans (many of them American citizens) are estimated to have returned to Mexico during the Depression, (though in this case not all left voluntarily. Many were illegally forced or pressured to leave by immigration officials, actions which were approved by President Hoover at the time as part of a crackdown on illegal immigrants, which continued well into the second administration of President Roosevelt. In 2005, the State of California passed an act apologising for the illegal expulsions). And in 1931, 100,000 Americans applied for jobs in Stalin's Soviet Union.

their fates. Others became more radical, and began to express bitterness at the system and the political leadership which had seemingly abandoned them. Alcoholism (notwithstanding Prohibition) became more common.

As the Depression progressed, the marriage rate fell; there were quarter of a million fewer marriages in 1932 than in 1929, as young people decided to postpone their marriage plans. The birth rate also declined (a 15 percent reduction being recorded between 1929 and 1933), partly due to the conscious decision on the part of some couples not to bring into the world children who would require feeding, but also because impotency on the part of unemployed men rose during the 1930s. This in turn damaged men's self-respect even more, and added to the strains of married life. Nevertheless, divorce rates also fell during the first few years of the Depression, as people found they could simply not afford to divorce (though the divorce rate rose during the second half of the decade). Instead, social workers began to record increasing numbers of cases of men leaving the family home, ostensibly to try their luck as migrant workers, and never being heard from again. Their abandoned families had to survive as best they could as the Depression ground on.

The Bonus Army

By the late spring of 1932, the inability of America's disorganised relief system to cope with the rising tide of unemployment was stimulating increasingly vocal demands for the provision of federal unemployment relief. This, of course, was something that Hoover stubbornly opposed on ideological grounds, and the attempts of his administration to label such demands as "un-American" and to paint those making such demands as "socialists" had been strangely effective during the earliest stages of the Depression. Now though, such arguments were becoming less convincing as the number of potential recipients of such relief continued to grow, and Hoover's successful establishment of the RFC led to charges that he was willing to provide relief for corporations but not for the starving unemployed. In addition, the American public now had the example before them of the New York Temporary Emergency Relief Administration (TERA), established at the behest of Governor Franklin Roosevelt in 1931, who had succeeded in persuading his Republican-dominated state legislature that the provision of relief directly to the unemployed was not a matter of charity but rather one of social duty. TERA went on to provide unemployment relief to approximately 10 percent of New York's families, and increasingly there were demands (not least from Governor Roosevelt) that it be replicated on a national scale using federal funds.

Even before the establishment of the RFC, champions of a federal relief programme were beginning to stand up in Congress to be counted. In late 1931, Republican Senator Robert La Follette Jr. of Wisconsin, Democratic Senator Edward Costigan of Colorado and Democratic Representative James Lewis of Illinois proposed a bill to create a Federal Emergency Relief Board, to be funded by $375 million of public money, whose task it would be to assist state relief programmes. Hoover, horrified at what he called an extravagant and destructive measure, bitterly opposed the bill and with the help of Southern Democrats in Congress who had their own concerns about the possible creation of a dependent welfare class, succeeded in ensuring that when the bill came to a vote in the Senate in February 1932, it failed by 14 votes.

The La Follette-Costigan-Lewis bill was followed by the Garner-Wagner relief bill, which would have created a federal public works programme as well as federal unemployment relief; Hoover vetoed this on 11th July. However, such was the political pressure being brought to bear on President Hoover that he was willing, reluctantly, to agree to a compromise in the form of the Emergency Relief and Reconstruction Act, sponsored by Democratic Senator Robert Wagner of New York and the Majority Leader of the House of Representatives Henry T Rainey, and which Hoover signed into law on 21st July. The Act authorised the RFC to spend up to $1.5 billion on public works, and to lend up to $300 million to individual states to assist with their relief efforts. It was the first major piece of national relief legislation passed during the Depression (and would be adopted and overhauled by President Roosevelt), but its enactment did little or nothing to assist Hoover's now dismal political prospects or (at least during the remainder of his term) America's unemployed.

Hoover's political prospects suffered a final battering just a few days after his enactment of the Emergency Relief and Reconstruction Act as a result of the expulsion from the nation's capital of thousands of unemployed First World

War veterans who had been protesting over the refusal of the US Government to make advance payments of bonuses that had originally been awarded to them (in the form of "compensation certificates") by Congress over President Coolidge's veto in 1925. Those bonuses were not due to be paid until 1945, but the original legislation had allowed veterans to borrow up to 22.5 percent of the value of their certificates against the sums that would eventually be payable to them. In 1931, faced with the sight of unemployed veterans homeless and begging in the streets, Congress had agreed to increase the borrowing limit to 50 percent over Hoover's veto. Now, in 1932, veterans were calling for the immediate payment of their bonuses in full, and nearly 20,000 of them gathered in Washington from all over the country during the spring and summer of that year to lobby Congress. Calling themselves the Bonus Expeditionary Force, the Bonus Marchers or the Bonus Army, the veterans were for the most part organised and disciplined, and camped out in Washington's parks and disused government buildings. Many, especially those accompanied by wives and children, settled down in a shanty town established on Anacostia Flats on the far side of the Anacostia River from the Capitol. "We'll stay here until 1945 if necessary to get our bonus" declared the veterans' effective leader, former Army sergeant Walter Waters.

The gathering of thousands of veteran soldiers in Washington raised military and political concerns; in particular, there were fears that the Bonus Army could be a prelude to some form of revolution, and before long there were rumours that a million men were poised to march on Washington. This was nonsense (though there were certainly some Communist agitators amongst the Bonus Army who would have been pleased to cause such trouble if they could - most veterans opposed them and expelled them from their camps whenever they were identified); the vast majority of the veterans were ordinary men desperate for financial help for themselves and their families. Nevertheless, the presence of the veterans and supporters proved increasingly disruptive for the city's officials and its ordinary inhabitants, and tensions grew on all sides as Congress prepared to debate the issue of the veterans' bonuses.

Against this background, the House of Representatives agreed to the demands of the veterans,[63] but President Hoover declined to meet the veterans' leaders and the Senate, when it debated the matter, refused to pass the requisite legislation (not least because they feared that acceding to the veterans' demands would require much-needed funds earmarked for the federal unemployment relief legislation then under consideration). Disappointed, many of the veterans packed up and returned home (some assisted by a grant of $100,000 provided by Congress at President Hoover's request), but several thousand lingered on in Washington even after Congress adjourned for the summer on 16th July. Asked to leave by the District of Columbia's commissioners, Walter Waters refused, telling a reporter: *"We didn't ask Hoover if we could come here and we won't let him tell us when to leave."* The government then announced that measures would be taken to clear squatting veterans from certain government buildings on Pennsylvania Avenue that had been scheduled for demolition or renovation, and on 28th July the District of Columbia's police began to try to evict the veterans in accordance with the government's instructions. A riot ensued, and two bonus marchers died. Others temporarily seized control of Eleventh Street Bridge which would have allowed reinforcements from the Anacostia Flats encampments to flood into the city and the police appealed to President Hoover for assistance. Hoover called in federal troops under the command of General Douglas MacArthur, Chief of Staff, to restore order. Under MacArthur's personal direction (and against the advice of his aide, Major Dwight D Eisenhower), the regular troops not only cleared the marchers from the streets of Washington and from the Eleventh Street Bridge but also crossed the river with cavalry (under the command of Major George S Patton[64]), machine gun tanks, bayonets and tear gas, and (under the gaze of the press) promptly set out clearing and burning down the shanty town on Anacostia Flats by force. By the end of the day, one

---

[63] The veterans' champion in the House was Democratic Representative Wright Patman of Texas, who a few months before had led attempts to try to impeach Andrew Mellon upon tax evasion and corruption charges, which had led to Mellon's resignation as Treasury Secretary.

[64] Who, during the subsequent fighting, was knocked off his horse by a flying brick.

soldier was dead but the shanty town was destroyed, and the remnants of the Bonus Army (including Walter Waters) had been scattered from the city.

Hoover and his administration tried to justify the actions of MacArthur's troops by blaming the veterans, suggesting they were *"hoodlums and communists"* and had threatened the US Government itself (a view that MacArthur shared to the end of his days). The public, appalled, were not convinced. The scenes they saw on the newsreels and read about in their newspapers depicted actions they might have expected from the blackshirts of Mussolini's Fascist Italy, Stalin's soldiers in the Soviet Union or the brownshirts of Hitler's Nazi Party, but even after three years of the Depression, most ordinary Americans were unprepared for the sight of American troops assaulting American citizens in America's capital city. MacArthur had been acting on his own initiative (and contrary to Hoover's express command) when he ordered his troops across the river but this didn't prevent Hoover from being held responsible.

The Battle of Anacostia Flats (as the sorry debacle came to be known) effectively marked the end for President Hoover. Any remaining political support steadily leached away from him over the next few weeks and months and now most people were counting the days until the next presidential election, scheduled for 8th November, when they would be given the chance to put the country on a new course. And Hoover knew it.

Chapter 8 A New Beginning

"Vote for Roosevelt and make it unanimous."

Telegram allegedly sent to President Hoover by an Illinois voter on 7th November, 1932

The Defeat of President Hoover

Herbert Hoover faced the presidential election of 1932, scheduled to be held on 8th November, a political corpse. Less than four years before, he had been elected to the White House in a landslide, receiving 58 percent of the popular vote and having carried 40 of the 48 states. Now, in the fall of 1932 his popularity had vanished and he was one of the most derided figures in the country. Frustrated and disappointed, still convinced that his policies held the key to economic salvation if only people would give them a chance, but aware that his allotted time was fast diminishing, to many observers he now seemed prematurely aged, his clothes frequently wrinkled, his hair unkempt, his skin sallow and his mood often morose and testy. He had grown to dislike the post of President and had little appetite for a political campaign that was apparently doomed from the start and yet he allowed his name to be put forward for re-nomination as the Republican Presidential candidate. There was little competition for the role, and at the Republican National Convention held in 1932, Hoover was re-nominated on the first ballot with 98 percent of the vote. Charles Curtis, Hoover's Vice-President was nominated as his running mate.

With the Presidential nomination in his pocket, Hoover at first did little actual campaigning preferring to leave the preliminary skirmishing to his aides and cabinet colleagues. Then in early October, he began a series of trips to various cities and towns across America, speaking in auditoriums and stadiums to audiences who listened gravely yet attentively as he sought to justify his actions and those of his administration, appealed for the maintenance of traditional American ways and values, warned of the dangers of radical change and declared his faith in the future of the country if only his advice was heeded. His speeches were intelligent and logical but they were the speeches of an administrator, not a politician. Some commentators thought that when he spoke, he was trying to justify his Presidency and his actions to future generations rather than to win the votes of Americans who would be entering the voting booths within a few weeks. Nevertheless, his first speeches seemed to some observers to be surprisingly well received by his audiences, especially the first speech in the series which he gave in Des Moines. Such a perception was an illusion; the audiences which appeared so supportive had been largely handpicked by local Republican Party officials from those who could be relied upon not to make public protest. Outside in the streets, the general public often delivered another message of open derision and contempt; on occasions mounted police and secret servicemen had to intervene to keep the President safe from the baying crowds. No previous President, some claimed, had ever been faced with such open public hostility and as the series of speeches went on,[65] it became harder for Republican officials to gerrymander audiences so they comprised only die-hard Hoover fans (or at least dyed in the wool anti-Democrats). Hoover became accustomed to delivering his speeches to a cacophony of boos and catcalls.

He decided to await the results of the election at his family home in Palo Alto, California, and so it was there that he received the news that he and the Republican Party had been swept out of power by a Democratic landslide, greater even than that which had borne him to the White House in 1928. Hoover received 15,761,254 votes (39.65 percent of the popular vote), carrying only 6 states and 59 electoral votes. His Democratic opponent Franklin D. Roosevelt received 22,821,277 votes (57.41 percent), winning 42 states and 472 electoral votes. So great was the scale of the Democratic victory that Hoover's telegram of concession was dispatched to Roosevelt shortly after nine in the evening before many of the votes on the West Coast had even been counted. With that telegram, Herbert Hoover effectively stepped out of the political limelight forever.

The New President

As the American people hoped and suspected, FDR was a man very different from his Republican predecessor. Herbert Hoover had been, fundamentally, a

---

[65] In themselves, Hoover's speeches were something of an innovation. Before the 1932 presidential election campaign, it was unusual for incumbent Presidents to actively campaign across the nation for re-election.

President Warren G. Harding

Charles Evans Hughes while Governor of New York

Down and out on New York Pier, 1931

Soup kitchen, also of 1931.

DARK REALITIES

Run on the American Union Bank in 1931.

"Scuse me, Buddy, is this the bread-line or a run on a bank?"

A cartoon from 1931, illustrating the relationship between personal and institutional uncertainty.

DARK REALITIES

The Tennessee Valley Authority, part of the New Deal, being signed into law by Franklin D Roosevelt on 18th May 1933.

"FDR and the alphabet soup agencies", by Cliff Berryman, Washington Evening Star (1938).

A less sympathetic view of FDR and his relationship to the Supreme Court.

FDR visits a farming community in the Oklahoma Panhandle suffering during the Dust Bowl years.

DARK REALITIES

At the time of the Louisiana Flood, by Margaret Bourke-White, 1937

Government worker with farmers

skilled engineer and administrator; though he had been living at the centre of American political life since the days of the First World War, he was not, at heart, a politician, and lacked many of the social skills and instincts of an experienced and tested practitioner in that field.[66] As such, he tended to approach problems logically and methodically, drawing on his own considerable practical experience, but also he approached problems rigidly, generally refusing to countenance any course of action that would lead to him straying outside the parameters dictated by his own beliefs and principles, and without always appreciating the political cost of his actions, or recognising the need to cultivate political allies and to placate potential foes. Perhaps most importantly of all, in the final analysis he failed to display the most important and basic aspect of leadership, namely the ability to persuade people to follow him. While a willingness to stand firm to one's principles even in the face of almost universal condemnation and opposition may be an admirable personal trait, a practice of displaying such integrity on a regular basis regardless of popular opinion or actual circumstances does not bode well for someone who desires a long-term career as a popular leader, as President Hoover discovered.

By way of contrast, popular leadership was a trait that FDR displayed in abundance and in the 1930s there were few people whose political skills could match his (and there have been very few since). Those skills, and the experience that had honed them, came from a lifetime of political activity and effort, and his steely determination to succeed, frequently masked by a velvet veneer of smooth camaraderie, had been tested and polished in the face of considerable personal and professional difficulties. As many commentators have noted, he was never really a conviction politician – his principal aim was to ride the winds of public opinion rather than to seek to change them abruptly – it was vitally important, he believed, not to be too far ahead of public opinion, or too far behind (though he was prepared to recognise exceptions to this general rule, as his later career demonstrated). Thus he learned early in his political life to proceed with caution when expressing views or proposing initiatives, and preferably without giving explicitly detailed public commitments

---

[66] The Presidency was Hoover's first elected post – in none of his previous political roles had he been directly appointed by a public mandate.

to any cause or person. Couple this tendency with apparent (often genuine) joviality and friendly manners, and set against his background of wealth inherited rather than earned, and it is easy to see why so many of his political rivals, then and in the years to come, misjudged and sometimes underestimated him. It is also easy to see how so many people could conclude a conversation with him believing they had gained his express and fervid support for one cause or another, only to find in the cold light of day that he had given no express support at all, or that such promises of assistance as he had given were so often surrounded and tempered by caveats and conditions as to render them, in practice, almost worthless.

The descendant of Dutch immigrants who had emigrated to New Amsterdam in 1650, he was born on 30th April 1882 at Springwood, his family's home on the outskirts of the town of Hyde Park, 90 miles north of New York City. The Roosevelts were by now wealthy and influential landowners and businessmen. In later years, some of his political opponents would sometimes castigate him as a scion of privilege and breeding, which must have come as a refreshing change to other accusations levelled at him during the years of New Deal by some members of the wealthier sections of society who accused him of being a traitor to his class.

Educated first at home and then at Groton, an elite private school in Massachusetts, and finally at Harvard, FDR had developed an interest in politics by his late teens, partly because his father had dabbled in local Democratic politics, but largely as a result of the example of his distant cousin Theodore Roosevelt[67] who had rapidly climbed the political ladder in the 1890s, as a Republican, to become Vice President to President McKinley in 1901. When President McKinley was assassinated by an anarchist, Leon Czolgosz, on 14th September 1901, Teddy Roosevelt was sworn in as the 26th President of the United States.

Leaving Harvard in 1904, FDR initially studied law and practised as a lawyer (though he showed little enthusiasm, or indeed aptitude, for a legal career). His political career commenced in January 1910 when he was elected to the New

---

[67] Technically they were fifth cousins

York State Senate. He served as a State Senator for nearly three years, making a name for himself as a politician sympathetic to the interests of ordinary (and often rural) voters, and an opponent of corrupt city-based politicians, a stance that earned him few friends in Tammany Hall.[68] He was then was appointed Assistant Secretary of the Navy (Teddy Roosevelt's old post) following President Wilson's victory in the presidential election of 1912.

FDR remained Assistant Secretary of the Navy for seven years, during years of peace and during the years when America fought in the First World War. He was closely involved in efforts to expand the US navy and as a consequence began to develop a national reputation. However, the immediate post-war years saw the country steadily swinging towards the Republicans and the embrace of isolationism. FDR knew that there would be no place in Washington for him under a Republican administration, and decided to seek the Democratic Vice-Presidential nomination for the presidential election of 1920, which he duly won, thus becoming the running mate of Democratic Presidential nominee James Cox. However, on Election Day, he and Cox went down to spectacular defeat at the hands of Warren Harding and Calvin Coolidge. FDR retreated to New York where he practised law in a somewhat desultory fashion and served as vice president of an insurance company as he pondered his next move.[69]

---

[68] It was during this time that he first met Louis Howe, a reporter who helped him gain re-election to the State Senate in 1912 when FDR was confined to bed with an attack of typhoid. Howe had made it clear from the outset that he considered FDR to have a brilliant political future, and was not at all averse to helping him to achieve it. Time would show Howe to be a brilliant political strategist from whom FDR would learn much, and the two men would go on to develop a remarkably close personal and political friendship that would one way or another last effectively until Howe's death in 1936. This friendship and political alliance would occur despite the fact that Howe was disliked and mistrusted by many of Roosevelt's other friends, colleagues and family (including initially Roosevelt's wife Eleanor, although as the years went by, she mellowed somewhat in her views of Howe, especially after she discovered how useful his politically astute advice could be to her personally).

[69] The question arises as to why FDR wanted to run for the Vice Presidency in an election which almost every political poll predicted would result in a Republican landslide and knowing (as he was warned by several close friends) that even in the

However, he then suffered a significant personal setback. While on holiday in August 1921, he complained of feeling tired, with strange intermittent pains in his limbs but nevertheless forced himself to swim and to sail in the cold waters of the Bay of Fundy. His sense of exhaustion grew and by the evening of 10th August he was obliged to go to bed in the early evening – he thought he was suffering from lumbago. When he awoke the next morning, he found that he could barely move his left leg; shortly afterwards his right leg failed him too. He was diagnosed as having contracted poliomyelitis;[70] he would never walk unaided again.

Franklin Roosevelt spent the next 35 months adapting to his new disability and struggling towards a semblance of semi-recovery, while maintaining his links with the Democratic Party. By the time of the Democratic National Convention in July 1924, he had recovered sufficiently to be able to make an appearance (on crutches) at the Convention where he nominated Governor Al Smith as the Democratic presidential candidate (though Smith did not win the nomination), and that appearance has generally been regarded as signalling FDR's return to national politics. He again nominated Al Smith at the 1928 National Convention, this time appearing without crutches but on the arm of his son Elliott. When Smith won the nomination (in part at least thanks to FDR's stirring speech in support), he suggested that FDR to run for the governorship of New York (one reason for this suggestion being that Al Smith suspected FDR might be a weak governor and thus allow Smith to retain a

---

event of a Democratic victory, simply running for the Vice Presidency could result in his name being tainted with the stain of second-rate mediocrity. Part of the attraction seems to have been that Teddy Roosevelt had proceeded from the post of Assistant Secretary to the Vice Presidency, and if possible FDR wanted to emulate his cousin. Moreover, FDR was now a recognised national figure and yet still a young man; he and Howe calculated he could bounce back from a failed Vice Presidential campaign. Furthermore (and this was an important factor in the mind of Louis Howe), a national campaign would allow him the opportunity to build what he had so far been lacking, namely a network of personal followers in key states that he could exploit in future political campaigns, and this is indeed what happened.

[70] Though in recent years, it has been suggested that he may have contracted Guillain-Barré Syndrome, a disease of motor and sensory nerves that shares several of the symptoms of polio, but was little known at the time.

degree of influence behind the scenes). FDR agreed to run despite widespread predictions (including those of Louis Howe) that 1928 would again be a year in which the Republicans would overwhelmingly dominate at the polls. Although the pollsters were generally shown to be correct, and Al Smith went down to spectacular defeat in the presidential election, failing even to win his own state in the process, FDR succeeded where Smith failed, defying the national trend and beating Republican gubernatorial challenger Albert Ottinger by 25,564 votes out of the 4,234, 822 cast in total.

Governor of New York

Franklin Roosevelt became Governor of New York on 1st January 1929 with a reputation for being reform-minded but with no particular programme of reform in mind. Nevertheless he successfully resisted somewhat clumsy attempts by Al Smith to retain a vestige of influence in the Governor's mansion at Albany. By way of example, Smith tried to insist that his close political adviser and principal secretary, Mrs Belle Moskowitz, write FDR's inaugural address and was less than pleased when FDR announced he had written his own – shortly thereafter Mrs Moskowitz effectively found herself out of a job. FDR sought to enhance his reformatory credentials by launching a series of well-reported initiatives. These included revising the state's penal system, seeking to establish a commission to investigate state-wide old age pensions and challenging what he considered to be monopolistic behaviour on the part of New York's power companies. His relations with Tammany Hall had improved since the days when he had served in the state legislature, and to the disappointment of some of his more radical supporters, he was reluctant during his first term in office as Governor to launch an open attack against the corruption that still emanated from New York City, now under the control of the notorious Jimmy Walker, the latest in a long line of morally dubious city mayors. However, when the Republicans began to make corruption the central theme of their campaign in the run-up to the gubernatorial election of 1930 (the gubernatorial term of office for New York then being two years) FDR asked the courts to launch a grand jury investigation into the sale of judicial offices, and quietly began to apply pressure upon Walker leading eventually to Walker's resignation in 1932 and well overdue departure from public life. Roosevelt went on to win re-election in November 1930 with ease, carrying

New York City by over half a million votes, and the remainder of the state by over 150,000.

He was now one of the most prominent Democrats in the country, eclipsing Al Smith who couldn't quite believe that he was now overshadowed by the man sitting in a wheel-chair in the executive mansion in Albany, a man who he himself had persuaded to run as Governor. Smith never forgave Roosevelt, whom he seemed to regard as having committed an act of *lèse majesté*, and over time he became one of Roosevelt's most bitter opponents within the ranks of the Democratic Party. Al Smith's increasing antagonism was however less important to Roosevelt and his closest advisers[71] than the fact that FDR was now an obvious candidate for the White House. Roosevelt's campaign for the Democratic presidential nomination in 1932 effectively began the moment that the results of New York's gubernatorial election of 1930 were announced.

In the meantime though, there was the Depression to be fought. While President Hoover in the White House argued that primary responsibility for securing economic recovery and relief from hardship ultimately rested on the shoulders of American businesses and the American people themselves, Roosevelt – himself now dependent on others for assistance in daily life thanks to his crippled legs – was far more sympathetic to the notion that people in trouble deserved assistance from more fortunate members of society, and especially support from their government and its institutions. In a speech he gave in 1931, he explained his views thus: *"I assert that modern society, acting*

---

[71] Louis Howe, for all that he was still close to FDR, was by now no longer his only close adviser and perhaps not even his closest; amongst those who now joined him in the inner circle was renowned labour expert Frances Perkins (who would go on to join FDR's cabinet as Secretary of Labor, becoming the first woman to enter the presidential line of succession in the process) and Samuel Rosenman, who became one of Roosevelt's principal speechwriters and went on to become the first official White House Counsel (and ultimately a judge). A later recruit would be Harry Hopkins, who joined Roosevelt's inner circle in 1931 and in due course would become Secretary of Commerce, a much valued advisor to President Roosevelt on international affairs and one of the principal architects of the New Deal. Howe was not at all happy discovering that he now had to share close access to Roosevelt but found he had no choice in the matter.

through its government, owes the definite obligation to prevent the starvation or the dire want of any of its fellow men and women who try to maintain themselves but cannot."

As in the case of the Federal Government, the State Government lacked the machinery to help with the newly unemployed and homeless; FDR set out to do what he could with the resources at his disposal, often against a background of bitter opposition from Republicans (who dominated the state legislature) and big business interests. He authorised the housing of the homeless in National Guard armouries and barracks. He launched a commission to investigate the possibility of unemployment insurance and another to seek ways of reducing unemployment by shortening the working day. But perhaps his greatest achievement as Governor was to persuade the state legislature (and it took some persuading) to establish a new state agency, the Temporary Emergency Relief Administration (TERA), which was intended to alleviate unemployment by creating a $20 million state-wide public works programme financed by an increase in state income tax. TERA's Chairman was Jesse Straus, the president of Macy's; it was he who hired Harry Hopkins as TERA's Executive Director, thus bringing Hopkins to Roosevelt's attention. Under Hopkins' efficient administration, TERA would eventually provide much needed unemployment relief to ten percent of New York's families. It was the first such state-sponsored programme in the country and attracted widespread favourable attention.

Roosevelt assembled a first-class campaign team in early 1932 in anticipation of the forthcoming presidential election, and as the months progressed, it became apparent that he was attracting widespread support across the country. However, for all of his popularity, the Democratic presidential nomination did not simply fall into his pocket at the Democratic National Convention held in Chicago between 27th June and 2nd July 1932. Although he had won most of the Democratic primaries, he was unpopular with certain factions within the Party, and at the Convention he faced two major contenders each in their own way representative of distinct constituencies. These were firstly John Nance Garner of Texas, Speaker of the House, hard drinking and tough talking, firmly on the conservative wing of the Party, with strong regional support in the South and West, a man with little love for the liberals of the Party (or vice versa). Secondly, there was Al Smith, convinced that that the nomination was (or should be) his by right, and representative of many traditional urban, often immigrant voters, many of whom were inclined to regard Roosevelt's supporters as potentially dangerous radicals. These were powerful opponents, and it took four ballots, and considerable negotiation and horse-trading behind the scenes before FDR could claim victory. This required accepting Garner as his Vice President, which turned out to be a smart move, as it proved to be popular with conservative Democrats in the rural South.

Al Smith, seeing his presidential hopes ground into dust once more by a man he was now coming to despise, deserted the Convention in fury before Roosevelt's victory had been formally announced, his political credibility irretrievably shattered.[72] Roosevelt for his part decided to break with tradition and accept the nomination in person, flying to Chicago to address the now rapturous delegates who rose to give him a standing ovation. In response, Roosevelt delivered a speech written for him by Sam Rosenman during which he uttered a phrase, one that wasn't original but would come to define the coming era: *"I pledge you, I pledge myself, to a new deal for the American people."*

Now in the depths of the third year of the Depression, the American people yearned above all else for that new deal. Rejecting all that President Hoover stood for, they would give Franklin Roosevelt the presidential election victory he wanted, but then it would be time for Roosevelt to deliver...what exactly? Throughout his campaigning from the time of the Convention to Election Day, Roosevelt talked much of the need for change, of the responsibility of the state to support its citizens and the responsibilities citizens bore to one another, and the desire to build a new and better America. But he was surprisingly vague on detail as to what his plans actually were (as the Republicans tried to point out, but now no one was listening to them). On the morning after the election, when ordinary Americans woke to find they had a new President-elect, they believed with justification that they had been promised that better America. What they didn't know was how that new America would come into being.

---

[72] Although Smith did eventually consent to campaign for Roosevelt during the 1932 presidential campaign.

　　　　　DARK REALITIES

Chapter 9 One Hundred Days

"Our greatest primary task is to put people to work."
Excerpt from President Roosevelt's First Inaugural Address, 4th March 1933

The Banking Crisis of 1933

Franklin D Roosevelt's first presidential inauguration took place in a cold and grey Washington on Saturday 4th March 1933, in the midst of the turmoil of yet another banking crisis. This one had started in early February when the governor of Louisiana had been obliged to declare a banking holiday to save one of the state's largest banks from a bank run; this was followed on 14th February by the governor of Michigan declaring an eight-day banking holiday to protect the faltering banks in his state. The next day, while Roosevelt was visiting Miami, a mentally deranged bricklayer called Giuseppe Zangara, who had come to believe that all Presidents, Kings and capitalists should be killed, fired five shots at him. Zangara missed the President-elect, but struck a number of bystanders, including Mayor Anton Cermak of Chicago with whom the President-elect had been talking; Cermak died a few days later, as did Zangara on 20th March, strapped to the electric chair in the Florida State Penitentiary. The combination of the banking holidays in Louisiana and Michigan and the assassination attempt caused bank runs across the country, and more and more states were forced to declare banking holidays as they attempted to preserve their beleaguered banks. Gold deposits began to be shipped out of the country once more at an alarming rate, ordinary Americans began to hoard such currency as they had and on Wall Street, share prices began to fall.

President Hoover, eking out the last days of his Presidency wrote to Roosevelt begging him to issue some form of reassuring statement, in the process claiming that his own policies had begun to work in the summer of 1932, and ascribing the latest economic crisis to a variety of causes including the uncertainties posed by Roosevelt's election, fears of inflation, socialism, rising unemployment, the potential abandonment of the gold standard , the lack of a balanced budget and even the prospective imposition of a dictatorship.

Roosevelt was less than amused by Hoover's unwanted advice, privately regarding it as cheeky[73], and even Hoover later admitted that if Roosevelt had responded as Hoover wished, this would have amounted to an effective endorsement of Hoover's economic policies and an abandonment of the *"so-called New Deal"* before it had even been born. Roosevelt delayed replying to Hoover until a few days before the inauguration, and when he finally did, he contrived to do so without making any concessions or pronouncements as to his future intentions at all. Hoover, now an extremely impotent lame duck President, could only sit and wait for the inauguration that would remove the last vestiges of political power from his hands as the country slid deeper into a new economic morass.

By the morning of the inauguration, more than half the banks in the country had closed their doors, some temporarily, others permanently. Industrial investment had declined by 90 percent since the heady days of 1929; automobile production had declined by 75 percent. Unemployment was rising once more, soup kitchens and other relief stations were shutting down due to a lack of funds. Food riots were increasingly common, as was crime generally. International trade was moribund. The New York Stock Exchange and the Chicago Board of Trade had closed as had many other lesser exchanges; across the nation factories stood idle and silent and economic activity had ground to a halt as Americans waited for the change in leadership and direction that so many desperately wanted. Yet even now, very few people had any real sense of what Roosevelt's plans were, other than in the loosest sense that change was urgently needed.

It isn't clear that President Roosevelt had a detailed overall plan at that time as to how the country's economic woes should be tackled; rather he simply considered that the country had a series of individual problems each of which needed urgent attention. He had a distinct advantage over Hoover in that (unlike Hoover) he had no deeply held political, economic or social ideology or doctrine that might cause him to dismiss out of hand possible solutions to problems simply because they appeared to clash with ingrained beliefs. He had

---

[73] It did not help that Hoover's secretary when typing the letter managed to misspell Roosevelt's name.

spent the months since the election gathering together into his prospective administration (either officially, or as informal advisers) a disparate body of men and women most of whom favoured (as he did) practical rather than theoretical solutions to economic and social problems. These included many whose names would become almost synonymous with Roosevelt and the New Deal, men and women such as Frances Perkins, the incoming Secretary of Labor, Cordell Hull, who was to be Secretary of State, William Woodin, Treasury Secretary, Harold Ickes, Secretary of the Interior, Jim Farley, the Postmaster General and Henry Wallace, Secretary of Agriculture. Not all of Roosevelt's appointees were brilliant; some were merely adequate and appointed primarily for political reasons, but some such as Frances Perkins and Cordell Hull were genuinely talented individuals who were anxious to ensure that the new administration succeeded in improving the state of the nation and the everyday lives of its citizens and were keen to play central roles in that task.

When seeking to address the country's problems, for FDR and his closest advisers, the key question would be whether something worked, or might work, or might at least give the impression of working. If an approach didn't succeed or if it couldn't be implemented in practice, it was to be rejected without lament and something else tried. The important point was not to stop trying. This was a philosophy that FDR would demonstrate again and again throughout his Presidency and its spirit would inculcate much of the New Deal.[74]

President Roosevelt had a real sympathy for people who were suffering, and believed firmly that the American prosperity depended on Americans working together with the active support and encouragement of their government to solve their problems. As a legacy of his own personal difficulties, he had an absolute belief in his own abilities, and had faith in the resilience of America's people and her political and social institutions. He knew too that a key component of any recovery process would be the need to re-establish public

---

[74] Indeed, in a speech he gave on 22nd May 1932, prior to gaining the Democratic nomination, FDR openly stated that: "…the country demands bold, persistent experimentation. It is common sense to take a method and try it. If it fails, admit it frankly and try another. But above all, try something."

confidence in those institutions, and that being seen to act decisively was perhaps even more important, at least in the beginning, than delivering results. From this developed the concept of Roosevelt's "First One Hundred Days", the first three months of his Presidency, during which time he and his new administration set out to pursue a new course for America.

Three Emergency Measures

The One Hundred Days began on 9th March 1933, when a special session of Congress was convened at the President's request. Roosevelt had initially meant for Congress to do little more during the special session than to consider, debate and hopefully pass three "emergency measures" bills, intended to address the most pressing of the country's problems, but the 1932 congressional elections had seen Democratic candidates overwhelm their Republican opponents, with the result that the Democrats now held commanding majorities in both the House of Representatives and the Senate. FDR seized the opportunity that this state of affairs presented and a flurry of bills (fifteen in all) had been signed into law by the time the special session ended on 16th June. These bills were largely rubber-stamped by Congress, sometimes on the same day they were received, often without any detailed debate or argument, even from the almost completely demoralised Congressional Republicans. Unsurprisingly, Roosevelt was accused by opponents of behaving like a dictator and over time, he would find it harder and harder to bend Congress to his wishes; but for the moment such was the national hysteria and stress that Congress gave him their unequivocal support. As for the new legislation itself, which formed the statutory essence of the New Deal, the need for haste, in order to take maximum advantage of the exceptional support offered by Congress, meant that much of it was drafted hastily, and some of the new legislation would require amendment and refinement in due course. That said, it is notable how well much of the new legislation met the needs of the country and answered the wishes of a majority of its citizens at that time.

The first matter of business was the banking crisis. On Sunday, 5th March, FDR had convened a meeting of the cabinet, and announced emergency measures intended to halt the bank runs and the flood of gold out of the country. Using powers under the Trading with the Enemy Act of 1917, he halted all transactions in gold, thus providing much-needed relief for the gold reserves held by the Federal Reserve. At the same time, he announced a nationwide four-day banking holiday, during which time bankers and treasury officials scurried to assemble a banking bill that would restore confidence in the country's banking system and bring the bank runs to an end. The bill was barely ready when the House of Representatives assembled at noon on 9th March, and printed copies were not available for every representative. Some representatives were still trying to find their seats in the chamber when debate on the bill began, a debate which ended less than three quarters of an hour later with many representatives still not having seen the bill; nevertheless, the bill was passed unanimously by the House. That afternoon, the Senate passed it with only seven dissenting votes, and President Roosevelt signed the Emergency Banking Relief Act of 1933 into law that evening.[75]

The Act was by no means the full blown attack on the American capitalist system that some extreme left-wingers had been hoping for, and many right-wingers had feared. It validated the actions the President had taken in seeking to invoke powers under the Trading with the Enemy Act without which, Roosevelt's actions in halting gold transactions using the powers of that Act might well have been illegal. It also gave the President the ability to declare a national emergency, during which he was to be given absolute control over the nation's finances, it gave the US Treasury the power to take control of banks in the United States and in American overseas territories, and to lay down

---

[75] One month later, on 5th April, FDR would issue Executive Order 6102 which effectively made it illegal for US citizens to own more than a small amount of gold coins and bullion (historic gold coin collections and gold used by industry, artists and dentists were exempt). Owners of gold were ordered to sell their holdings to the US Government at the rate of $20.67 per troy ounce by 1st May 1933. The Order was later amended several times but essentially remained in force until 1975. Both the executive order and the declaration of a bank holiday were measures that President Hoover had been urging Roosevelt to announce in the weeks leading up to his inauguration. Interestingly, the original Order may not have been legal; the Emergency Banking Relief Act which provided the statutory authority under which the Order was issued stipulated that such orders should be signed by the Secretary of the Treasury, not the President.

regulations by which they had to operate, and expanded the ability of the Federal Reserve to issue currency and loans. Crucially, it allowed for banks to be re-opened under government supervision, and Roosevelt made it clear in a radio broadcast on 12th March (the first of his so-called "fireside chats") that banks would only be re-opened if the Treasury was satisfied that they were "sound". If the Treasury had concerns about any particular bank, the Government would work with the bank, its investors and shareholders to encourage measures that would restore its soundness, such as recapitalisation and merger. State banks which were not part of the Federal Reserve system would nevertheless receive similar support. During the course of his radio address, Roosevelt observed that when the banks re-opened, it was possible that a very few people would try to withdraw their savings, but he added that it was his belief that hoarding during the past week had become an exceedingly unfashionable pastime in every part of the nation. In fact, when the banks began to re-open on 13th March, it quickly became clear that the Americans had decided to place their faith in the new banking measures. Bank runs did not materialise, and reassured depositors began to return their savings to the banking system. By the end of April 1933, 70 percent of America's banks had re-opened their doors for business. The problem of the lack of public confidence in the US banking system, which had existed even in the early days of the Republic, but which had been acute since the onset of the Depression had, for the moment at least, been solved, and within only a few days of Roosevelt taking office as President. His actions in dealing promptly and resolutely with the banking crisis made him a hero in homes across America and persuaded the vast majority of Americans, far more than mere words could ever have done, that he was the man to lead them out of the Depression.[76]

---

[76] Further important structural reforms were introduced to the banking system on 16th June 1933, when President Roosevelt signed into law the Banking Act of 1933, commonly known as the Glass-Steagall Act of 1933 after its legislative sponsors (and not to be confused with an earlier Glass-Steagall Act passed the previous year). The new Act sought to discourage excessive speculative investment by introducing a sharp distinction between commercial and investment banking, and insisting on a strict separation of the two activities; henceforth banks would be either commercial

But many other problems remained. On 10th March, the President sent to Congress for its (hasty) consideration a second "emergency measures" bill drafted by Budget Director Lewis Douglas and intended to reduce government expenditure. Entitled *"A Bill to Maintain the Credit of the United States Government"*, under its provisions, the salaries of federal employees were to be cut by up to 15 percent, resulting in a saving of $100 million. Veterans' benefits too were to be reduced by $400 million and the defence budget slashed from $752 million in 1932 to $531 million in 1934. Despite some opposition (the reduction in veterans' benefits was opposed by some Democratic Congressmen but had considerable support in conservative ranks, while the US Army in the form of US Chief of Staff Douglas MacArthur bitterly predicted that America would lose its next war if the cuts to the military budget were implemented), the bill passed through the House and Senate and the President signed the Economy Act (as it became known) on 20th March. The savings generated by the Economy Act, though important, were less than had been hoped for ($243 million in the first year according to one estimate), and even this saving was lost the following year when Congress voted to increase federal wages and to grant a bonus to veterans; nevertheless, the Economy Act sent an important message that the pain of the Depression was to be shared by those working in government service as well as by those in the private sector. President Roosevelt himself took a voluntary pay cut and was widely regarded as setting a good example.

The third "emergency measures" bill was also passing through Congress at that time. During the 1932 elections, Roosevelt and the Democratic Party generally had promised to abolish the federal laws underpinning Prohibition, and Congress had passed a bill to repeal the Eighteenth Amendment (whereby Prohibition had been introduced) in February 1933; it was now being debated

---

(depositary) banks or investment banks, with the former effectively prohibited from selling investment banking services to deposit holders. The Act also created the Federal Deposit Insurance Corporation, providing federally-backed insurance for bank deposits. It remained in force until 1999, when Congress succumbed to pressure from the banking community and overwhelmingly voted for its repeal which was effected by President Clinton. Critics have argued that the repeal of the Glass-Steagall Act played a major role in creating the sub-prime lending and credit crisis of the last few years.

in various state conventions throughout the country, and would eventually be ratified as the Twenty First Amendment by the requisite three-quarters of all states on 5th December 1933, with national Prohibition formally ending on 15th December.[77] In anticipation, at Roosevelt's urging, the Beer-Wine Revenue Act was passed by Congress and signed by him on 22nd March, permitting the sale (and taxation) of beer and wine with an alcohol content of less than 3.2%. The new Act came into force on 7th April, and in those states that chose not to maintain Prohibition on a state-wide basis, men and women began to gather outside bars and breweries early in the morning of that day, anxious to taste their first (legal) beer since January 1920. Celebrations erupted spontaneously in cities and towns across the land and lasted long into the night. Although the importance of the re-legalisation of the sale of weak beer and wine might seem almost trivial when set against the gravity of the country's economic and social problems, it constituted an important facet of the New Deal in its earliest years. Not only was the re-legalisation itself almost universally popular, triggering a surge of hope (and indeed happiness) in Americans across the country at a time when such emotions were in distinctly short supply, but the taxes levied on beer and wine represented a new (and potentially valuable) form of revenue for the Federal Government. Moreover, the repeal of Prohibition led to the creation of new jobs in the drinks and entertainment industries generally as well as in related industries such as transportation (some estimates of the time predicted that as many as half a million new jobs would eventually be created as a result of repeal). Particularly welcome was the expectation of an increased demand for grain from the beleaguered farming sector. Perhaps most importantly of all, the repeal of Prohibition was seen by most Americans as definitive proof that their new government, under FDR's firm leadership, was able and determined to improve their everyday lives, and the effect of this on the public morale was noticeable.

Relief for Farmers

One of the most serious problems to be addressed under the New Deal legislative programme was the agricultural depression that had been plaguing

---

[77] Though the repeal of Prohibition was almost universally popular, several states were to remain "dry" even after ratification occurred.

America since the early 1920s. It was exacerbated in the 1930s not only by the onset of the Great Depression but also by steadily worsening drought conditions, particularly in the mid-western and southern plains states, which helped to give rise to such phenomena as the dust bowl of Oklahoma. At the heart of the problem lay the simple fact that American farmers were producing more food than was needed at home or could be sold at a profit abroad, but were unable to agree collectively to cut back production to any significant extent. This led to a steady decline in food prices generally, which in turn increased the financial pressure on farmers.[78] By the time of Roosevelt's inauguration, many farmers were finding that their farm incomes were insufficient to cover their costs, let alone produce profits, and stories of banks foreclosing on mortgaged farmers were commonplace. The rural population had begun to decline as dispossessed farmers and labourers and their families abandoned the countryside and began to seek opportunities in cities and towns. Throughout the 1920s and during the Hoover years, there had been various attempts to address the problems posed by the agricultural depression, but none had shown more than transitory success.

The principal weapon that Roosevelt and his advisers deployed against the agricultural depression was a new federal agency – the Agricultural Adjustment Administration (AAA)[79] which was established under the auspices of the Agricultural Adjustment Act of 1933. That Act, primarily drafted by Roosevelt's Secretary of Agriculture, Henry Wallace (who would go on to become Vice President of the United States during FDR's third term as President) did not pass quite as smoothly through Congress as some of the other New Deal legislation. One potential policy for dealing with the country's agricultural problems long advocated by a powerful (and growing) group of representatives and senators was that of deliberately encouraging inflation, so that farmers' debts would simply be inflated away (after all, many people reasoned, that was essentially what had happened to Germany's debts during the hyperinflation of the early 1920s – though others grimly pointed to the

---

[78] Agricultural incomes had declined by approximately 60 percent during the years of the Hoover administration alone.

[79] The New Deal gave birth to a plethora of new institutions and projects known by their initials – the AAA was the first.

disadvantages of excessive inflation, also as exemplified by what happened in Germany following the end of the First World War). A leading proponent of inflationism, Senator Elmer Thomas of Oklahoma, added an amendment to the Agricultural Adjustment Act, just before it was sent to Roosevelt for signature, which authorised the President at his discretion to devalue the dollar by as much as 50 percent (by reducing its gold content), and to inflate the money supply (by printing up to $3 billion worth of paper currency or coining silver). Many of Roosevelt's economic advisers were horrified at the amendment (one of them declared that the amendment, if adopted, would represent "the end of western civilization"), but the President decided that acceptance of the amendment was the political price he would have to pay in order for the Act to be passed within the Hundred Days. In fact, President Roosevelt was by no means as opposed to the idea of allowing debts to be inflated away as were some of his closest advisers; in practice the powers created under the Thomas Amendment were used sparingly. President Roosevelt did however announce on 19th April 1933 that he was taking the dollar off the gold standard, which coupled with the new restrictions on the overseas transfer of gold, led to a weakening of the dollar on the foreign exchanges, and helped to push up the prices of imports (such as there were in 1933). However, in itself, this did little to help the beleaguered farmers of America, who were to receive more practical (if sometimes controversial) help from the AAA.

Broadly speaking, the remit of the AAA was to stabilise the prices of farm produce and to encourage greater diversification in the farming sector by persuading farmers to reduce their production of staples such as wheat, cotton, tobacco, rice, milk and pigs, in exchange for subsidies from the Federal Government. The cost of this exercise was to be met by the imposition of a tax on processed foods. Unfortunately, the timing of the Act's passage through Congress and its signing into law meant that implementation of the acreage reduction programmes of the AAA in the first year would require the destruction of cotton plants already sown, and the slaughter of piglets already born, something that many farmers initially found difficult to reconcile with their natural instincts of preserving their crops and animals at all costs. Many ordinary Americans too questioned whether it was right to destroy farm produce in a world of shortages; nevertheless in 1933, American farmers ploughed up 10 million acres of cotton plants (perhaps a quarter of all the cotton plants planted in the country that year), and slaughtered six million piglets. Farmers might well also have been required that first year to destroy a substantial proportion of America's wheat and corn production, were it not for worsening drought in the Great Plains which severely affected the American wheat and corn harvests that year. 1933 was the only year in which crops and animals were actually destroyed; thereafter careful planning under the direction of the AAA's local agents meant that such drastic and unorthodox steps were unnecessary.

Initially, and ostensibly, compliance by American farmers with the AAA's acreage reduction programmes was voluntary; in practice, considerable pressure was brought upon farmers by local "production control" committees set up under the auspices of the AAA to encourage their cooperation (and in any event, most farmers needed the subsidy payments cooperation brought if they were to survive). By 1934, supporters of the AAA had succeeded in persuading the government to introduce compulsion in the cotton and tobacco sectors, with the imposition of punitive taxes imposed on farmers who exceeded specified quotas. Unpopular though the programmes of the AAA were with some, and though they were to give rise to fierce legal battles in the future, they did achieve some success during FDR's first term: wheat prices reached 86 cents a bushel in 1934, having risen from 38 cents a bushel in 1932, while corn prices rose from 32 cents a bushel to 82 cents a bushel during the same period. And cotton prices improved from 7 cents a pound in 1932 to more than 12 cents a pound in 1934. These price rises had an inevitable impact on net farm income, which rose by approximately 50 percent between 1932 and 1936.

Welcome though the rises in prices and income were on America's farms, the programmes of the AAA in the early years were not without significant drawbacks. Unsurprisingly, the farmers with the bigger farms tended to receive the largest subsidy payments; once the larger farmers had grown used to regular subsidy payments and had tackled their most urgent financial problems, they tended to use the payments to purchase new farm equipment, and especially tractors, and then lay off farm workers they no longer required, increasing rural unemployment. This problem was particularly acute in the cotton belt in the south of the country, where most of the workers in the cotton fields were sharecroppers and poor tenant farmers, who owned no land of their own but effectively "rented" land from the larger landowners in exchange for a share of their crops. Sometimes they were also dependent upon the landowners for seeds and farm tools, and even clothes and food. It was rare that a sharecropper or tenant farmer could make sufficient money to allow him to escape from this system which effectively had been in operation since the end of the American Civil War and which quite rightly has been described as neo-feudalism. By the early 1930s, it was a system that had ensnared more than 1.5 million households (one-third of them – the poorest of all – being African American). The acres that landlords selected to lie fallow in exchange for subsidies were typically those which they had hitherto rented to sharecroppers and tenant farmers (the subsidy payments being more valuable than the "rents" that could be levied from the landless workers). Landlords were supposed to share the subsidy payments they received for not working those fields with their tenants and sharecroppers but few did so, and far too often the sharecroppers and tenants were simply turfed off the land and left to make their way to the cities and towns to search for such relief as they could find, or simply wander the roads and highways, joining the legions of dispossessed there who had already discovered they had nowhere else to go. Eventually attempts would be made to help dispossessed farm workers and their families (in 1935, in the form of the Resettlement Agency, which tried to help farm workers relocate to areas of farm labour shortage, and in 1937 in the form of the Farm Security Administration, which tried to provide social services and financial assistance to tenant farmers so that they could buy their own land), but the new agencies were underfunded and in the South faced serious opposition from local politicians and large agricultural interests who objected in particular to assistance being provided to black sharecroppers. While the new agencies did eventually provide some much needed assistance to several thousand landless farming families, the vast majority of the dispossessed farm workers received little or no help, and the problem of extreme rural poverty persisted throughout the decade and beyond.[80]

---

[80] It has been estimated that for every dollar spent by the Resettlement Agency and the

The Tennessee Valley Authority

Further – and dramatic – long-term assistance for rural agricultural life was provided in the form of the Tennessee Valley Authority (TVA), which was established by Congress at Roosevelt's urging on 18th May. During the early Depression years, the problems facing the states of the Tennessee Valley, that is, the drainage basin of the Tennessee River – Virginia, North Carolina, Tennessee, Alabama, Mississippi and Kentucky – were significant. Many of the forests of the area had been destroyed by excessive deforestation, particularly in the years following the Civil War. Farmland had been overplanted, causing soil quality to plummet, and catastrophic flooding was almost a perennial occurrence. The farming methods adopted by many local farmers exacerbated the problems – one report commented that the farming methods used in some places were little more advanced than those of the early colonial farmers, with crop rotation and the use of fertilizers being effectively unknown. Soil erosion was so bad that there were genuine fears that it might prove impossible ever to restore the fertility of the land in many counties. Unsurprisingly, rural poverty throughout the Tennessee Valley was acute, as bad as if not worse than could be found anywhere else in the country at that time and malnourishment (particularly of children) was commonplace. Thirty percent of the population suffered from malaria; tuberculosis, pellagra and trachoma were also rife.

More than 50 percent of the population in the Tennessee Valley lived on farms; nearly all of them (97 percent according to some estimates) had no access to electricity. Yet the potential for the generation of hydroelectric power in the Valley was immense. During the First World War, a major hydroelectric plant (and two nitrate plants for the production of ammunition and explosives) had been built at Muscle Shoals, Alabama, and there was the potential for other hydroelectric plants to be built, holding out the promise of cheap electricity that could not only power the farms of the area but could also encourage the development of industrial centres throughout the Valley and provide a major boost for the economies of the Valley's states. Unfortunately, this dream, which was shared by Republican and Democratic progressives

Farm Security Administration on dispossessed farm workers, ten dollars were paid to larger farmers under the auspices of the AAA and other federal agencies.

alike, had been frustrated for years, partly due to a lack of interest by the Coolidge and Hoover administrations, and partly because of the absence of a unifying planning authority capable of operating on a trans-state basis throughout the Valley. Exacerbating the problems was the debate as to the extent to which federal and state authorities could and should become involved in issues of power production, rather than leaving such matters in the hands of private producers. Those arguing for the need for the public regulation – and even public ownership – of utility companies alleged that many private utility companies exploited their positions in breach of the anti-monopoly laws, overcharged their customers, generally provided a poor service and were unwilling, and in some cases, unable, to expand the supply of electricity to areas where it was badly needed; supporters of the private utilities feared public regulation of the power companies as constituting a step on the road to socialism, arguing it would not only provide State and Federal Governments with unwarranted and unjustifiable additional power over the lives of ordinary Americans, but would also constitute a direct attack on the fundamentals of capitalism itself.

Roosevelt had paid a visit to Muscle Shoals in January 1933, and had since his days as the Governor of New York been interested in the debate relating to the public control of the private utility companies. Genuinely moved by the plight of the poor families he saw in the Valley, forced to light their homes by kerosene lamps and simple candles, and to cook their meagre meals by wood fires, he now publicly supported the establishment of a trans-state regional authority (in the form of a public corporation), one capable of operating throughout the Tennessee Valley and empowered to address the problems of the area on an integrated basis, arguing that the advantages such an authority could bestow would far outweigh its disadvantages. Congress agreed, and the TVA was established with a wide remit to generate and distribute hydro-electric power not only from Muscle Shoals, but also from new generating plants to be established. This in turn would require the construction of new dams, and it was natural to extend the authority of the TVA to include responsibility for flood controls throughout the Valley. The TVA also assumed responsibility for the improvement of farm lands, sending advisers to teach farmers modern farming techniques, providing them with low-cost fertilizers, advising them on how to address problems of soil erosion, encouraging reforestation and the conservation of wildlife. The TVA's programmes were not implemented without some difficulty (the creation of the new dams led to the deliberate flooding of hundreds of thousands of acres of farm land, and the displacement of over 15,000 families), but generally speaking, the establishment of the TVA was greeted with considerable enthusiasm by most of the inhabitants of the Valley, particularly once cheap electricity began to flow to the rural farms. Farm productivity began to rise and new jobs began to be created, not only by the TVA itself but also by the new industries that began to be attracted to the area. Recovery of the Tennessee Valley did not come overnight, but the TVA had proved its worth within a few years of operation, and would go on to play a major role in the industrialisation of the South. It continues to operate to this day, one of President Roosevelt's greatest legacies.[81]

The Unemployed

One of the most important challenges facing President Roosevelt's new administration was that of unemployment, which by the early months of 1933 had reached almost 25 percent (having been perhaps 3.2 percent before the Great Crash). Reinvigorating American businesses and creating new jobs were thus at the top of the President's list of primary objectives for the New Deal, and in typical Roosevelt style, these objectives were pursued simultaneously by a number of disparate measures.

Roosevelt's first direct legislative assault on unemployment reached Congress on 21st March in the form of a proposal to create a Civilian Conservancy Corps (CCC) which would employ young (unmarried) men aged between 17 and 24 whose families were on relief (eventually veterans and Native Americans would also be employed by the CCC) in a variety of different areas such as forestry, flood relief, and the conservation and use of natural resources in lands owned

---

[81] The fame, and the example of the TVA, would spread far beyond America. On a personal note, the author can recall being taught about the creation of the TVA during a geography lesson in an English grammar school during the early 1970s; it was presented as one of the greatest social and industrial achievements of the Depression Years.

by the federal and state governments. Congress passed the Civilian Conservation Corps Reforestation Act on 31st March 1933; it was signed into law by President Roosevelt the same day and the new agency came into existence on 5th April 1933. The CCC was an unusual agency for the New Deal in that it was never intended to be permanent; nevertheless, during the nine years of its existence, it proved to be extremely popular with the general public. Service with the CCC was voluntary and much sought after, and within two years of its establishment, the CCC was providing employment for half a million men.

Living in camps run by reserve US army officers (there were over 2,500 camps), CCC workers were provided with accommodation, food and free medical care, and moreover paid $30 a month ($25 of which they had to send home to their families). In the creation of the CCC, the President was essentially seeking to repeat on a larger scale a similar project he had initiated in New York while Governor, and in so doing, he created one of the most popular institutions of the New Deal. By the time the CCC was disbanded in 1942, more than 3 million men had worked for it, in the process having planted nearly three billion trees, created hundreds of parks and dramatically improved the public infrastructure of the national parks by the construction of new roads, lookouts, bridges and firebreaks.

At the same time as he proposed the creation of the CCC, Roosevelt also persuaded Congress to agree to the creation of the Federal Emergency Relief Administration (FERA). FERA, supervised by Harry Hopkins, a close personal friend and associate of FDR (and who would in the future become the Secretary of Commerce), was given the mandate of providing and coordinating $500 million-worth of federal unemployment assistance to the various individual states and local agencies in the form of grants (rather than loans) for local work-relief projects. Grants were provided on the basis that every federal dollar advanced would be matched by three dollars from local city or state coffers. Despite opposition and difficulties in some quarters (some southern local authorities objected to what they considered to be the provision of "too generous" relief for destitute African Americans, while elsewhere it proved surprisingly difficult to persuade what were described as "former white collar workers" to register for such relief as could be provided[82]) and despite (legitimate) criticism that the FERA relief efforts were often haphazard and sometimes wasteful, FERA working with local authorities ultimately provided work and other forms of support by one means or another for more than 2.5 million people before it was replaced in 1935 by two new agencies – the Works Progress Administration and the Social Security Administration.

Nevertheless, welcome though such measures were, they were insufficient in themselves to have a significant effect upon the nation's unemployment rate. Further action would be required; however, before President Roosevelt and his administration could present any detailed proposals, Congress announced proposals of its own on 6th April, in the form of a bill sponsored by Alabama Senator Hugo Black, which broadly speaking sought to "share" such work as was available with the unemployed by reducing the working week of industrial workers to 30 hours. The senators supporting the bill announced that they hoped 6 million new jobs might be created by such a measure as businesses sought to hire additional employees to carry out the work that existing employees would otherwise have carried out during the course of a longer and harder working week; it was accepted that the incomes of workers might shrink somewhat, but this was deemed an acceptable price for the expected reduction in unemployment.

Roosevelt and his advisers were unenthusiastic about Black's bill, fearing that it would simply prove unworkable in practice in the factories and on the farms; they questioned the financial viability of the plan, and whether the cost of an additional 6 million workers (even allowing for reductions in the wages of

---

[82] This reluctance to register for assistance, despite often dire need, was reported as being largely due to feelings of personal pride which persisted for many even after several years of unemployment and hardship. One unemployed former insurance clerk when interviewed by a FERA official confessed that *"we had been living on bread and water for three weeks before I could make myself do it…"* (that is, claim relief when it was offered). Another claimant reported *"I simply had to murder my pride."* Part of the problem was that to qualify for FERA assistance, an applicant had to undergo a means test administered by local administrators who were often condescending and sometimes prejudiced against people forced to seek support; the test itself was generally regarded as intrusive and humiliating.

existing workers) could be met by American businesses. There was also concern about the likely responses of existing workers who would suddenly be asked to cut back on their overtime and to take home less pay. Finally, Homer S. Cummings, Roosevelt's first US Attorney-General, suggested that the proposals set out in Black's bill were unconstitutional. Roosevelt therefore felt unable to support the bill, but this simply meant that he and his administration needed rapidly to come up with proposals of their own, which after some hurried thinking and mutual horse-trading by different groups among Roosevelt's advisers, materialised in the form of proposals for a National Industrial Recovery Act (NIRA) which was announced to Congress on 17th May and subsequently enacted.

At the heart of the new Act were three broad areas of legislation. The first, which soon became widely referred to as Section 7(a), gave the Federal Government power to regulate wages and working hours and (perhaps even more importantly) gave employees the right to *"organise and bargain collectively through representatives of their own choosing…"* and to be free *"…from interference, restraint, or coercion of employers of labor, or their agents, in the designation of such representatives or in the self-organization or in other concerted activities for the purpose of collective bargaining…"*. Section 7(a) was a major milestone in the development of the American labor movement and the subsequent exercise of the rights it created was to have a momentous impact on American industry generally, and particularly those industries such as steel and automobile manufacturing which for decades had been fiercely resisting attempts by employees to organise themselves. Hereafter, the right of workers to organise would be supported by the Federal Government (although this did not prevent industrialists such as Henry Ford from continuing to seek to exclude unions from their factory floors for several years to come). Simultaneously, the right of employers to require that their workers abstain from forming a union or only join a company-sponsored union as a condition of their employment was abolished.

Secondly, NIRA created a new federal agency, the National Recovery Administration, or NRA. The NRA's principal task was to encourage business recovery by a myriad of different ways (which were ultimately spelt out in 557 different codes of fair practice). Under its auspices, industrial production was subject to government control by means of the introduction of production quotas and minimum prices, wages were fixed (and where possible, raised), maximum working hours were imposed, and the anti-monopoly legislation largely suspended.[83] The ultimate aim was to stimulate business recovery by encouraging efficiency and eliminating unfair competition. When the NRA first appeared, many businesses rushed to announce their compliance with the new rules (which in turn allowed them to display the NRA's symbol, a blue eagle, with its bold motto "We do our part" indicating their willingness to help in bringing about national recovery). Not every business submitted willingly to the directives of the NRA; Henry Ford in particular refused to cooperate, while many small businesses complained bitterly about the plethora of new red tape that they now had to contend with simply to do business. Nevertheless within a few months of the NRA's inception, more than 22 million workers were employed under the NRA codes, prices and wages began to stabilise and the relentless rise in unemployment which America had suffered since 1929 was first brought to a halt, and then slowly began to reverse itself. For the first time in years, Americans began to wonder if the worst of the Great Depression might now finally be over, and whether better days might, after all, lie ahead.

Thirdly, NIRA created the Public Works Administration (PWA), (called the Federal Emergency Administration of Public Works until 1939). The PWA's mandate (under the direction of Secretary of the Interior Harold Ickes) was to create a wide-ranging public construction programme with a remit to spend $3.3 billion in its first year of operation. In a sense, the creation of the PWA represented something of a compromise with Congress as far as President Roosevelt was concerned; although not averse to public spending (as evidenced by his creation of the CCC and its predecessor programmes while Governor of New York), broadly speaking he was inclined to support it for reasons other than economic, for example, because it was the *"right thing to do"* (as exemplified by his support for relief for the unemployed which he justified

---

[83] The NRA's rules could be detailed and explicit; it had regulations, for instance, which dictated what tailors could and could not sew, and what they could charge for repairing specific items of clothing. In one instance, a tailor was fined under the NRA guidelines for repairing a suit for less than the NRA-mandated price.

as a charitable measure).[84]   As a general rule, at least during the first few months of his first administration, he was as determined as President Hoover had been that any large scale public works programme should in the medium to long term be self-financing. Ever since his inauguration, there had been calls from some of the more progressive members of Congress for the instigation of a large-scale public works programme funded by $5 billion of federal funds and deliberately intended to create work for the unemployed. Roosevelt initially resisted such calls, warning reporters that talk of any such programme using public money was "wild", but eventually he was obliged to succumb to Congressional pressure (and pressure from those in his own administration, such as Frances Perkins, who supported widespread public spending as a way of restarting the economy and reducing unemployment) and agree to the inclusion of the PWA within the scope of the NIRA legislation.

The PWA did not itself generally employ workers directly; rather it placed orders with private contractors. Under its direction, a wide variety of federal public work projects were initiated, including the building of highways, tunnels, dams, bridges (including the Triborough Bridge in New York), federal buildings and even warships. At a state level, in conjunction with state authorities (who had to find 70 percent of the required funds), hospitals, schools, public water and public sewage facilities were constructed. By the end of the decade, the PWA had spent $6 billion on public works in way or another, creating over 600,000 jobs in the process, most of them (perhaps unsurprisingly) in the construction sector. This was impressive in itself, but the PWA was in the final analysis less successful in tackling unemployment and stimulating the economy by encouraging the growth of new businesses than some of its supporters had hoped. This was partly due to Roosevelt's reluctance to countenance deficit spending by means of the PWA on the scale that the PWA's supporters had hoped (and which if provided might well have had a more dramatic impact on the unemployment rate), but it was also partly

---

[84] Not that he was averse to supporting public spending plans for political reasons. One of the reasons he supported unemployment relief while Governor of New York was specifically because it would reduce the dependency of unemployed voters on the Tammany political machine. *"People on relief would have no use for Tammany's services"* he once observed to an aide. *"They'd be independent."*

due to the simple fact that many of the PWA's projects (and ultimately there were thousands of them across the country) took time to plan and to implement and thus time for the PWA to deliver demonstrable results. Nevertheless, the PWA did at least help to provide crucially needed employment in the construction sector when all other construction activities had virtually ground to a halt, and it did represent the first attempt to provide large-scale federal funding to multiple projects on a nation-wide scale. In that light, the PWA must be regarded as a success.[85]

The End of the Hundred Days

The end of the Hundred Days Congress ended on 16th June marked the end of one of the most remarkable periods of legislative activity in the history of the United States (and, indeed, in the history of any nation). As President Roosevelt signed the final bills sent to him from Congress, the basic elements of the New Deal were falling into place, and there were already some achievements to celebrate. The problem of perennial banking crises had, for the foreseeable future at least, been solved, and public confidence in the American banking system had been restored. The Agricultural Adjustment Act and ancillary legislation was poised to deliver real, urgently needed assistance to American farmers (albeit that the rendering of such assistance would in due course create other problems that would have to be addressed). The National Industrial Recovery Act would help to rationalise American business practices

---

[85] As a demonstration of what could be done with adequate funding for the task at hand and enthusiastic support from the White House, we have the example of the Civil Works Administration (CWA). In November 1933, frustrated at the apparent lack of progress by the PWA, and faced with the prospect of high unemployment during the cold winter months, FDR "liberated" $400 million from the PWA's budget and arranged for the creation of the CWA under the auspices of FERA and the guidance of Harry Hopkins. During the winter of 1933/34, the CWA instigated scores of public work projects ranging from street paving exercises to the building of schools and airports, in the process providing temporary work (and pay in the form of the minimum wage rather than unemployment relief payments) for more than 4 million people and much needed boosts to local economies across the country. Costs concerns (and a belief that the economy was finally reviving) led to the abolition of the CWA in the spring of 1934.

by discouraging harmful competition and overproduction while at the same time introducing legal protections for workers as regards both working conditions and wages. There was, in the form of the PWA, the promise of large-scale public works and the hope that this would kick-start the motors of the American economy and help to reduce unemployment. The Tennessee Valley Authority promised to set an example of planned regional development on a scale that had hitherto never been attempted. And these were merely the principal achievements of the Hundred Days – other pieces of smaller, ancillary legislation intended to supplement and complement the principal legislative achievements had also been passed during that period, helping to create the legal and social and economic edifice that was the New Deal as it existed in the summer of 1933.

Never before in American history had the Federal Government intruded so far into the day-to-day economic and social lives of ordinary Americans. Some objected, regarding the new legislation as an assault on the ancient liberties of the American people and on the system of capitalism itself. There were those who alleged that FDR was hellbent on introducing a new tyranny to the United States. Others however welcomed the changes that Roosevelt was introducing, arguing that desperate times demand desperate measures. Journalist Walter Lippmann, who initially had evinced no great enthusiasm for FDR, was later moved to write of the Hundred Days: *"In the hundred days from March to June we became an organised nation confident of our power to provide for our own security and to control our own destiny."* There were many who shared Lippmann's sentiment. And more than that, for some (including Lippmann), one of the most striking aspects of the Hundred Days was the rise in the apparent stature of FDR himself; even some of those who voted for him and knew him were surprised by the degree of moral and decisive leadership that he contrived to display during this time – to an even greater degree than had been seen during the pre-election period, Roosevelt's optimism and fortitude now seemed to be infusing the spirit of the nation.

But for all the excitement of the New Deal, and the new glow of energy and optimism now emanating from the White House, the stark fact remained that the country was still embroiled in the dank miasma of the Great Depression. The New Deal of 1933, with all of its myriad policies and projects, was just the beginning of the campaign to extract the nation from the Depression's grasp. Few foresaw how long that campaign would last. But at least, now, it had started.

Chapter 10   Dark Realities

"Only a foolish optimist can deny the dark realities of the moment"
Excerpt from President Roosevelt's First Inaugural Address, 4th March 1933

Roosevelt's Bombshell

With the abandonment of the gold standard in April 1933, the United States (like Great Britain before her) was effectively renouncing the use of one of the standard methods of restraining inflation. There was a considerable body of opinion that believed that a surge in inflation might be a useful weapon in the fight against the Depression; admittedly prices of imports would rise but the cost of American exports would fall, which in turn would help to stimulate the American economy. Moreover, debt burdens (including those incurred to help to pay for the New Deal) would be reduced by the simple expedient of allowing them to be satisfied by the payment of inflated dollars. Many of the policies and programmes underpinning the New Deal, such as the NRA's price and wage controls and the AAA's plans to stimulate US agriculture demanded a measure of inflation if they were to work.

Nevertheless, the abandonment of the gold standard sent a shiver of dismay through the more cautious economists, politicians and businessmen, both at home and abroad and when FDR first announced that the United States was taking this step, he had sought to appease critics by implying that it was little more than a temporary measure. Indeed, he went further and suggested that not only was there hope that the United States would in time return to the gold standard, but also that it was desirable that the whole world should return *"to some form of gold standard…"*, although not necessarily the specific standard that had held sway before the Depression. Towards the end of April 1933, during discussions with British Prime Minister Ramsay MacDonald and French Premier Edouard Herriot, FDR effectively reiterated that message by indicating that the forthcoming World Economic Conference (scheduled to be held in London in mid-June and July and attended by the representatives of 66 nations) should lead to an opportunity to stabilise international exchange rates and the potential re-establishment of a gold standard. He repeated this once again in mid-May.

Unsurprisingly, the Conference delegates expected that America would take a leading role in the discussions, and play a major part in the global fight against the Depression. Their surprise and shock was therefore all the greater when, without warning, President Roosevelt sent a "bombshell message" to the conference on 3rd July 1933 in which he effectively declared that for the foreseeable future, the United States would not be a party to efforts to stabilise international exchange rates. Nor would the United States return to the gold standard – nor indeed any gold standard. Effectively, FDR's statement was a declaration that the United States would fight the Depression alone.

Why did President Roosevelt intervene as he did? There were, it seems, several factors at work. To begin with, Roosevelt had only ever been lukewarm about the conference – it had after all originally been proposed by President Hoover. Moreover, he was not alone in his lack of enthusiasm – Congress was divided as to what it could and should expect from the conference, as were the delegates America sent to London. Indeed, strife within the US delegation led to the political downfall of one of its key members, Assistant Secretary of State Raymond Moley, hitherto one of Roosevelt's strongest supporters and an ardent advocate of the New Deal. Moley had agreed to attend the delegation believing that Roosevelt sincerely wanted some form of stabilisation and had initiated a series of talks and proposals with other representatives at the conference on this basis. Roosevelt's message of 3rd July undermined his position, something Moley bitterly resented, and which led to serious arguments with Cordell Hull, the Secretary of State and a worsening of Moley's relationship with the President. In due course, Moley would resign, and go on to become a Republican and a trenchant critic of both the New Deal and the President. With division on all sides at the time of the World Economic Conference, President Roosevelt was understandably reluctant to commit himself to a course of action that could lead him into difficult political waters and perhaps jeopardise the New Deal itself.

Secondly, there was a mismatch between America's view of its financial relationship with the rest of the world and how the rest of the world viewed that relationship. Immediately prior to the Great Crash, America had been responsible for one-sixth of the world's exports and one-eighth of its imports; yet foreign trade before the Crash amounted to perhaps 5 percent of America's

GDP. In other words, at a time when the rest of the world needed America to function as a global economic and financial powerhouse if world trade was to begin to flow freely and profitably once more, America's economy, to a very great extent, was self-sufficient – America needed the world less than the world needed it. Yet despite this disparity in needs and power, and for all their talk of mutual interests and the advantages of financial cooperation, the European delegates to the conference, consciously or unconsciously, were talking in terms of setting exchange rates (particularly the pound/dollar exchange rate) at levels that undervalued the dollar, something that was manifestly unfavourable to the United States. Roosevelt himself pointed out the dangers to America of adopting such an approach, declaring that the United States should not "...*reduce the value of the dollar so that foreign governments could trade it at bargain prices in other markets...*" Combining this view with the suspicion (shared by Roosevelt and at least some of his key advisers) that the currency stabilisation proposals (particularly as advanced by the French, who continued to cling to the gold standard) were really little more than a crude attempt by the debtor nations to try and wriggle out of their responsibility for paying their war debts to the United States, and it is unsurprising that Roosevelt backed away from any specific formal commitment towards a policy of international currency stabilisation which could potentially damage America's economic recovery before it had even commenced.[86]

Thirdly, America was still, largely, a nation of isolationists. Criticised though he was by some of those who favoured a swift return to the gold standard and

---

[86] President Roosevelt's accordance of priority to the need to secure national recovery over international economic cooperation should not have come as a surprise to the other nations attending the conference. In his inaugural address of only a few months before, he had declared that Americans should "*... address ourselves to putting our own national house in order and making income balance outgoings. Our international trade relations, though vastly important, are in point of time and necessity secondary to the establishment of a sound national economy. I favor as a practical policy the putting of first things first. I shall spare no effort to restore world trade by international economic readjustment, but the emergency at home cannot wait on that accomplishment.*" This was a view he reiterated firmly in his message of 3rd July: "*The sound internal economic system of a nation is a greater factor in its well-being than the price of its currency in changing terms of the currencies of other nations....*"

who supported international economic cooperation, Roosevelt's decision was nevertheless broadly popular both in Congress and with ordinary Americans, and Roosevelt was never averse to courting popularity. Even more importantly however, acceptance of the conference's stabilisation proposals and a return to the gold standard would have meant abandoning any possibility of making use of inflation as an anti-Depression tool, something which Roosevelt was increasingly unwilling to do as the summer months of 1933 passed.

Roosevelt's message to the World Economic Conference was to have world-wide consequences. It effectively brought the conference to an end (though delegates continued to linger in London until 28th July). In announcing the non-participation of the United States in any attempt to coordinate a global response to the Depression, FDR in practice had ensured that no such global response would be attempted; henceforth it was every nation for itself (although the nations of the British Empire and Commonwealth did attempt to maintain some degree of mutual cooperation). Most disturbingly, the President's apparent continuing embrace of traditional American isolationism was read by many abroad as extending beyond the economic arena – in Germany, Adolf Hitler who in January 1933 had seized the German Chancellorship (and who a few weeks after that became the effective dictator of the country) concluded that America would allow Germany to do as she wished in Europe, without any sanction or reprisal.[87] In the Far East, the Japanese took note with interest of America's apparent abrupt retreat from the world stage. In several European countries (particularly France), the image of America as a benign world leader and a reliable ally suffered serious damage from which it never really fully recovered. By way of example, during the Second World War, General Charles de Gaulle was said to have cited Roosevelt's intervention during the conference as support for de Gaulle's proposition that America could have prevented the fall of France to the Nazis

---

[87] Hjalmar Schacht, President of the Reichsbank, later appointed by Hitler as Reich Minister of Economics, praised Roosevelt for his intervention at the conference, declaring him to be an economic nationalist in the same mould as Hitler and Mussolini. Having said that, John Maynard Keynes also praised President Roosevelt's pronouncement (virtually the only British economist to do so), saying he was *"magnificently right"*.

in 1940 if she had really wished to do so. Even in Great Britain, Prime Minister Ramsay MacDonald believed he had been *"personally betrayed"* by Roosevelt; complete trust between the two men was never fully restored. King George V too, apparently felt upset on MacDonald's behalf, telling courtiers that he would not have foreigners *"…worrying my Prime Minister this way…"*

Yet for all the international criticism of President Roosevelt's actions at the time (and since – economic historians continue to argue over whether Roosevelt was right to act as he did), the President's constitutional first duty was to the United States and her citizens; embracing the proposals of the conference would have meant the United States retreating into the straitjacket of the gold standard and being forced to accept the loss of financial flexibility that such a step would have entailed. It would have been widely regarded as a backward step by many of the President's supporters, would have cost him popular and political support, would probably have jeopardised the New Deal even before it had properly commenced and quite possibly would have delayed economic recovery for several years. And while the international community may have benefited to a degree from America's agreement to the conference's proposals, in the long run, they had more to gain from seeing a genuine recovery in America's economy – an economically strong and resurgent America would have helped to pull her trading partners out of the Depression (and, indeed, this is ultimately what happened).

Trouble with the NRA

President Roosevelt and his advisers (and indeed, much of the country) spent the remainder of the summer and early autumn of 1933 looking for signs that the various New Deal agencies were beginning to deliver results, and of all those agencies, perhaps none loomed larger in the eyes of the general public than the NRA. At its head was a former brigadier general, Hugh Johnson, who had administered the draft during the First World War and served on the War Industries Board, but who had resigned his commission in 1919 to go into industry. Energetic, hard-working, chain-smoking, more than capable of profanity and fond of alcohol, Johnson quickly captured people's imagination as the public face of the NRA (he was named Time magazine's man of the year of 1933). It was he who suggested the design of the NRA's Blue Eagle, and (with FDR's approval) he consciously modelled the NRA on the War Industries Board of the First World War, arguing that the spirit of cooperation that had united industries and workers during the war could once again be tapped during the crisis of the Depression if the country was to overcome its problems. President Roosevelt, when announcing the creation of the NRA on 16th June 1933, had himself stressed the importance of Americans banding and working together *"as one great team to victory"*, and Johnson envisaged that team moving forward under the banners of the NRA. As previously noted, within a few months, the influence of the NRA was making itself felt throughout the country; by September 1933, over 500 codes of fair practice had been issued and many businesses had rushed to declare their compliance with the new rules (and thus earn the right to display the Blue Eagle).

But the NRA was by no means popular with everyone. Henry Ford had opposed it from the start, won a considerable degree of public sympathy for his stance (he was seen as an individual standing up for his rights against governmental interference) and saw his share of the automobile market rise in 1934 as a result. Chrysler and General Motors, in contrast, meekly submitted and displayed the Blue Eagle. Nor was Ford the only person who complained about the NRA, and the number of detractors grew rapidly as the months passed. Many objected to the increased bureaucracy that the NRA imposed (certainly a legitimate complaint; the NRA itself eventually hired over 4,000 employees to draft, administer and implement its codes and practices, and within two years had issued over 13,000 pages of codes) while others complained that in practice, the NRA favoured larger businesses and unfairly (and possibly illegally) discriminated against smaller entrepreneurs. Some claimed that NRA codes were not enforced uniformly across the country (which was true) and consumer groups grumbled that the NRA was pushing up the prices of food and other essentials in the shops (also true). Union leaders declared that too little was being done to prevent employers from circumventing the provisions of NIRA and the NRA codes relating to trade union membership while employers began to have second thoughts about the NIRA provisions relating to independent trade unions and procrastinated about implementing them, encouraging instead company-sponsored unions and complaining when NRA officials intervened. Exacerbating the situation was the fact that NIRA represented a golden moment for America's trade union movement, and its leaders did not hesitate to take advantage of their new freedom to recruit members, telling would-be recruits that joining a union was patriotic and the President wanted them to do so. Such techniques worked; the membership of the United Mine Workers increased by more than 100,000 during June 1933 (by the end of the year, the union's membership had increased from 100,000 to more than 400,000) and thousands of other workers joined unions in other industries over the summer months. Employers responded to this increase in independent union activity by sacking workers for union-related activities, the number of strikes began to rise and industrial relations between employers and workers worsened noticeably.

By early 1934, public criticism of the NRA had reached such a level that Johnson felt obliged to arrange for the Department of Commerce to hold a public convention which ordinary members of the public could attend and at which they could raise their concerns. The convention opened on 27th February with more than two thousand people swamping the halls and great auditorium of the newly built Department of Commerce Building in Washington DC[88], all eager to list the many perceived deficiencies of the NRA. It rapidly became clear that in the view of many, not only was the NRA failing in its duties under NIRA but was actively hostile to the interests of small businesses and that it did too little to protect the rights of ordinary workers. Similar complaints were now being raised in Congress. In early March, in response to the criticism, President Roosevelt ordered the creation of a National Recovery Review Board, chaired by veteran lawyer and civil libertarian Clarence Darrow, to investigate and report upon the complaints being levied against the NRA. Darrow, regarded by many (including himself) as a staunch defender of "ordinary Americans", enthusiastically plunged into the investigation, and on 20th May, under his leadership, the Board published its preliminary report that supported the view that the NRA favoured large businesses to the detriment of smaller ones, that it encouraged monopolistic

---

[88] Re-named the Herbert C Hoover Building in 1981. When it was first completed in 1932, it was the largest office building in the world.

practices, and that it turned a blind eye to employers seeking to circumvent the rights of workers to establish and join independent trade unions.

Darrow's report was by no means accepted uncritically, and it generated considerable controversy, many of its critics charging that the Review Board had not fully assessed all the evidence presented to it and had not been objective in its approach to the investigation. These were legitimate criticisms (though Darrow sought to rebut them with characteristic gusto); nevertheless, the general feeling (at least amongst Roosevelt supporters) was that steps had to be taken to provide further protections for American workers. However Roosevelt took no action, even persuading Senator Robert Wagner of New York (a strong supporter of legal rights for workers and the New Deal generally) to drop his labour disputes bill that would effectively have banned any management interference with trade unions and encouraged independent collective bargaining arrangements, on the grounds that the bill's objectives could be met within the framework of existing legislation. Progressive Democrats and Labour leaders throughout the country felt a sense of betrayal and disappointment, and a series of major strikes promptly erupted across the country, some so serious as to require declarations of martial law. For the moment, Roosevelt did nothing to seek to improve industrial relations, and throughout the hot spring and summer months of 1934, the country seemed to be quivering on the edge of industrial anarchy.

In the meantime, Hugh Johnson's behaviour was giving rise to increasing concern. His drinking had become more pronounced through the summer and autumn of 1933, and it began to affect his ability to do his job. Seemingly oblivious of the impression it gave, he would frequently disappear for days at a time on drinking expeditions; when he did turn up for work, he sometimes deeply insulted people he met. His relationship with his secretary Robbie Robinson (who was also his mistress) gave rise to public criticism, although according to some accounts, she was one of the few people who could help him to control his drinking. By the late summer of 1934, it was clear to everyone except himself that he could no longer continue at the helm of the NRA. President Roosevelt tried to allow him the opportunity to depart gracefully by suggesting he be appointed to a mission to Europe to study economic conditions there, but presumably misreading the President's intentions, he firmly refused to go, later telling the press that the President wanted him to *"stay right here with my feet nailed to the floor. That's what I am going to do."* Eventually, Roosevelt had little choice but to fire him and he departed on 1st October. No one replaced him; instead the NRA continued to operate in the midst of a sea of public criticisms and legal challenges under the general direction of a team of senior executives reporting directly to FDR. But by then, its days (at least in the form of its original incarnation) were numbered.

Set a Thief to Catch a Thief

Roosevelt and his fellow New Dealers were not content merely to kick-start the American economy while providing urgently needed relief for the victims of the Depression; they also wanted to minimise, as best they could, the likelihood of another Great Crash in the future. This meant looking for the causes of the current economic calamity. In the eyes of most Americans (including Roosevelt himself), much (if not all) of the blame for the Crash and the Depression rested with the speculators of Wall Street and their practices. This was an impression that seemed to be vindicated by a Senate enquiry into the causes of the Crash held between 1932 and 1934[89], which uncovered and publicised numerous abusive Wall Street practices (such as pool operations, tax evasion and active disregard of conflicts of interest) and shocked a watching and vengeful American public.

It was clear to all that institutional reform of Wall Street was badly needed, and would be implemented by Roosevelt no matter how much Wall Street squealed in protest, which indeed it did at the prospect of new, federally mandated regulation. Richard Whitney, the President of the New York Stock Exchange, signally failed to reassure critics of Wall Street when he claimed to investigators that the Pecora Commission's accusations of malpractice and incompetence on the part of at least some Wall Street practitioners were misplaced, that reform was not needed and that the Exchange was *"a perfect institution"*. In an attempt to avoid new regulation, the governors of the New York Stock Exchange themselves voted to ban some of the more outrageous practices such as the

---

[89] Commonly known as the Pecora Commission after its fourth (and most effective) chief counsel, Ferdinand Pecora.

operation of investment pools and dealings using insider information; however, this was too little, too late, and on 6th June 1934, the Securities Exchange Act of 1934 was signed into law. This new legislation (predictably described by one Wall Street apologist as designed to push the nation *"along the road from Democracy to Communism"*) built on the success of the Securities Act of 1933 (passed during the Hundred Days) which had introduced federal regulation of the issue of new securities. The Securities Exchange Act now sought to extend federal regulation to all the US stock markets, by regulating the trade of securities such as stocks, bonds and debentures. To make and enforce the new rules, a regulatory body was created, the Securities and Exchange Commission (SEC), with widespread powers to intervene and prevent corporate abuses.

The SEC was to be governed by a board of five commissioners with a chairman who would, in practice, lead the SEC. To the astonishment of almost everyone, in July 1934 Roosevelt decided to appoint Joseph P Kennedy[90] who in the 1920s had gained notoriety and a considerable fortune as both a Wall Street speculator and a Hollywood moviemaker. There were also dark rumours that he owed at least part of his fortune to bootlegging during the Prohibition, and that he enjoyed close ties to gangsters. Nevertheless, he had also been an early and prominent supporter of Roosevelt's Presidential campaign, and had been disappointed not to receive a Cabinet post. Roosevelt was well aware of Kennedy's disappointment, and was anxious not to turn him into a political enemy if this could be avoided. Offering Kennedy the Chairmanship of the SEC was therefore a way for Roosevelt to assuage Kennedy's wounded pride and keep his political support.

However, there was more to the offer than the simple settlement of political debts. Roosevelt genuinely wanted the SEC to succeed. Critics of the Securities

---

[90] Strictly speaking, President Roosevelt was not empowered to appoint the chairman, this being a matter for the Board of Commissioners itself. But he made sure that the other Commissioners, who included Ferdinand Pecora and James Landis (who later succeeded Joe Kennedy as Chairman of the SEC, and subsequently appointed Dean of Harvard Law School and Special Counsel to President John F Kennedy, but was ultimately jailed for tax evasion) were aware of his wishes and willing to carry them out.

Act of 1933 had alleged that the new regulations were being interpreted in such a way as to hamper legitimate business activities. The number of new stock issues had plummeted following the passage of the Act, thanks critics claimed, to the cumbersome form-filling that the new legislation now required. This in turn was affecting the ability of companies (and particularly smaller companies) to refinance themselves and thus potentially was delaying economic recovery. Roosevelt, anxious to avoid similar accusations being made about the Securities Exchange Act and the SEC, believed that Kennedy as a practical business man would be able to deliver the much needed stock market reforms without imposing unnecessary red tape upon American businesses. Then too, concerns had been voiced by many liberal reformers that the wicked speculators of Wall Street might yet prove more than a match for the officials of the SEC. But Kennedy was seasoned in the ways of Wall Street and could stand up to even the wiliest speculator. *"I'm setting a thief to catch a thief"* is how Roosevelt is said to have responded to one critic who questioned the advisability of the appointment.

However, news of Kennedy's appointment was greeted by a torrent of criticism by corporate reformers and New Deal enthusiasts alike, both within and outside the administration.[91] The New York Post declared that of the five Commissioners, Kennedy was the least fit to serve as Chairman. Newsweek pointed out the apparent incongruity in the appointment by commenting acidly: *"Mr Kennedy, former speculator and pool operator, will now curb speculation and prohibit pools"*. The New Republic described Kennedy as *"...that worst of all economic parasites, a Wall Street Operator..."* and commented that in selecting Kennedy, President Roosevelt had *"gone to the bottom of the heap"*. Even the Washington Daily News, usually a firm supporter of President Roosevelt warned that the President *"...cannot with impunity administer such a slap in the face to his most loyal and effective supporters as that reported to be contemplated in the appointment of Joseph P Kennedy..."* Within the heart of the administration, Harold Ickes, Secretary of the Interior, expressed doubts about the appointment in the privacy of his diary: *"The President has great confidence in him....but I have never*

---

[91] Though the Journal of Commerce reported that brokers on Wall Street were pleased, feeling the appointment would be helpful to their interests.

known any of these cases to work out as expected...", while Jerome Frank, general counsel at the Agricultural Adjustment Administration (and himself destined to serve as an SEC Commissioner in due course) described it as being akin to *"...setting a wolf to guard a flock of sheep..."* In the Senate, there was so much doubt over the appointment that Kennedy himself suggested that the Senate postpone his confirmation in the post for six months until he had shown that he had *"come through".*

In fact, Joe Kennedy confounded his critics (and disappointed many brokers) during the 15 months that he held office as SEC Chairman by doing an excellent job (and the Senate confirmed his appointment without debate in January 1935). He assumed his new duties immediately, and on 3rd July made a radio broadcast and issued a press release in which he emphasised that legitimate business had nothing to fear from the SEC, but promised a sharp crackdown on unethical practices. A few weeks later, in a speech before the National Press Club, he reiterated this message, emphasising that the SEC would seek to encourage normal and proper business activities and restore business confidence.

The first tasks facing the SEC under Kennedy's leadership were to establish rules for the registration of stock exchanges and temporary rules for the registration of securities traded on those exchanges, and to reduce the burden of over-regulation where this was hampering business activity to no purpose. To this end, registration forms were designed with the twin aims of being (relatively) easy to complete while at the same time worded so as to highlight potential irregularities. With a view to stamping down on insider dealing, and to ensure as far as possible that all potential investors had access to the same basic relevant information, stock exchanges were required to furnish statistical data, and company officers controlling more than 10 percent of their company's shares were required to declare their ownership. Stock exchanges were also required to publish their constitutions and by-laws and to expel any member breaking the law or otherwise indulging in dubious practices. At the same time, the SEC reviewed and reduced the administrative burdens created by the Securities Act of 1933 (which as previously noted dealt with the issue of new securities). When the new rules and forms were published in January 1935, it was clear to Wall Street and Washington alike that they were a dramatic improvement on what had been in place before. Kennedy openly expressed the hope that the new regulations would result in a resumption of new stock offerings. *"The charge has been made that the Act has been holding back the flotations."* Kennedy observed. *"Well, this is our answer."* The new system was indeed simpler and cheaper to operate than its predecessor and within months, the number of companies refinancing themselves by issuing new shares began to rise. The SEC, and Kennedy, had scored a notable triumph.

Having fulfilled Roosevelt's expectation that he could create a regulatory framework in compliance with the Securities Act of 1933 and the Securities Exchange Act without imposing an unnecessary burden on American businesses, Kennedy and the SEC then turned their attention to tackling abuses on the stock exchanges in a common sense and practical manner. Some progress in this regard had already been achieved by the new rules but now, in mid-April of 1935, the SEC, after consultation with officials of exchanges across the country, issued a series of 16 rules or guidelines for the regulation of trading that exchanges would be required to implement, either in the form recommended by the SEC or as amended with the approval of the SEC. They included prohibitions on exchange members trading for their own accounts on a scale that was excessive in view of the financial resources available to that member (Rule 1) and while in possession of information of unexecuted buy or sell orders from customers (Rule 5). Rule 6 included a prohibition on exchange members selling stocks at successively lower prices (or buying them at successively higher prices) *"...for the purpose of creating or inducing a false, misleading or artificial appearance of activity in such security, or for the purpose of unduly or improperly influencing the market price of such security, or for the purpose of making a price which does not reflect the true state of the market in such security."* Rule 9 required members to maintain written records of orders transmitted to the trading floor, while Rule 16 restricted the ability of members to short-sell a security at a price below that security's last sale price on the exchange.

The 16 rules were well received (the New York Stock Exchange adopted them immediately) and Kennedy and the SEC had scored a second triumph. For the SEC, this double success went a long way to reassuring Wall Street and the general American public that the SEC was capable of carrying out its mandate, that is, of improving the regulation and administration of the country's securities markets. Joe Kennedy had succeeded in demonstrating that he was more than a successful Wall Street operator, that he was capable of assuming positions of responsibility in the public service; in the years to come the Kennedy name would increasingly be linked to the concept of public service (most often of course, but not exclusively) in the field of politics. For the moment, it was time for Kennedy to move on, and he resigned as Chairman and Commissioner of the SEC on 23rd September 1935 (being replaced as Chairman by James M Landis). President Roosevelt congratulated him for ensuring the SEC administered the laws *"...so effectively as to win confidence of the general investing public and the financial community...."* As for the press, the Washington Post bluntly stated that *"... opinion is widespread that Kennedy has done one of the best jobs of anyone connected with the New Deal...."* while New Republic, eating its words of approximately a year and a half before described Kennedy as *"...a most useful member of the Commission."*

Kennedy gravely accepted such praise as his due and temporarily departed the scene while keeping his eyes open for the next public service opportunity. In the meantime, President Roosevelt and much of the New Deal legislation itself was facing a series of attacks of unprecedented severity, ones that – if successful – might have proved capable of ripping the heart out of the New Deal, and of costing FDR the Presidency. The enemy this time was not the unions, the bankers, the stock exchange brokers, or even the unemployed and destitute, but the nine justices of the Supreme Court of the United States.

Chapter 11   Nemeses

"Tell the President that we're not going to let the government centralize everything. It's come to an end."

Comment made following the ruling in the Schechter Poultry Case, 27 May 1935 by Associate Justice Louis Brandeis of the US Supreme Court (1856 – 1941)

The Kingfisher

By the beginning of 1935, notwithstanding the excitement of the New Deal initiatives, and the very real progress that had been made in laying down the legal and financial foundations for eventual financial recovery, some of the glamour that had enveloped Roosevelt and his administration following the presidential election had ebbed away and both the President and his policies were now under increasing attack from a number of different directions. FDR himself was still personally popular across much of the country, indeed, under his leadership, the Democrats had only recently scored a notable political triumph in the mid-term congressional elections of 1934 by gaining nine seats in the Senate[92] and a further nine seats in the House, refuting the generally held political wisdom that the party in power will always lose seats in mid-term elections. Nevertheless, though the Republican presence in Congress had never been so threadbare (following the mid-terms, they held barely a quarter of the seats in each of the Senate and the House), opposition to FDR's policies from the political right was beginning to intensify, as Republicans began to coordinate their attacks with those of business leaders and newspaper editors who claimed that the ultimate consequence of Roosevelt's administration would be to deliver the country into the arms of the communists.

This was expected by Roosevelt and his colleagues, but as long as they held a clear mandate from the people, such attacks could be cheerfully brushed aside. President Roosevelt and his political allies were more concerned about the challenges from the political left, for some of these at least were being made by politicians and activists who might have persuaded a sufficient number of

---

[92] One of the newly elected senators being Harry S Truman.

Americans that the New Deal initiatives were not radical enough, thus damaging FDR's political standing.

One of the most potentially dangerous of these opponents was Huey Long, nicknamed "the Kingfisher" after a cartoon character of the day, a man who was already an established politician in his own right, having served as governor of Louisiana from 1928 to 1932, and as a senator from that state thereafter. Politically controversial (while governor, he had survived an impeachment attempt in the Louisiana state legislature, had continued to serve as governor for more than a year after winning his senatorial seat so as to deny the governor's mansion to his lieutenant-governor (a political enemy) and had eventually seen that same lieutenant-governor dismissed from office on a technicality of election law), he was an unabashed proponent of left-wing populist policies, including extreme wealth redistribution measures in the form of punitive taxation of wealthy individuals and corporations (though he favoured property tax reductions for ordinary working men and women), and extensive public works programmes to stimulate the economy. He was a fierce critic of the Federal Reserve, whom he blamed as being principally responsible for the Depression. His opponents often accused him of acting like a dictator (some likened him to Hitler), and some of the methods he used to achieve his goals (such as securing the firing of state employees who were relatives of his political enemies, requiring state workers to contribute to his election war chests and bribing potential supporters with offers of jobs and patronage) were less than parliamentary. Probably at no time in American history has one man alone so effectively controlled the political machinery of a state. Nevertheless he enjoyed a genuinely solid core of support amongst Louisiana's poorest voters, of whom there were many. Initially he had been a supporter of FDR (though thinking little of FDR personally), but he withdrew his support when it became clear that FDR would not adopt the extreme "tax the rich" policies that Long was advocating.

In early 1934, he proposed a wealth redistribution programme (which he popularised as a "Share the Wealth" Society) under which every American family would have a "household estate" of $5,000, and a minimum guaranteed annual income of $2,500. College education would be provided free of charge. The working week would be cut to 30 hours and older citizens would receive state funded pensions as of right. The programme would be paid for by sharply increased income and inheritance taxes; no one would be allowed to pass on more than $5 million to their heirs or earn more than $1.8 million.[93] Critics rapidly pointed out flaws in Long's mathematical reasoning, not least the fact that he had seriously underestimated the cost of his proposals (in order to provide the promised household estates for every family in America, for example, the inheritance tax threshold would have to be set at approximately $7,000 rather than $5 million); nevertheless, Long continued to advocate his Share the Wealth proposals at length in radio broadcasts, public speeches and in political pamphlets. He also began to attack the basic tenets of the New Deal itself, charging that it was responsible for creating homelessness (which to an extent was arguably true), and that it favoured big businesses over the unemployed.

By January 1935, it was clear that Long was beginning to attract considerable public attention in some of the southern and western states. He was now openly contemptuous of the President, describing him as being little more than a superficial rich man's son who was more concerned with maintaining wealth inequality than genuinely alleviating poverty and it was obvious to most informed observers that Long had his own ambitions for the White House. *"I can take him"* Long said to a friend about Roosevelt. *"He's a phony...he's scared of me...I can outpromise him and he knows it... People will believe me and they won't believe*

---

[93] Some aspects of Long's Share the Wealth proposals were superficially similar to those made in 1933 by a hitherto obscure Californian physician called Francis Everett Townsend who proposed that all Americans aged over 60 should be paid $200 a month, provided they agreed to retire from employment and spend the money they received. Townsend argued that adopting his plan would stimulate employment amongst the young and generate economic growth, and proposed that the cost of the programme should be met by a special sales tax. Unfortunately, it was swiftly demonstrated that Townsend had woefully underestimated the true cost of his programme – if implemented, it would have absorbed half of the nation's income and required a doubling of taxes. Townsend's proposals proved very popular (though economically unworkable), and within a few years, he was claiming he had the support of 25 million voters. A bill incorporating some of Townsend's proposals was even introduced to Congress, where it found no support but arguably did influence some aspects of the Social Security bill that the Roosevelt administration was then drafting.

him…" On another occasion, he declared to reporters that *"Franklin Roosevelt will not be the next President of the United States".* It was rumoured that Long was seriously contemplating running in the 1940 presidential election as a third party candidate. In the meantime, his public opposition to FDR could cost the President many much-needed Democratic votes in the South in the 1936 presidential election (one poll suggested that he could carry as much as 12 percent of the popular vote in 1936, which might have been enough to snatch eight or nine southern states from the President's grasp, possibly giving the Republicans the chance to retake the White House).

For the moment, there was little that Roosevelt could do to silence Long's criticisms; he chose not to respond personally in kind to Long's outspoken attacks on his character and policies. He did instruct Louis Howe to monitor Long's activities, and steps were taken to restrict Long's ability to attract federal subsidies to his state. Treasury officials were dispatched to Louisiana to discreetly search for signs of possible tax evasion by Long (Long was too clever for them – they found nothing of substance that they could use to discredit him). On 4th March 1935, Hugh Johnson (still a Roosevelt enthusiast despite having been forced to step down from the chairmanship of the NRA) made a nationwide broadcast on NBC in which he warned of the dangers of demagoguery, naming Huey Long as an architect of potential revolution in America; millions listened to him, but millions also listened to Long's rebuttal of Johnson's attack which was broadcast across the nation a few days later.

It was clear that it would take more than a few radio broadcasts by Roosevelt supporters to deal with the menace posed by Long, and Roosevelt might eventually have been obliged to engage personally with Long. As it happened, this proved unnecessary. On 8th September 1935, Long was attending a session of the Louisiana State Capitol in Baton Rouge where he was attempting to secure the removal from office of a political opponent, Judge Henry Pavey. As he walked through a corridor, an assassin, identified in most reports as Judge Pavey's son-in-law, approached and shot him in the stomach before himself being gunned down by Long's armed bodyguards. Mortally wounded, Long died two days later, aged 42. His last words were reported as being *"God, don't let me die. I have so much to do."* With his death, support for his policies nationwide faded away, though his political organisation in Louisiana continued to be a force in state politics for several decades afterwards.

Father Coughlin

To complicate matters, Long was not the only popular demagogue with whom Roosevelt had to contend; one of FDR's most outspoken critics during the mid-1930s was a Catholic parish priest based in Detroit named Father Charles Coughlin. Coughlin, a Canadian by birth and of Irish Catholic ancestry, had become the parish priest of the Royal Oak suburb of Detroit in 1926. His parish was mainly composed of automobile workers (many of them soon to become unemployed) and Coughlin genuinely worried about them, especially after the Great Crash. *"I knew..."* he later reflected, *"that the little people, the average man, was suffering. I also knew no one else had the courage to tell the truth about why the nation was in such mortal danger."* He began to fill his sermons with vague demands for Christian "social justice" and fretted about the possible growth of communism amongst his congregation, something to which he was vehemently opposed.[94] He was an extremely gifted orator, having according to Pulitzer prize-winning writer Wallace Stegner: *"... a voice of such mellow richness, such manly, heart-warming, confidential intimacy, such emotional and ingratiating charm, that anyone tuning past it on the radio dial almost automatically retuned to hear it again".*

He had swiftly identified the newly-developing technology of the radio as a means of spreading his opinions to a much wider audience than that which dutifully attended his small church every Sunday, and as early as October 1926, he had arranged for his sermons to be broadcast across Detroit by a local radio station. Within three years, just as the Depression began to bite hard, his talks were being regularly broadcast as far as Chicago and Cincinnati, and then in 1930, CBS agreed to broadcast his sermons from coast to coast. He quickly became a celebrity – the "Radio Priest" – and tens of millions of Americans across the country regularly tuned in to hear him speak. Indeed they did more than that, they wrote thousands of fan letters to him and sent him cash – so much so that he had to hire dozens of clerks and secretaries (one estimate

---

[94] He also opposed the Ku Klux Klan. This was unsurprising as they had greeted his arrival in Royal Oak by planting a burning cross in his front yard.

places the number he employed at over a hundred) to deal with his correspondence. He used some of the cash sent to him (estimated to be in the region of half a million dollars a year) to rebuild his church. The rest proved useful when CBS decided not to renew his contract in 1931 (on the grounds that he was too inflammatory and political); he simply established his own radio network which before long was broadcasting from 30 stations across the country.

Initially, he had largely restricted his broadcasts to religious topics, expressed his views in a religious context; before long however, he began straying into the wider political world, castigating not only godless communism but also the supposed evils of matters as diverse as birth control and the gold standard as well as the dangers posed by international bankers. He advocated widespread nationalisation, first of the American banking system and then whole swathes of American industries. He was also a firm believer in the advantages of pursuing inflationary policies. A fierce opponent of President Hoover, he had initially supported FDR's bid for the Presidency and the New Deal. *"...The New Deal is Christ's deal..."* he had solemnly declared to millions of listeners, and he told a Congressional Hearing in January 1934 that *"God is directing President Roosevelt."* Unsurprisingly, during the 1932 presidential campaign, Roosevelt had looked kindly (if cautiously) upon the outspoken priest, at least to the extent that he felt Coughlin could act as a useful bridge to Roman Catholic voters whom Roosevelt himself might otherwise have found difficult to persuade to vote for him. Once the victory was won, however, Coughlin's clumsy attempts to promote the interests of individual Catholics by turning up at the White House and suggesting them for various diplomatic and political posts, coupled with some of his more extreme utterances such as his demands for widespread nationalisation, began to irritate the President.

In turn, Father Coughlin's enthusiasm for the President began to wane once he realised that Roosevelt was intent on overhauling and improving the American banking system rather than simply nationalising it. Roosevelt's failure openly to endorse the use of inflationary policies constituted to Coughlin's eyes another error on the part of the President and he began to view the implementation of the New Deal, which he had once endorsed so heartily, as dangerously close to his *bête noire*, communism. Messages of support for Roosevelt and his policies during the course of Coughlin's radio broadcasts began to disappear.

Then on 11th November 1934, declaring that capitalism was dead, Coughlin established the National Union for Social Justice, a loosely structured and somewhat disorganised society which called for monetary reform, the nationalisation of key industries and the banks, extreme taxation of the wealthy, increased labour rights and the right – indeed the obligation – of the government to intervene so as to eradicate "individualism" in business. According to the NUSJ, private businesses should have licences before they could establish and operate factories, and the output of those factories should be regulated by the government "for the public good." The views of the NUSJ were soon regularly expressed in a weekly magazine, National Justice, which eventually attracted a million subscribers.

In their appeals for monetary reform (and particularly the demands that the US currency should operate on a basis of bimetallism[95]) Coughlin and the NUSJ were consciously trying to tap into the populist legacy left by the Free Silver movement of the 1890s. In their demands for nationalisation and the operation of surviving private businesses for the supposed public good as determined by the government, they were dangerously close to some of the policies that were then being adopted by the fascist regimes in Europe (and Coughlin must have been aware of this) though this was a time when it was still possible to maintain that for all their faults, the fascists had some good

---

[95] Whereby, broadly speaking, the dollar was to be valued by reference to specific quantities of both gold and silver – by this time, of course, the United States had already abandoned the gold standard (under which the dollar was valued by reference to a specific amount of gold alone). Bimetallism and "free silver" had been at the heart of a major populist movement in the Mid-West in the 1890s, championed by William Jennings Bryan and (for a while) by elements of the Democratic Party. The cause of free silver had effectively been lost when Bryan was defeated in the 1896 presidential election by Republican William McKinley (who had supported the gold standard). Since that time, the championing of bimetallism had largely been seen as the preserve of cranks and monetary obsessives, though it retained some support in farming communities, who continued to hope that its adoption would help to stabilise agricultural prices and reduce rural poverty.

ideas that could bear examination and even adoption in western democracies without facing public disdain. Be that as it may, the NUSJ struck a chord in at least some American hearts, though the disorganisation of its record-keeping makes it hard to determine just how many people supported its aims to the extent of becoming fully paid-up members; some contemporary estimates placed NUSJ membership as high as seven to eight million. In any event, sufficient numbers listened to Coughlin's views (which to some observers became increasingly pro-fascist, pro-isolationist and anti-Roosevelt with every year that passed) for Roosevelt and his political allies to take seriously the possibility that Coughlin might leach votes away from Democratic candidates to third party challengers, allowing the Republicans to benefit from a splitting of the votes. This possibility continued, and Father Coughlin remained a potential thorn in Roosevelt's side, for the rest of the decade and even (to an extent) into the early 1940s.

The World Court

By mid-January 1935, Coughlin had almost entirely broken away from Roosevelt (in March 1935, he would declare that he could no longer support the New Deal as it simply protected "plutocrats and communists"). Then, on 16th January, the issue of America's affiliation to the World Court in the Hague[96] arose once more. Just as the United States had refused to join the League of Nations following the end of the First World War, so too had she refused to submit to the jurisdiction of the World Court, though some Americans served as judges of the Court, including (briefly) Charles Evans Hughes before he became the Chief Justice of the United States. From time to time since the Court's creation in 1922, various half-hearted attempts had been made to secure America's membership of the World Court by those who favoured America taking a more open and active part in world affairs (Harding, Coolidge and Hoover had each supported America's membership, at least in principle, at one time or another) but all such attempts had failed to overcome the conservatism of an isolationist Congress. Now on 16th January

---

[96] Formally, the Permanent Court of International Justice, established following the creation of the League of Nations, and not to be confused with the International Court of Justice established under the Charter of the United Nations in 1945.

1935, President Roosevelt, who was increasingly concerned about the international situation, and keen following his bombshell at the World Economic Conference in London to demonstrate to the rest of the world that America had not completely closed her doors to international cooperation, asked the Senate to consider passing a treaty which would secure America's affiliation to the Court.

On the face of it, it should have been easy for President Roosevelt to get his way; he required a two-thirds vote of the Senate, and the Democrats with 69 senators controlled more than two-thirds of the seats by themselves. In practice, news that the Roosevelt administration was seeking to secure American membership of the Court galvanised not only right-wing isolationists (such as publisher William Hearst whose editorials denounced the proposals mercilessly, and Senator Hiram Johnson, a leading voice of the isolationists on the Senate floor) but also those on the left, with Father Coughlin (and Huey Long) leading the charge[97] to oppose American membership at meetings and in radio broadcasts across the country. Opponents of the treaty were pushing against an open door; most ordinary Americans, even those who would normally have supported Roosevelt on any other matter, were still too steeped in the dream of isolationism to do anything other than oppose the latest membership bid, and to heed the commands of Coughlin, Long and other opponents of the World Court that they should make the strength of their feelings known to their representatives and senators. And they did; according to some estimates, more than 50,000 telegrams denouncing membership of the World Court were sent to the Senate alone in the days leading up to the vote. Thousands of letters also made certain that senators and representatives were under no illusion as to the strength of feeling of the American public on this issue.

---

[97] Coughlin was noticeably increasingly sympathetic to Long during the last few months of Long's life, though Coughlin had little good to say about Long's Share the Wealth programme, considering it to be little more than communism in disguise. Nevertheless, they were united in their opposition to the World Court, and their campaign of opposition to America's prospective membership of the Court may have been the first time they worked closely together on a national issue.

When the Senate came to vote on the issue on 29th January 1935, with seven senators mysteriously absent from the chamber, only 52 voted in favour of American membership of the World Court, with 36 senators voting against. Roosevelt had failed to obtain his two-thirds majority. Publically, he was calm and dignified in the face of defeat; privately, he railed against those senators who had voted no. *"As to the thirty six senators who placed themselves on record against the principle of the World Court"* he wrote angrily to Senate majority leader Joseph Robinson *"I am inclined to think that if they ever get to Heaven they will be doing a great deal of apologising for a very long time – that is if God is against war – and I think He is."* To a friend, he commented *"the radio talks of people like Coughlin turned the trick against us."* Roosevelt could complain all he liked; the fact was that he had just suffered the worst defeat of his Presidency to date, and he had proof of the dangers posed by being too far ahead of popular opinion, and the threat created by left and right-wing opponents working in concert against him. Father Coughlin now had a triumph he could crow about in his radio broadcasts. And to make matters worse, the Supreme Court was now stirring and about to deliver its own bitter blows against Roosevelt's Presidency.

Legal Challenges

The most serious challenges to the New Deal, and the Presidency of Franklin Roosevelt, arose not in the political arena, but in America's courts, as the constitutionality of the various pieces of legislation comprising the New Deal began to be questioned, not only by disgruntled businessmen but also by conservative bodies such as the American Liberty League. As much of the New Deal legislation had been rushed onto the statute books, many of the new laws contained serious flaws, some only apparent with the benefit of hindsight. Moreover, some of the new provisions certainly seemed to sit uncomfortably within the constitutional framework of the United States. As a consequence, Roosevelt's opponents in the early years of his Presidency had a considerable degree of success in challenging the constitutionality of those laws in the lower federal courts, many of whose judges had been appointed by Republican presidents precisely because they favoured a conservative interpretation of the US constitution and laws. By the spring of 1935, hundreds of injunctions had been issued by the lower federal courts against the New Deal legislation, and speculation was mounting in both political and legal circles that sooner rather than later, the entire edifice of the New Deal would face its ultimate test in the Supreme Court of the United States. Given that four of the nine justices sitting on the bench of the Supreme Court (Sutherland, McReynolds, Butler and Van Devanter - collectively known as "The Four Horsemen of the Apocalypse") were known for their extremely conservative interpretations of the Constitution, while three other justices (Stone, Brandeis and Cardozo) were known to be particularly sensitive to the need to protect civil liberties from excessive federal legislation, it was not clear that the outcome of contest when it finally arose would be a victory for Roosevelt and the New Deal.[98]

Initially, when the first legal challenges to the New Deal began to reach the Supreme Court, to a litany of complaints from conservative circles, the Court had issued majority rulings favourable to the New Deal. For example, in 1934, the Court had upheld both a New York state law allowing the state government to prescribe minimum prices for milk and a Minnesota law imposing a mandatory delay before home owners could lose their homes by way of mortgage foreclosure. Moreover, to the surprise of some commentators, the Court had (reluctantly and again by majority ruling) supported measures passed by Congress at Roosevelt's urging invalidating provisions in both private and public contracts that required that payments be made with gold (rather than paper) dollars. However, on this occasion Mr Justice McReynolds, who together with the other three Horsemen had issued a minority opinion denying that Congress had the requisite constitutional authority to ban "gold clauses", was moved to liken President Roosevelt to the tyrannical Roman emperor Nero, and warned that *"...as for the Constitution, it does not seem too much to say that it is gone."* In fact, the Constitution was very firmly in place, and functioning as intended, as McReynolds and his fellow justices were about to demonstrate.

---

[98] The remaining two justices (Chief Justice Charles Evans Hughes and Owen Roberts – both Hoover appointees – tended to act as "swing votes" when judicial opinion was divided between the Four Horsemen on one side and Stone, Brandeis and Cardozo on the other. Unfortunately while Hughes at least also genuinely cared about civil liberties, both he and Roberts had voted with the conservative faction often enough in the past to make it difficult to predict how they would vote in any particular case.

In one sense, they had already done so. A little over a month before the Supreme Court's ruling in the gold clause case, on 7th January 1935, in an 8 -1 decision (with only Mr Justice Cardozo in disagreement), the Supreme Court had declared section 9(c) of the National Industrial Recovery Act (popularly known as the "hot oil provisions", which permitted the President to prohibit interstate shipments of oil and gasoline products in excess of specified limits) to be unconstitutional on the grounds that it delegated too much decision-making power to the executive wing of the government. Then, on 6th May, by a majority vote, the Supreme Court declared that Congress could not require railroad companies to establish mandatory pension schemes for its employees. This decision took even some conservatives by surprise, as Congress had been prescribing rules for railroads in minute detail almost since the first piece of railroad track had been laid in the United States. Nevertheless the Court declared the provisions of the Railroad Retirement Act of 1934 to be unconstitutional.

However, from the perspective of the New Dealers, worse was to come. On 27th May, the Supreme Court issued a volley of decisions, in the process striking down the Emergency Farm Mortgage Act of 1934 (which had been one of the pieces of legislation passed during the Hundred Days intended to help struggling farmers refinance their farm mortgages with borrowed federal funds) on the grounds that it was unfair to farmers' creditors. The Supreme Court also held that the President did not have unlimited power to remove officials of the Federal Trade Commission from office. Most importantly of all, the Court issued its ruling in the Schechter Poultry case, one of the most dramatic rulings in the Court's long and eventful history.

Problems with Poultry

As so often occurs with momentous legal judgments, the origins of the case of *Schechter Poultry Corporation v the United States* were humble and mundane. Four brothers in New York operated a small poultry business, principally supplying kosher chickens to local Jewish customers. As such, they found themselves subject to the NRA live poultry code[99] which not only sought to dictate working conditions within the poultry business (such as minimum wages and maximum working hours) but also contained long and complex rules intended to prohibit the purchase and sale for human consumption of poultry products that were unfit for that purpose – a worthy enough aim in itself. However, the rules also prohibited "straight killing", which in effect meant that while a customer could buy a coop (or half a coop) of birds, they could not choose an individual bird of their choice, but had to accept one selected at random. This immediately put the code at odds with Jewish food rituals (as well as the wishes of customers) because a principal aspect of running a kosher poultry business was the right of customers themselves to select individual birds. The brothers, like many other small business owners, found that strict compliance with the code's draconian regulations was impossible if they wanted to stay in business.

The Schechter brothers themselves, whose family had only recently immigrated to the United States, had little interest in the rights and wrongs of the NRA code; they were simply trying to run a kosher poultry business. Their customers apparently had no complaint about the quality of the birds they were selling; nevertheless, in the summer of 1934 the Justice Department began to investigate alleged violations of the NRA live poultry code by the Schechter brothers, arguing that because many of the chickens that the brothers sold were originally raised outside the state and then shipped to New York's poultry markets (where the brothers bought them), they were effectively running an interstate commercial business and thus were subject to key aspects of the NRA codes which (deriving from federal law) applied solely to inter-state commerce. In due course, the brothers were found guilty in the District Court for the Eastern District of New York of having breached the code in various ways, including non-compliance with the wage and working hours regulations, the filing of inaccurate reports, fixing prices, avoiding inspections by the local health authorities, selling to unlicensed purchasers and selling unfit and uninspected poultry.[100] They were fined and given short

---

[99] Strictly speaking, the *Code of Fair Competition for the Live Poultry Industry of the Metropolitan Area in and about the City of New York*.

[100] The latter charge originated from an inspection of ten chickens, of which three were suspected to be ill. When submitted to autopsy, only one of the three suspect

prison sentences, and duly appealed. The circuit court swiftly rejected their appeals in December 1934, and the brothers appealed to the Supreme Court. The Justice Department, anxious to take an apparently unloseable case to the Supreme Court so they could affix that court's sanction to the constitutionality of the NRA, and by implication, to the New Deal as a whole, supported the brothers' request for an appeals hearing, and the Supreme Court agreed. The appeals were scheduled to begin on 2nd May 1935.

In his opening argument, Donald Richberg, one of the lawyers appearing on behalf of the NRA, seeking to pre-empt accusations that the NRA codes were unconstitutional, at least insofar as applied to the Schechter brothers, tried to argue that the NRA had been created out of the crisis of a national emergency, and that its rules and legal decisions based on those rules should therefore be judged against the fact of that emergency. The NRA, declared Richberg, *"…cannot be considered wholly disassociated from the conditions which brought about the Act."* This was tantamount to arguing that the NRA, indeed much of the legislation of the New Deal, should not be subject to the same assessment of constitutionality as other areas of federal law, but rather should be judged by constitutional standards unique to itself. If successful, this argument would have made it very difficult in the future to challenge any aspect of the NRA (and the wider New Deal) on the grounds of unconstitutionality.

The justices of the Supreme Court were less than impressed with this plea for special treatment. They were astonished to learn that customers were unable to select the individual birds they wanted (*"And it is for this that your clients have gone to jail?"* Mr Justice McReynolds asked the Schechter's lawyer, James Heller) and they mercilessly probed the NRA's assertion that a Brooklyn-based poultry business buying its chickens and selling them on to customers in New York constituted interstate business. They noted Heller's assertions that key aspects of the codes were unworkable in practice, and that the wage, hours and pricing

---

chickens was found to be ill, and then of a condition that could not have been discovered without an autopsy – and thus could not have been identified by any of the brothers, the potential customers the rabbis or ritual slaughterers employed by the brothers to ensure that their products complied with Jewish dietary laws. Nevertheless, the authorities insisted on bringing the charge of selling unfit birds.

regulations, though supposedly intended to eliminate unfair competition, often failed to operate fairly at the local level, as they tended to favour larger businesses (which could afford to comply with the code's demands and remain in operation) at the expense of smaller ones (which could not).

When the justices of the Supreme Court issued their judgment in the case on 27th May 1935, the decision was unanimous in favour of the defendants. Mr Chief Justice Hughes, reading out the majority opinion, declared that *"Neither the slaughtering nor the sales by the defendants [of poultry] were transactions in interstate commerce"* immediately placing any violation by the Schechters of the NRA's wage and hour rules and the sick poultry regulations beyond the reach of NRA's codes. Furthermore, addressing the NRA's pleas for special treatment, he declared that *"Extraordinary conditions may call for extraordinary remedies. But the argument necessarily stops short of an attempt to justify action which lies outside the sphere of constitutional authority. Extraordinary conditions do not create or enlarge constitutional power."* In a separate opinion, Mr Justice Cardozo, speaking on behalf of himself and Mr Justice Stone issued a barrage of legal criticism about the ability of Congress to delegate law-making to mere regulators. The Schechter case, he declared demonstrated *"an attempted delegation not confined to any single act nor to any class or group of acts identified or described by reference to a standard. Here, in effect, is a roving commission to enquire into evils and upon discovery correct them."* This, Cardozo declared, was *"delegation running riot"* and was unconstitutional. He concluded by declaring that as a consequence of the Court's rulings, the NRA code must collapse completely. At a stroke, the National Industrial Recovery Act, and the NRA which it had spawned, were nullified, its codes of no effect and there were now grave doubts about the ability of other regulatory bodies such as the SEC to make rules and regulations.

Roosevelt's first reaction when he received news of the Supreme Court's decision was incredulity, demanding to know where the liberals on the bench had stood on the question of the NRA's constitutionality. *"Where was Brandeis…Cardozo….Stone…?" "With the majority…"* came the answer. Anger swiftly followed, and four days later Roosevelt gave a press conference at which he criticised the decision, complaining that the Supreme Court had imposed a *"horse and buggy definition of interstate commerce"* on the nation. The Attorney-General, Homer Cummings, shared Roosevelt's anger: *"I tell you Mr*

President", he declared, *"…we must find a way to get rid of the membership of the Supreme Court"*. But that was easier said than done.

For the moment, however, the court's ruling had to be obeyed, and during the month of June 1935, the NRA was effectively dismantled, leaving behind little more than a government information gathering service. The administration salvaged what it could from the wreckage – several key aspects of NIRA were to be saved by more carefully drafted pieces of legislation, and in any event, it was quietly conceded that the NRA's days had been numbered ever since the departure of Hugh Johnson in 1934. Nevertheless, it was a bitter blow to Roosevelt to see one of the centrepieces of the New Deal unceremoniously thrown aside by the Supreme Court, particularly with the 1936 presidential election drawing near. From the time of the decision in Schechter, Roosevelt and many members of the administration began to regard the Supreme Court as their greatest obstacle to pursuing the New Deal, their antipathy towards the court growing over the months that followed as the Court repeatedly struck down key components of the New Deal legislation, including, in January 1936, the Agricultural Adjustment Act, which was held to breach states' rights. Then, in June of that same year came the Court's ruling in the case of *Morehead v New York ex rel Tipaldo*, by which (with a five to four majority) a New York minimum wage law was held to breach freedom of contract rights. For New Dealers, the Tipaldo case was the ultimate blow; hitherto the Court's assaults on the New Deal legislation had all focussed on restricting federal powers, but the Tipaldo case constituted an assault on the regulatory powers of the individual states themselves. The result, as Roosevelt himself noted, was to create a *"no man's land where no government – state or federal – [could] function."* This was clearly unacceptable to the White House, and there was now the very real danger that the entire New Deal might be rejected by the Court as being unconstitutional. And to make matters worse, the dangers posed by the Court's rulings were arising just as Roosevelt and his administration were trying to push a series of new laws through Congress, including a revised labour relations bill, a social security bill, a new banking bill and a new (and draconian) tax bill. With so many bills in such a short time, contemporaries referred to them as constituting a second New Deal, and passing the legislation for which was believed to be essential by Roosevelt supporters if the

President's victory in the 1936 presidential election was to be assured. But with the first New Deal now apparently under mortal attack from the Supreme Court, was it likely that the second New Deal would fare any better?

DARK REALITIES

Chapter 12   The Second New Deal

"When a calm and fair review of the work of this Congress is made, it will be called a historic session…"

Excerpt from a letter to Congress from President Roosevelt upon the adjournment of Congress on 26th August 1935.

Strike!

A substantial amount of President Roosevelt's time during the first half of 1935 was spent persuading Congress of the importance of passing the Second New Deal legislative programme, much of which was intended to refine and improve the laws passed during the original Hundred Days (and given the imminent demise of significant parts of the legislative framework underpinning the New Deal thanks to the rulings of the Supreme Court, the new legislation was needed urgently). As in the case of the bills passed during the Hundred Days, this second batch of legislation was wide-ranging, covering important banking and tax matters as well as seeking to improve working practices on the factory floors and the farms. Importantly, the bills sought to avoid the flaw of excessive reliance upon the delegation of legislative powers to administrative agencies that had so aroused the ire of the Supreme Court.

One of the most important of the new bills was the Labor Relations bill. The need for new labour legislation was growing acute; 1934 had seen a dramatic increase in strikes and other forms of labour unrest across the country, as workers tried to improve their pay and working conditions (which had generally worsened dramatically since the onset of the Depression) and organise independent unions, while employers sought to oppose them. In a number of cases, the unrest swiftly escalated into civil disorder. A graphic example of this occurred in Toledo, Ohio in May 1934, when a strike organised by the American Federation of Labor (with support from the American Workers Party) at the premises of the Electric Auto-Lite Company led to the presence of thousands of protesting strikers on the streets and attempts to storm the Company's factory and the calling out of the National Guard. Before the strike ended (as a result of government-sponsored arbitration) two men had been killed and dozens seriously injured.

Around the same time, striking dockyard workers in California protesting about the way work assignments were awarded succeeded in closing the port of San Francisco for nearly two months; an attempt by an association of employers to break the strike by force led to several days of violence and the death of two more men. This, in turn, led to a general strike by union workers in San Francisco that lasted several days. Dockworkers also went on strike in Oakland (California), Portland (Oregon) and Seattle (Washington), severely disrupting the transport of goods to and from those ports. A violent strike that summer by the Teamsters union members in Minneapolis which lasted for several months also led to deaths and transport disruption and ultimately forced the state's governor, Floyd Olson, to declare martial law. In September 1934, textile workers affiliated with the United Textile Workers Union went on strike in more than 20 states (the largest strike in American history) demanding that employers comply with provisions of the Cotton Textile Code issued by the NRA relating to working hours, wages and collective bargaining; within days, in many places, the strike degenerated into riots, provoking fierce, sometimes deadly responses (especially in the South) from local police forces, National Guard units and thugs hired by mill owners to break the strike. Before the union called the strike to a halt in October, nine men had been killed and once more dozens had been injured.[101] And there were other violent strikes and protests in industrial centres across the country.

For many Americans, the apparently continual eruption of labour unrest and violence all across the country raised once again the old fears of communist conspiracies, and the belief that the strikes were being organised from Moscow; a sense of potential industrial anarchy pervaded the air. In Washington, the political authorities were (on the whole) better informed as to the cause of the strikes and violence, but nevertheless were determined that the

---

[101] Once the strike was over, the UTW tried to claim it as a victory, but it was a disaster for the union – many striking textile workers were blacklisted by the mill owners and permanently lost their jobs while the mill owners themselves largely failed to meet any of the union's demands. Perhaps even more importantly, many of the textile workers who retained their jobs in the South were so disillusioned by the UTW's performance that they abandoned the very idea of joining an organised union, so that union membership by southern textile workers remained low for several decades to come.

unrest should cease as soon as possible. For this to happen, the existing labour disputes legislation needed to be improved, and then firmly enforced.

With these aims in mind, Senator Wagner of New York had tried to introduce a labour disputes bill into Congress as early as March 1934 but had abandoned it at Roosevelt's request, on the understanding that labour issues would be addressed elsewhere. Now, in the form of the National Labor Relations bill, an attempt was to be made to strengthen the provisions of section 7(a) of NIRA guaranteeing workers the freedom to organise collectively without undue influence from hostile employers. Roosevelt himself, though privately thinking that some union leaders were little more than populist rabble-rousers, was conscious that many workers were being denied the rights of union membership to which they were entitled by law. There was, too, the need to meet the challenges posed by Long, Coughlin and the other demagogues and Roosevelt was not blind to the potential political benefits of linking his administration (and the wider Democratic Party) to an expanding and increasingly influential labour movement. President Roosevelt and other leading members of his administration (such as Labor Secretary Frances Perkins) therefore quietly supported Wagner's bill as it made its passage through Congress. That support was needed more in the Senate than in the House, where several powerful senators feared that the creation of yet more workers' rights and the recognition of genuinely independent unions might not only damage American industry, particularly in the low wage southern states, but also be unconstitutional; Wagner's critics urged that his bill should be delayed for at least a year (or even scrapped). For a while, therefore, President Roosevelt had to tread a delicate path of supporting Wagner and his fellow progressives without offending important senatorial allies. The decision by the Supreme Court in late May 1935 in the Schechter case that key aspects of NIRA and the NRA were unconstitutional allowed FDR to become more overt in his support for the new legislation, and following a brilliant defence of his bill by Senator Wagner in the closing stages of the debate in the Senate which effectively silenced the remaining critics, the President finally signed the National Labor Relations Act into law on 5th July 1935.

At the heart of the Wagner Act (as the new legislation was soon to be popularly named) lay an attempt to restrict the responses that private sector employers[102] could adopt when facing employees who wished to organise themselves into trade unions. Attempts by employers to restrict or coerce employees seeking to form independent unions or otherwise to associate for the means of collective bargaining in respect of wages and working conditions were declared to be unfair labour practices, as was any refusal to bargain collectively with workers' representatives. The sponsorship by employers of company unions to the exclusion of independent unions was banned. Employers were also prohibited from discriminating against workers who supported the creation of independent unions (or in favour of those who voiced opposition to such unions). The National Labor Relations Board (created to replace the National Labor Board established under the auspices of NIRA which had been struck down by the Supreme Court) was empowered to supervise the election of worker representatives (who were to be elected by secret ballots – a concept which appalled many employers) and to prosecute violations of the Act through the federal courts.

Predictably, the new Act was opposed vociferously by many employers, and the American Liberty League announced that it considered the new legislation to be unconstitutional, declaring that it was only a matter of time before the Supreme Court ruled it to be so. The American Chamber of Commerce pronounced the Wagner Act to be the end of free enterprise in America. In the meantime, some employers announced they would defy its provisions; others more cautiously paid lip service to the requirements of the Wagner Act but still refused to allow the creation of genuinely independent unions by their workers. Legal challenges as to the constitutionality of the new legislation began to mount almost immediately.

Unsurprisingly, industrial unrest did not diminish. Then, in November 1935, a group of union activists committed to more radical action in supporting workers' rights to organise than the leadership of the American Federation of Labor was then willing to countenance, walked out of an AFL convention in

---

[102] At least those to whom the Act applied. It did not apply to whole swathes of workers, including domestic and agricultural workers and some employees working within the transport industries such as the railroads and airlines. It also did not apply to government employees.

Atlantic City in order to form the Committee for Industrial Organisation (later the Congress for Industrial Organisation). The CIO, as the new body soon became known, was dedicated to organising workers in a myriad of American mass-production industries such as automobile manufacturing, mining, steel, rubber and textiles, all sectors of America's industry where employer opposition to the formation of independent unions had been most determined.[103] Within months of its creation, the CIO under the leadership of John L Lewis, the outspoken president of the United Mine Workers, was actively seeking to take advantage of the new legislation and to organise workers in factories and workshops across the country, usually in the face of bitter resistance from employers and management. The increasing militancy on the part of workers and unions increased Washington's desperation to bring the industrial unrest to an end as soon as possible. Not only did continual strikes threaten the tenuous economic recovery which was underway, thanks in no small part to the original New Deal[104], but the continuing industrial unrest also threatened to overshadow the forthcoming presidential election of 1936, an event that was increasingly in the minds of the President and his advisers. But President Roosevelt had no magic wand to wave over American industry to dampen down the unrest. It would end only when workers and their unions could successfully claim the new rights they had been granted, and when employers were persuaded that the creation of independent unions, the establishment of fair and sensible collective bargaining procedures and the introduction of reasonable pay and working conditions did not portend the end of capitalism or the introduction of godless communism, but rather could be good for business. It took some time for these simple truths to be appreciated.

---

[103] The American steel industry, for example, had been almost entirely union-free since 1892, when an attempt to introduce unions into the steel plants in Homestead, Pennsylvania owned by Andrew Carnegie had been spectacularly if bloodily defeated by the Homestead plant's managers with the assistance of armed Pinkerton agents.

[104] The unemployment rate, for example, which had peaked at 24.9 percent in 1933 (when approximately 12.8 million people of working age were seeking jobs) had been falling ever since the implementation of the New Deal and by July 1935 stood at 21.3 percent (approximately 10.9 million people) and was continuing to fall.

While serious strikes were to erupt throughout much of 1936 and beyond (and did indeed to an extent overshadow the presidential election), a turning-point of sorts had been reached (if only the protagonists had known it) in the relations between employers and workers by the creation of the CIO. Less hidebound in their approach and tactics than the AFL (which had responded to the creation of the rival body by expelling from its membership those unions who had elected to follow Lewis into the CIO), and surprisingly well funded, the CIO unions sought new ways to challenge employers which would lessen the likelihood of violence breaking out on the picket line and cost the unions much needed public sympathy. One tactic which worked surprisingly well was the development of the "sit-down strike" which was first seen (on a large scale) in February 1936 during a strike held by workers at the Goodyear Tire and Rubber Company's plant in Akron, Ohio, where workers were trying to secure recognition of their newly formed union (the United Rubber Workers) and an improvement to pay and working conditions. Traditionally, striking workers had sought to establish a picket line around their place of work, usually leaving the factory or industrial plant in the hands of the local managers, who would more often than not respond by trying to bring replacement "scab" labour into the factory to replace the striking workers. Not only did the successful use of scab labour weaken the strikers' negotiating positions, but transferring the scab workers across the picket lines was always a source of tension, and often gave rise to violence. In contrast, when the rubber workers at Goodyear's Akron plant went on strike, many of them simply sat down on the factory floor and refused to leave until an agreement had been reached with management.[105]

The sit-down strike proved to be an important weapon in the workers' arsenal. To begin with, it seemed less threatening than a picket line and there was thus less risk of alienating public support for striking workers (indeed some journalists covering strikes where the tactic was used wrote approvingly of its use in place of the traditional picket line). Moreover, by occupying the factory,

---

[105] There was nevertheless a picket line around the Goodyear plant at Akron; demonstrating their belief that the President was fundamentally on their side, striking workers nicknamed one of the picket line's strong points as "Camp Roosevelt".

the striking workers effectively made it impossible for management to use scab labour, while the police and local politicians were reluctant to intervene against strikers who were simply sitting on the floor next to their machines. Employers likewise, who would not have hesitated to unleash armed "security guards" to break their way through a picket line were reluctant to deploy such tactics when there was a risk of serious damage occurring to factory equipment.

To the surprise of many, the sit-down strike at Goodyear's Akron plant encouraged management to enter into serious negotiations with the striking workers within a relatively short period, and the strike was over by the end of the first week in March, with the employer having agreed to reinstate striking workers' jobs and to grant improved pay and working conditions. Admittedly, the strikers did not win all their demands; the employer still stubbornly refused to recognise the URW; full recognition was only finally granted in 1941. Nevertheless, the relative and speedy success of the sit down strike in forcing a degree of flexibility in the attitude of management did not go unnoticed by union leaders elsewhere in the country who were now visibly preparing for further strike actions, and it was clear that sit down strikes would be repeated in future disputes. As for those future disputes, many commentators of the time predicted that the next major strike would occur in the steel regions, and particularly in the steel plants of Pennsylvania, where union activists were keen to reverse the outcome of the Homestead strike so many years before. Unions and steel industry leaders thus spent the summer, autumn and winter months of 1936 bracing themselves for forthcoming conflict. In fact, the next major battle in the war for union recognition and the enforcement of workers' rights occurred not in the steel industry but in the heart of the automobile industry, at the industrial complex of General Motors, in the town of Flint, Michigan, where workers seeking satisfaction of the usual demands – recognition of their independent union, in this case, the United Auto Workers, and improved pay and working conditions – instituted a sit down strike at the end of December 1936 under the leadership of local union leader Walter Reuther, first in one plant and then (in defiance of court orders obtained by GM who predictably declared the strike to be the work of communists) in others, crippling GM's automobile production.[106] While there was a violent confrontation between striking workers and the local police during the seizure of one of the plants (a fight that became known as the Battle of the Running Bulls), the local state authorities made it clear that they regarded the strike was a matter for the workers and their employer to resolve – Michigan Governor Frank Murphy, in particular, emphasised that when he said he was willing to call out the National Guard "to keep order", he meant exactly that (albeit that the National Guard kept order at times with fixed bayonets). The state government, declared the Governor, would not "take sides".

The pressure on GM to reach a settlement with the strikers mounted rapidly; not only was the loss of car production financially crippling and allowing GM's principal competitors Chrysler and Ford to begin to eat into GM's market share (both rival companies took steps to increase their own car production in response to the GM shutdown), but President Roosevelt himself quietly urged the GM management to recognise the union. By 11th February 1937, GM could take no more. It agreed to recognise the UAW as the sole union representing workers in its car plants and the strike ended, although other union demands were for the moment rebuffed. Nevertheless, GM's recognition of the UAW represented a major breakthrough on the part of organised labour in the automobile industry. Chrysler Motors quietly followed GM's lead a few months later and recognised the UAW, leaving Ford for the

---

[106] Although during the period of industrial unrest in the mid-1930s, workers' demands varied between locations and industries, it is noticeable how broadly similar those demands were across the country regardless of the industries concerned. Workers' demands were not generally excessive, and focussed on independent union recognition, collective bargaining and the provision of reasonable wages and working conditions. Organised labour grew swiftly in both numbers and power within a few years. Some estimates place aggregate union membership in the US in 1933 at approximately 2.7 million; by the end of 1936, it was approximately 4 million and one year later, aggregate membership had risen to 7 million, and was continuing to rise.. Notwithstanding this dramatic increase in power, unions during the late 1930s on the whole behaved more responsibly than had been expected by many critics. Much of the blame for the continuing industrial unrest following the introduction of the NRA and the National Labor Relations Act must, therefore, be placed on recalcitrant employers.

time being as the only major car manufacturer which refused to recognise a union.

But even more dramatic was the response of the steel industry to the Flint strike, and to GM's swift surrender; recognising the power that the sit down strike gave to workers, and aware that the Roosevelt administration could not be relied upon to automatically support management, on 2nd March 1937 US Steel announced it was prepared to recognise the Steel Workers Organising Committee (a predecessor to the United Steel Workers of America), and to grant substantial improvements to the pay and working conditions of its steel workers. US Steel, the corporate leviathan at the very heart of the American industry, had yielded to the demands of its workers without a struggle. Though other parts of American industry tried to resist the demands of organised labour for several more years (the Ford Motor Company, for example, under Henry Ford's stubborn leadership, continued to refuse to recognise any independent union until 1941), it was clear that industrial workers could not be denied their unions (and especially CIO-affiliated unions).

Naturally, industrial strikes and disputes (and workplace-related violence) did not disappear overnight, or completely, but employers soon found that there were benefits in recognising unions. True, collective bargaining sessions could be painful, but one of the key fears of employers who had opposed union recognition, namely that once recognised, unions would then seek to interfere in the actual management of their businesses, proved to be unfounded. Union leaders on the whole were prepared to allow management to manage provided workers' pay and conditions were tolerable, and by and large, in unionised industries, both improved considerably after 1937. As a consequence, and as the supporters of the new labour laws had predicted and hoped, the involvement of the CIO-affiliated unions in the arena of the workplace actually helped to promote industrial peace and to increase industrial production, with sharp drops in absenteeism and employee turnover soon being reported across the country by businesses with recognised unions. Ultimately, organised labour, protected by the new labour legislation of the New Deal, played an important role in helping to bring about America's recovery from the Great Depression. And politically too, Roosevelt, and the wider Democratic Party, benefitted from organised labour's new found freedoms, as industrial workers in the cities, newly enrolled in unions which they trusted to protect them, and benefiting from improved pay and working conditions, identified the President as the author of their improved circumstances, and rewarded him by voting for him almost en masse in the presidential election of 1940.

The Big Bill

"The Big Bill" was Roosevelt's private name for the Emergency Relief Appropriations bill, which the 74th Congress approved on 8th April 1935 with surprisingly little trouble[107], considering that the bill called for $4 billion of public funds, the largest peacetime appropriation by the United States to date, as well as the re-allocation of $880 million of previously approved funding, to be used for work relief and public works construction. Underlying the new legislation was the concern, first identified by some economic observers (most notably John Maynard Keynes), that even when genuine economic recovery finally arrived, the American economy might prove to be incapable of providing real jobs for all of the current unemployed principally because on-going technological advances were rendering many forms of traditional employment superfluous as industrial machinery increasingly replaced human workers. Even as early as 1934, some of Roosevelt's closest advisers, including Harry Hopkins, then supervising the Federal Emergency Relief Administration (FERA), were arguing that a federally mandated support programme would be needed to help the long-term unemployed, and FDR himself, in a fireside chat broadcast on 28th June 1934, predicted that the Federal Government would be *"…engaged in the task of rehabilitating many hundreds and thousands of…families…for many years to come…"*

President Roosevelt and his advisers recognised a sharp distinction between the need to provide immediate relief for the unemployed with a view to alleviating destitution, perhaps coupled with token efforts of providing recipients with useful but temporary tasks such as cutting the grass in the public parks and removing refuse from the streets, and the provision of a coherent and effective longer term programme designed to create genuine work opportunities for those who simply could not find any other form of

---

[107] Though Huey Long did his best to derail its passage through the Senate.

employment but were capable of working. While there was no attempt to deny that immediate relief was urgently needed by many, concerns were openly expressed that the provision of simple relief alone over the long term could prove morally and spiritually destructive for the recipients, creating a benefits-dependent sub-culture which, if once allowed to establish itself, would prove difficult to eradicate (not to mention create very real resentment on the part of those in paid employment who would be required to pay high taxes to fund it). Indeed, in his second state of the union address on 4th January 1935, the President himself declared that the simple provision of unemployment relief alone was tantamount to administering *"...a narcotic, a subtle destroyer of the human spirit. It is inimical to the dictates of sound policy. It is in violation of the traditions of America. Work must be found for the able-bodied but destitute workers. The Federal Government must and shall quit this business of relief".* What instead was needed, declared President Roosevelt, was a federal programme that would make it possible for the United States *"to give employment to ... people now on relief.."* though he added that he hoped that such employment would only be required *"...pending their absorption in a rising tide of private employment".* The Big Bill was essentially the federal programme that Roosevelt had called for in his message to Congress[108] and it sought to tackle unemployment by a variety of means, partly working through existing agencies such as the Civilian Construction Corps and the Public Works Administration, and partly through the creation of new agencies.

One of the new agencies created was the Rural Electrification Agency which received authorisation from Congress in 1936 under the Rural Electrification

---

[108] In his message to Congress, Roosevelt emphasised that he believed that the federal programme should focus on the 3.5 million able-bodied unemployed on the relief rolls. There were a further 1.5 million people on those rolls who were unemployable through no fault of their own (for example, due to illness, age or physical handicap); the President said that he believed that they should continue to find relief under the existing relief systems established by local governments and charities (though he added that he stood willing *"...to help [those] local agencies to get the means necessary to assume this burden.'*). Moreover, the President's proposals did not extend to those who, for one reason or another, were not on any form of relief roll (and according to some estimates, there were 5 million people who fell within this description).

Act of 1936 to provide loans and other forms of funding to encourage the provision of electricity in rural areas, principally by co-operatively owned non-profit local power companies which the REA would help to establish. Between 1935 and 1945, thanks in large part to the REA, the ratio of rural farms with access to reliable electricity supplies increased from approximately 20 percent to over 90 percent. In the process, thousands of jobs were created, involving not only the installation of electrical circuitry in people's homes and other buildings, but also the creation of new electricity generating plants and sub-stations and the erection, stringing and maintenance of miles and miles of power cables that the new electricity networks required.

The most important and largest of the new agencies however (and one which would ultimately gather under its administrative wings many other agencies of various types) was the Works Progress Administration[109] or WPA, arguably the most important relief agency created under the New Deal. To run the new agency, Roosevelt selected Harry Hopkins, who had already cut his teeth administering earlier relief agencies such as TERA and FERA and knew how to deliver results. With an initial budget of $1.4 billion, in its first year it created job opportunities for more than 3 million people; by the time it was brought to an end in 1943, it had found jobs for 8.5 million people for a total cost of approximately $11 billion, and had by one means or another been responsible for the creation of more than half a million miles of new roads in rural areas, more than 2,500 hospitals, 5,900 schools, 350 airports, and numerous other public buildings including the Griffith Observatory in Los Angeles.

The WPA's influence extended into a wide variety of different fields. For example, in addition to sponsoring major construction projects, the WPA also spawned the National Youth Administration, which was intended to address the special needs of young people who, without relevant experience, often found it particularly difficult to gain employment. Under the NYA, funds were made available to create "work-study" jobs at colleges and universities, and part-time job training opportunities with local businesses. By 1938, more than 300,000 young people were continuing their education thanks to work-study

---

[109] After 1939, it was re-named the Works Projects Administration.

jobs; another 400,000 were in part-time employment under the auspices of the NYA.

To the surprise of many, and the objection of some but with the enthusiastic support of Roosevelt's wife Eleanor, the WPA was also willing to provide support for artists, musicians, actors, poets and other writers, theatre crews, editors, historians and archaeologists. These were people who could usually obtain little support in their chosen professions from more traditionally-minded relief agencies. The WPA created "Project One" (sometimes called "Federal One"). This gave rise to a number of sub-agencies including the Federal Theater Project (which encouraged the creation and performance of plays), the Federal Writers Project (which sponsored the creation of a wide variety of works including guidebooks to a number of American states and cities, roadmaps, local history studies and photographic surveys of the country from coast to coast), the Federal Arts Project (which broadly speaking aimed to support artists in the same way that the FWP supported writers) and the Federal Music Project (which as might be expected supported musicians). There was also the Historical Records Survey (originally forming part of the FWP, the smallest and generally regarded as the most efficient of the new sub-agencies) which was tasked with collecting and conserving historical records and testimonies throughout the United States, and whose work has often proved to be invaluable to later historians.

Project One and its sub-agencies received considerable criticism from many quarters, partly for its cost (local and state government were sometimes reluctant to provide their share of the cost – up to 30 percent of the various projects that were adopted, even after the relevant sub-agency had approved the release of federal funds). In fact, Project One and its various sub-agencies cost less than one percent of the WPA's total budget but many still objected to providing funding for intellectuals such as writers, artists and musicians, declaring they would prefer to see the money spent in support of people seeking "proper work". Other complaints alleged that some of the works being produced (and particularly many of the new plays being sponsored and performed under the auspices of the Federal Theater Project) were little more than communist propaganda[110], and such accusations were at least partially responsible for the gradual loss of congressional support for Project One, which finally led to the FTP being disbanded in June 1939 by an act of Congress. Most of the remaining agencies were also closed or had their funding severely curtailed over the next few years, and the WPA itself was terminated in 1943. Nevertheless, during their years of operation, Project One and its sub-agencies provided much needed employment for thousands of people, and led to the considerable enrichment of American cultural life.[111] Indeed, thanks to the activities of Project One, many Americans, particularly in rural areas, had their first opportunities to enjoy elements of "high culture" which had hitherto largely been the preserve of the privileged elite (according to some estimates, 60 percent of the audiences attending FTP productions for the first time had never before experienced a live theatrical production) and this helped Americans to maintain an image of themselves as a bastion of civilization despite the often harsh and drab realities of their everyday lives.

The Social Security Act of 1935

The third major piece of legislation of the Second New Deal was the Social Security Act of 1935. With Huey Long and Dr Townsend promoting their financially impossible but potentially vote-winning proposals for the elderly and unemployed, it was vital that the Roosevelt administration had its own plans for such matters in place before the commencement of the campaign season for the presidential election of 1936 began. The Wagner Act was intended primarily to provide immediate and medium-term assistance in the form of government-sponsored employment for those of the unemployed who were capable of working. With the Social Security Act, Roosevelt wanted to provide real long-term assistance for those who (for whatever reason) could not work (for example, single mothers with dependent children), and those

---

[110] Though it should be stressed that in addition to newly-commissioned material, the FTP also staged established works by playwrights such as George Bernard Shaw and the classics such as Shakespeare.

[111] Writers, actors and other artists who could claim that Project One had helped them in the crucial early stages of their careers included Orson Welles, John Steinbeck, Jackson Pollock, John Houseman, Burt Lancaster and John Cheever.

such as people over 65 who would probably be eager to remove themselves from the workforce (and thus release much needed jobs to younger unemployed workers) if they were able to support themselves adequately without working. He also wanted to provide some measure of (temporary) support for the unemployed who were capable of working and actively looking for work. Although the Act created a benefits system that was complex (and destined to increase in complexity over the years), broadly speaking the system Roosevelt was proposing[112] rested upon two concepts: unemployment insurance and government sponsored old age pensions, both of which Roosevelt had supported on a state-wide basis while he had been Governor of New York. Then, when framing the requisite legislation at state level, he had been assisted by Frances Perkins, now his Labor Secretary, and thus it was natural that in 1934 he assigned to her the task of chairing a committee that would prepare the necessary legislation for Congress. Other members of the committee were Henry Morgenthau, the Treasury Secretary, Agriculture Secretary Henry Wallace, Secretary of the Interior Harold Ickes and (almost inevitably) Harry Hopkins.

Not universally popular with all of her colleagues in the Roosevelt administration (one critic complained of her speaking as if she had *"swallowed a press release"*; others found her cool and distant in her dealings with the general public), she nevertheless brought a great deal of common sense to her role as Labor Secretary, and could usually count on the President's support for her various plans and proposals; in return, she was one of Roosevelt's most stalwart supporters in the cabinet.[113] Chairing the Committee on Economic Security (as the committee tasked with preparing the social security bill for submission to Congress came to be known) was a golden opportunity for

---

[112] President Roosevelt was involved in the drafting and passage of the bill that became the Social Security Act to a far greater extent than he had been involved in the case of the Emergency Relief Appropriations bill, where (as previously noted) he had largely been content to support the bill's passage through Congress from the sidelines.

[113] She had not only to cope with a degree of misogynist antagonism at the cabinet table; her home life was difficult. Her husband and daughter both suffered from mental illness, and her husband was eventually committed to a mental asylum; she was the family's sole source of financial support.

Frances Perkins and she and her fellow committee members eagerly seized the chance to promote ground-breaking social legislation.

At heart was the issue that the United States, virtually alone amongst the industrialised nations of the world, had no universal system in place to support the long-term unemployable or to provide pensions for the elderly. Germany, under the direction of Chancellor Otto von Bismark, had introduced various forms of compulsory social insurance legislation as early as the 1880s, and other European nations had followed Bismark's lead over the years that had followed. Until the advent of the Great Depression however, there had been little popular demand for a comparable system in America (indeed, some union leaders had actively opposed the notion, fearing government interference in social issues that they considered properly belonged to them). A few states had some form of publicly-funded pensions legislation on their statute books, but these were usually extremely limited in scope and once the Depression struck, were so underfunded as to be virtually worthless. Some pension support was provided for military veterans and public employees such as police, fire officers and teachers, but the vast majority of people had no pension coverage at all. Most expected to have to work until they died, unless they could find some form of haven in their old age either with their families or on some form of local welfare, eking out their existence with any savings they had. The majority of elderly Americans had no choice but to follow the first option. As for the long term unemployable, these received virtually no support at all, other than could be gleaned from their families or from charities.

It was clear that whatever proposals the Committee made, the resulting legislation would have to be far-reaching in scope, and would no doubt pose difficult financial challenges and face considerable opposition from conservative critics. Potentially complicating matters even further was the President's evident enthusiasm for the project; he intended if possible to make social insurance a campaign issue, which meant that in reality the Committee under Perkins' Chairmanship had only a few months to formulate policy and legislation that might help to shape the nation both socially and financially for generations to come. When discussing the matter with Perkins prior to the establishment of the Committee, Roosevelt had talked in terms of "cradle to grave" social security for everyone, regardless of their individual circumstances.

This was Roosevelt's ideal; both he and Perkins knew that in practice the Committee's proposals would be sharply constrained by political and fiscal reality, not least by the dangers of concentrating too much power over the social security system in the hands of the Federal Government. This would invite the Supreme Court to strike the legislation down for being unconstitutional but there were other more subtle dangers from such an approach. *"Just think what would happen if all that power was here, and Huey Long became President!"* FDR himself pointed out. From the start, the Committee was (somewhat unenthusiastically) convinced that the new social security system would have to be built on a platform of both federal and state laws and require a substantial degree of participation by the individual states in day-to-day operations.[114]

Cost was a restricting factor; it was soon obvious that the cost of universal cradle to grave social security would be so high as to render the whole programme unworkable, and Roosevelt was opposed to the Committee's initial proposal that the programme should initially be run in deficit, creating an ever-increasing funding liability for future generations to deal with. *"It is almost dishonest"*, Roosevelt declared, *"to build up an accumulated deficit for the Congress of the United States to meet in 1980. We can't do that. We can't sell the United States short in 1980 any more than in 1935."*[115] Clearly, cradle to grave coverage would have to wait. The Committee agreed (again reluctantly) that the scope of social security coverage should initially be restricted and in particular that various classes of workers such as domestic servants, farm workers, some teachers, government employees, librarians and employees in workforces comprising fewer than ten workers should be denied coverage under the Act. In practice, that meant that women and minorities (and particularly African Americans who constituted a substantial proportion of the nation's farm workers) were more likely to be

---

[114] Committee members also reluctantly excluded universal health care from the ambit of the new proposed legislation; primarily for fear that opposition from the medical profession might wreck the entire legislative package if it was included.

[115] Ironically, the Congresses of the United States convened during the 1980s showed far less fear of deficit spending than President Roosevelt demonstrated in 1935, and had little or no problem sanctioning massive increases to the level of federal debt during those years and leaving that debt as a problem for future generations to face.

excluded from the protections to be offered by the new system than white male workers.[116] Moreover, workers should be required to contribute at least something towards the cost of the programme.

Perkins and her colleagues were acutely conscious that the final form of the legislation, which was signed into law as the Social Security Act of 1935 by President Roosevelt on 14th August 1935 after a fairly bruising passage through Congress (one senator opposed to the legislation asked Frances Perkins: *"Isn't this socialism? Isn't this a teensy weensy bit of socialism?"*), fell far short of the initial dreams. Nevertheless, the social security programme introduced under the Act did provide for the first time at least some measure of social security protection for 26 million Americans, and Frances Perkins herself eventually conceded that the final version of the legislation was *"…the only plan that could have been put through Congress".* Under the Act, retirement benefits were to be provided for "retirees" (at age 65) as well as temporary support for those unemployed who were actively seeking work. The cost of meeting retirement benefits was to be met by contributions (essentially a new tax) paid by the worker and his or her employer. Support was also to be provided for families with dependent children (particularly important for those families in which the father had abandoned his wife and children during the nadir of the Depression) and by ancillary programmes, for people with disabilities which prevented them from working (such as blindness). The costs of these were to be met out of general taxation (but the money made available was passed to the individual states to distribute). As for unemployment benefits, whilst some federal funds were made available (paid for by another new federal tax on all but the smallest employers) an ingenious tax-offset programme was established which encouraged individual states to establish their own unemployment compensation programmes in exchange for a refund of up to 90 percent of the federal unemployment tax levied on employers in their state. This encouraged the individual states to play an active role in the general social security programme, but there was considerable variation between the states as regards the generosity of the state-wide programmes that were eventually established,

---

[116] Over the decades that followed, the scope of the social security system was slowly extended to cover many of the groups initially excluded.

so that (for example) in 1939, it was reported that a poor child in Massachusetts could receive $61 of monthly support, while a poor child in Mississippi only received $8 a month, despite both states receiving the same amount of subsidy from the Federal Government. In addition, by involving the states, the likelihood of a successful challenge before the Supreme Court over the constitutionality of the new legislation could be reduced.

Naturally, the new system had its critics, particularly amongst Republicans and Southern Democrats (who were widely regarded in liberal circles as being ultimately to blame for the exclusion of so many African Americans from the scope of the new legislation; the NAACP protested bitterly on this point). Right wing critics declared that the new system would breed sloth and ignorance, and impose a *"crushing burden on industry and labor"*; one congressman declared that it would *"...pull the pillars of the temple down upon the heads of our descendants..."* Another (perhaps predictably) declared it to be *"un-American."* Former President Herbert Hoover was appalled and declared that *"...economic and social security should not be attained through the regimentation of the mental and spiritual health of our people..."* and refused to apply for a social security number, declaring he did not wish to be *"numberfied"* (he was issued with a social security number anyway).

Nevertheless, despite the critics, a new bureaucracy was born in Washington DC, the new federal taxes intended to fund the programme began to be collected in 1937 and the first monthly social security cheque was paid to Ida M Fuller of Vermont on 31st January 1940. That first cheque was for $22.54.[117]

The Tax Bill

Another key component of the Second New Deal was Roosevelt's tax bill, which ultimately became the Revenue Act of 1935. Dubbed a "soak the rich" package by its critics and supporters alike, from the President's perspective, it had two principal aims, namely to increase the revenue available to the Federal

---

[117] Miss Fuller, who had worked as a legal secretary, paid a total of $24.75-worth of social security contributions during 1937, 1938 and 1939, and retired in November 1939, two months after her 65th birthday. She lived to be 100, and during her retirement received in aggregate $22,888.92 in the form of social security cheques.

Government, and to counter the more extreme demands for a redistribution of the nation's wealth being proposed by Huey Long, Father Coughlin and Dr Townshend and their supporters. The tax proposals embodied in the bill surprised even some of Roosevelt's own supporters; in his budget speech of 7th January 1935, he had stated that he did not think it advisable to increase tax rates or introduce new taxes during the 1936 fiscal year. By mid-June he had clearly changed his mind, principally for political reasons[118] for on 19th June, in a special message to Congress, he called for increased federal taxes on large personal incomes, inheritances and gifts, as well as increases to the tax rates applicable to corporations and a levy on inter-corporate dividend distributions. The bill, hurriedly prepared by Treasury Secretary Henry Morgenthau and his team, was debated by Congress for ten weeks, during which some of the more extreme proposals contained in the original draft (such as a graduated corporate income tax) were dropped or modified, before the bill was finally signed into law by the President on 30th August 1935.

Under the new legislation, the maximum corporate income tax rate was increased by 3 percent, to 16.75 percent. Personal incomes exceeding $50,000 were to be taxed at a new rate of 75 percent (and ultimately a rate of 79 percent was imposed on incomes over $5 million, though it was claimed that only one person, John D Rockefeller, actually paid tax at the top rate[119]). However, as aggressive as these new tax rates appeared when reported in the press, on closer examination, many wealthy tax payers and their advisers discovered that the apparently confiscatory nature of the new legislation was considerably mitigated by loopholes and tax concessions, and indeed, in its final form, the bill was only intended to raise an additional $250 million. Most Americans were unaffected by the new tax measures; the basic income tax rate

---

[118] Treasury Secretary Morgenthau admitted as much to an aide, stating that the tax bill was essentially a campaign document for the forthcoming presidential election.

[119] Rockefeller had by now passed the bulk of his wealth to his son, retaining a "mere" $25 million, so it seems unlikely that his income exceeded $5 million in the mid-1930s. Rockefeller's personal fortune may have fallen to $7 million during the early years of the Depression (though it recovered substantially before his death in 1937). The thought of a fortune worth only $7 million later prompted one of his grandchildren to comment: *"For Grandfather, that was practically broke!"*

remained at 4 percent, but the incomes of most American households (19 out of 20 according to some estimates) were such that they fell below the minimum threshold and they paid no federal income tax at all. As a genuine "soak the rich" measure, the Revenue Act of 1935 was a failure; as a piece of pre-election propaganda seeking to steal voters away from Huey Long and the other demagogues demanding extreme wealth redistribution, it was more successful, though the cost for Roosevelt personally was an intensification of the contempt felt for him by many fellow members of the "wealthy class". All of the available evidence suggests that this was a price that Franklin Roosevelt was willing to pay in exchange for retaining the keys to the White House in the presidential election of 1936.

Chapter 13   Moving Forwards

"Governments can err. Presidents do make mistakes, but the immortal Dante tells us that divine justice weighs the sins of the cold-blooded and the sins of the warm-hearted on different scales. Better the occasional faults of a government that lives in a spirit of charity than the consistent omissions of a government frozen in the ice of its own indifference."

Extract from the acceptance speech for renomination for the Presidency made by President Roosevelt to the Democratic National Convention held in Philadelphia, Pennsylvania on 27th June 1936

"Reform if you would preserve..."

Approaching the presidential election of 1936, there was little doubt that the Democratic presidential nomination was Franklin Roosevelt's for the taking, and take it he did, at the Democratic National Convention held in Philadelphia on 27th June 1936, without even the need for a roll call. Vice President John Nance Garner was equally smoothly confirmed as the President's running mate. With those matters decided, the President settled down to the task of being re-elected.

FDR and his campaign advisers were conscious that much had changed since the election held in 1932. Then, almost the entire country had been demanding urgent change and was willing to believe that Roosevelt was the man to rescue the nation without actually knowing much of what Roosevelt as the President would do. Now, four years later, the political landscape was more complex. During those years, there had unquestionably been change, on the whole for the better in the eyes of many voters in the middle and on the moderate left of the political spectrum. Public faith had been restored in the American banking system. Unemployment, a key barometer of the state of the nation for many during the Depression, and which had peaked at approximately 12.8 million on the eve of Roosevelt's first inauguration, had been falling more or less steadily ever since then, so that by the autumn of 1936, it stood at approximately 9 million (or 16.9 percent of the workforce). The nation's gross national product, having collapsed during Hoover's presidency to approximately $56 billion at the end of 1932, had grown so much that by early 1936, it stood at around $73 billion. New legal measures had been introduced to improve working conditions and to protect the rights of workers to organise and bargain collectively. And the general morale of many Americans, who believed that their government was now at least trying to help them, was certainly higher than it had been during the Hoover years.

But not everyone viewed Roosevelt so positively. Since 1932, he had lost potentially important supporters in the business, financial and legal sectors, who now feared that the measures contained in the New Deal and the Second New Deal were little more than communism in disguise, and quite possibly unconstitutional. There were those who genuinely thought that another term of President Roosevelt might see the quashing of the US constitution and the implementation of a Roosevelt dictatorship.[120] Never before (with the possible exception of the Civil War years) had the presence of the Federal Government been so obvious in everyday life – the WPA alone now employed 7 percent of America's workforce, and the power of the "men from Washington" to interfere in the lives of ordinary people was resented in some quarters just as much as the jobs created by the New Deal were appreciated in others.

Furthermore, many of the President's own social class (relatively few in number, but articulate when they wished to be and well placed to make their views known) were now implacably united in seeing him as a traitor to themselves and their country as they perceived it, and felt little hesitation in saying so. On the other side of the political spectrum, there were those who felt that the New Deal did not go far enough and that Roosevelt was doing all he could to protect the wealthy from the social justice they so richly deserved. Indeed, just as Roosevelt was being confirmed as the Democrats' presidential nominee, Father Coughlin, Dr Townsend and a self-appointed successor to Huey Long, preacher and political organiser Gerald L K Smith, were in the process of establishing a new political party, the Union Party, with a view to denouncing Roosevelt and his policies and promoting in their place a "share the wealth" programme modelled upon that popularised by Huey Long before his assassination. During the election campaign, the President showed little sign of concern about opposition from the wealthy and privileged but the prospect of a Union Party presidential nominee snatching vital votes from left-

---

[120] A Gallup poll at about this time indicated that 45 percent of respondents thought that Roosevelt's policies might lead to dictatorship.

leaning voters, and in the process allowing a Republican to win the White House worried him and his campaign staff as much as the prospect of Huey Long running for President had worried them the year before.

For taxpayers of a more financially-inclined state of mind, especially those who favoured a balanced budget, the cost of the New Deal and the abandonment of the gold standard was troubling – the Federal Government was now spending more than 9 percent of the nation's GDP and the federal deficit was in excess of $4.5 billion and rising, seemingly promising a prospect of ever-increasing (and ever more wide-ranging) taxes if the New Deal were allowed to continue. With so many different factions and interested parties attempting to sway the electorate in the run-up to the presidential election, it was therefore by no means clear that President Roosevelt would necessarily be granted a second term and many political commentators, supported by a plethora of polling data, predicted a very close race in November 1936.

The Republican leadership, still reeling from the debacles of the elections of 1932 and the mid-terms of 1934, was well aware of the old adage that he who controls the middle of the political spectrum is well positioned to win the victory, and concluded that they needed to field a candidate who could challenge Roosevelt on this vital political ground where he was unquestionably popular. At the Republican National Convention of 1936 held in Cleveland Ohio in June, there was no shortage of potential candidates seeking the nomination[121] but only two serious candidates ultimately emerged, Governor Alfred Landon of Kansas and Senator William Borah of Idaho, both of whom could legitimately claim at least some credibility with middle-ground voters.

Landon was a wealthy former businessman who had spoken up in favour of the need for the government to provide day-to-day social support at times of crisis, a stance which cost him the political support of President Hoover in 1932 during his first gubernatorial campaign – and which probably helped him to gain the governorship, despite the general Democratic landslide during the elections of that year. He then retained the governorship in 1934, when he was

---

[121] Candidates who failed to gain the nomination that year included car manufacturing tycoon Henry Ford, Theodore Roosevelt Jr (son of the former President), aviator Charles Lindbergh and former President Herbert Hoover.

the only Republican governor that year to be re-elected to office. Landon was nevertheless also fiscally conservative enough to appeal to many Republican delegates and believed where possible in reducing taxes and balancing the budget (his supporters billed him as the "Kansas Coolidge").

Borah, an attorney by training, had gained a reputation as an isolationist earlier in the century. He had vigorously opposed President Wilson's plans for the League of Nations – indeed he opposed a wide range of things, including many of the deeply held beliefs of the conservative wing of his own party, giving rise to his nickname "The Great Opposer". Like Landon he too supported some aspects of the New Deal and had refused to endorse Hoover during his re-election campaign of 1932. Indeed Borah's tendency to adopt political positions at odds with the views of many within his own party gave rise to suggestions that he might bolt from the Republicans and become a supporter of Roosevelt. He never abandoned the Republicans however, and his willingness to be outspoken for the issues in which he believed ensured his personal popularity with many of his constituents. Ultimately, it was Borah's poor relationship with the conservatives in his party which cost him the nomination; when the convention's delegates were ask to choose between the two men, they overwhelmingly voted for Landon by 984 votes to 19. Editor and publisher Frank Knox (destined in due course to become Secretary of the Navy during Roosevelt's fourth term despite his Republican affiliations) was chosen as the Republican's Vice-Presidential nominee.

President Roosevelt responded to the challenge of Landon and Knox by effectively ignoring them, save to contradict them when they indulged in malicious scaremongering. Instead, in a series of speeches commencing on 29th September in Syracuse, New York, he chose to emphasise the progress that had been made since he had taken office, claiming (with considerable justification) that many Americans would recall *"...that starvation was averted, that homes and farms were saved, that crop prices rose, that industry revived, and that the dangerous forces subversive of our form of government were turned aside"* during the years of his first term. Turning on those who accused him of being little more than a communist,[122] he argued that the forces of communism were best helped by ignoring the circumstances that would allow that political faith to grow, and charged that this was exactly what had been happening under the last Republican presidency: *"Conditions congenial to communism were being bred and fostered throughout this nation up to the very day of March 4, 1933. Hunger was breeding it, the loss of homes and farms were breeding it, a ruinous price level was breeding it. Discontent and fear were spreading through the land. The previous national administration, bewildered, did nothing."* And he warned that the Republicans had little to offer but maintenance of the status quo – they had, he asserted, little interest in bringing in new legislation that would help the average citizen face the difficulties of economic depression, and help to safeguard the institutions of the Republic in a difficult and changing world. Indeed, he claimed, *"...out of the strains and stresses of these years, we have come to see that the true conservative is the man who has a real concern for injustices and takes thought against the day of reckoning. The true conservative seeks to protect the system of private property and free enterprise by correcting such injustices and inequalities as arise from it. The most serious threat to our institutions comes from those who refuse to face the need for change. Liberalism becomes the protection for the far-sighted conservative."*

The message *"reform, if you would preserve..."* became one of the central planks of Roosevelt's re-election campaign, and in speeches across the north-east of the country throughout that autumn, he hammered that message home, warning that *"...the old enemies of peace – business and financial monopoly, speculation, reckless banking, class antagonism, sectionalism [and] war profiteering..."* were rising up to challenge further reform, and to cast down much of what had already been achieved. *"Never before in all our history have these forces been so united against one candidate as they stand today...they are unanimous in their hate for me..."* he somewhat histrionically but graphically claimed to an audience packed into New York's

---

[122] Among the people who accused him of this stood Father Coughlin, who now also declared him to be a "liar", "anti-God" and a "scab President" – eventually this proved too much for Coughlin's superiors in the Church who ordered that he apologise publicly to the President – which Father Coughlin did. Thereafter, the Church kept a closer eye on what their outspoken parish priest was up to. Eventually (in 1942) he was ordered to cease his political activities and confine himself to his duties in his parish, an order which (by and large) he obeyed until his retirement in 1966.

Madison Square Gardens on the evening of 31st October, before adding *"...and I welcome their hate."*

Such utterances delighted the packed crowds who thronged to hear him wherever he went, but appalled many ordinary businessmen who might otherwise have been inclined to support him and even some of his own close advisers wondered if his attacks on the business community went too far. What mattered, however, was that he retained control of the centre of the political spectrum, which he did, thanks in part to thoroughly lacklustre campaigns on the parts of Landon and Knox. Particularly crass were Landon's attempts to smear the new social security system, warning workers that they would never see their contributions again (and failing to acknowledge that employers as well as employees were required to pay into the new system), and alleging that it would be necessary for the government to issue everyone with metal dog-tags if the system was to have any hope of working at all, allegations that Roosevelt took great delight in demolishing. Scaremongering apart, it seemed that Landon and Knox had little new of substance to offer the American people.

Nevertheless, even as Roosevelt was speaking at Madison Square Gardens, there came a warning that even the President should not take the support of the American people for granted. The journal Literary Digest, an influential and venerable magazine that had been in circulation since 1890, published the results of a major poll it had carried out, claiming to have sampled the voting intentions of over 2.3 million voters (having sent out 10 million ballot papers). The Digest had successfully predicted the results of the presidential elections of 1916, 1920, 1924, 1928 and 1932; now it was openly predicting that the election to be held on 3rd November 1936 would see a Landon victory, with the Republican presidential candidate gaining 57 percent of the popular vote and 370 electoral votes (Roosevelt was predicted to gain only 41 percent of the popular vote). Moreover, this followed the results of the gubernatorial, state and congressional elections held in Maine a few weeks before,[123] which had

---

[123] At the time, Maine took pride in holding its state-wide and congressional elections in September rather than November like other states (presidential elections took place in November at the same time as the rest of the country), and had gained a reputation

seen a series of Republican victories, giving hope to Republicans and dismay to Democrats across the country who believed that the country would follow Maine's lead. To add still further to the concerns of the Democratic leadership, the results of a Gallup poll were published in which 53 percent of the people polled declared themselves to be "conservative" rather than "liberal by nature".

Could Landon and the Republicans seize the White House after all, despite everything, especially the spectre of Hoover's failure which still tarnished the reputation of the Republicans? Just possibly, yes, particularly if the Union Party split the votes on the left so as to fatally weaken Roosevelt's position (and some polls carried out by the Democratic Party suggested the Union Party might attract enough support from Irish Catholic voters to achieve exactly that result). But the Digest's poll was the only one of the final set of major polls to predict a victory for Landon; all the others published in the last few days before the election predicted victory for Roosevelt and Garner, albeit in a fairly tight race. Roosevelt himself was said to have believed he could gain 360 electoral votes while Landon secured 170; even he, however, jovially dismissed a prediction by James Farley, the Postmaster-General, (Roosevelt's campaign manager and one of his closest political advisers at the time, Louis Howe having died a few months before), that he would win every state except for Maine and Vermont.

Yet when the votes came to be counted, that was exactly the result that emerged. The presidential election of 1936 was an overwhelming landslide for President Roosevelt, who won 46 states and 523 electoral votes, compared to Landon's two states and eight electoral votes. Moreover, Roosevelt had won 61 percent of the popular vote (27.48 million votes); Landon had won 37 percent (16.68 million votes). The Union Party, whose presence in the race had genuinely been a matter of concern for the President, barely registered on the

---

as a bellwether state, since for many years, the results of its state elections had pre-figured those of subsequent presidential elections, giving rise to the saying: *"As Maine goes, so goes the nation".* Once the presidential election results for 1936 became known, the slogan was rewritten (by James Farley): *"As goes Maine, so goes Vermont."* Maine's reputation as a politically predictive state never recovered.

voting scales at all, attracting only 882,000 votes, and ceased to be politically relevant overnight.

Roosevelt's triumph was repeated in congressional, gubernatorial and state-wide elections throughout the country – the results for the Democrats were even better than they had achieved in the congressional elections of 1934. After 3rd November, the Democrats held 331 seats in the House of Representatives (the Republicans had 89 seats); in the Senate the Democrats held 76 seats while the Republicans held only 16. There were so many Democratic senators that there was insufficient room for them on the Democratic side of the aisle in the Senate chamber, and some had to sit on the side traditionally reserved for the Republicans. The Democrats also held 39 of the country's 48 state governorships; the Republicans held only six, with a further three being held by independents.

Roosevelt and the Democratic Party had clearly won a resounding new mandate from the American people to continue with the policies of the New Deal. That said, when the political advisers began to delve through the voting data, some interesting facts began to emerge. It was clear, for instance, that Roosevelt had been right to focus his attention on wooing voters in the middle and left of the political spectrum, while risking the antagonism of the right and the business community generally. He had gained immense support from the inner city wards of the great industrial cities, particularly in the industrial north-east of the country, largely in response to the assistance the New Deal policies had provided in those districts, where traditionally many people had previously been reluctant to vote. Despite the threat posed by the Union Party, but with widespread labour union endorsement, he had overwhelmingly attracted the support of the industrial working classes, and particularly the Irish Catholic vote; similarly, many African Americans (where they were able to vote – disenfranchisement in the southern states remained a serious problem) had voted Democrat despite the fact that since the end of the Civil War, African Americans had usually supported the Republicans, the party of Abraham Lincoln. Thereafter, the Republicans were unable to take the African American vote for granted, as historically they had tended to do.

There were some aspects of the results that warned thoughtful observers that despite rhetoric to the contrary from extreme Roosevelt supporters, the election should not be regarded as tantamount to the crowning of a new American monarch. Admittedly, Roosevelt's share of the overall popular vote had increased since the 1932 elections (increasing from 57 percent to 61 percent), but one in three Americans had voted against him and the policies of the New Deal and his share of the popular vote actually fell in 14 states (particularly mid-western states). In the most populous states which he had taken (including New York, Pennsylvania, Michigan and New Jersey) the rise in his share of the vote was largely due to his extreme popularity in the big cities but the position was not as clear-cut in rural districts of those states. In the state of New York, for example (political territory that Roosevelt might have expected to hold without difficulty given his long-standing historic association with the state), he had failed to carry many of the rural counties and had retained the state's 47 electoral college votes only because of the vice-like political grip he held on New York City itself. This was a state of affairs repeated throughout the nation – results showed that outside the South and the big industrial cities, Roosevelt had struggled to achieve a majority of the votes cast, especially in the small towns of the mid-west. Nevertheless he had won the election; he could now settle down to craft and pursue the policies of his second administration, policies which he had promised the American people would help to secure and advance the economic recovery of the nation.

It later transpired that the eve of election poll by the Literary Digest which had so definitely and so inaccurately predicted a Landon victory, had polled individuals whose names were on lists of automobile owners and telephone subscribers, and had thus focused largely on the wealthier voters who were more likely to vote for Landon and the Republicans. Moreover, of those polled it was the Republican-leaning voters who were more likely to complete and return the poll's ballot papers. The poll therefore unwittingly oversampled Republican voting intentions and no attempt was made to correct this bias. The reputation of the Literary Digest's polls plummeted after the 1936 election, and the debacle was claimed by some commentators as being at least partly responsible for the demise of the journal two years later.

Showdown with the Supreme Court

When Franklin Roosevelt stood on the East Portico of the Capitol shortly after noon on 20th January 1937 to deliver his second inaugural address, he was able to report to the American people that *"our progress out of the depression is obvious"*. The nation's GNP had finally recovered and had even modestly surpassed the level of 1929. Industrial production figures were rising and fast approaching levels last seen in the giddy months before the Great Crash. Exports were increasing; by early 1937 in dollar terms America was exporting nearly twice as much as she had in 1932, although export levels were still well below those seen in mid-1929 in large part thanks to the continuing and complicated tangle of trade barriers erected by America and the world's other major trading nations which acted as a brake on the world's economic recovery. The modest economic recovery in turn meant that the number of people unemployed was continuing to fall, though as Roosevelt himself admitted in the course of his address, there were still millions of people who were *"..ill-housed, ill-clad, ill-nourished…"* Much remained to be done to help those still suffering economic and social hardship. Nevertheless, there was a palpable sense of recovery in the air, a general feeling that at least a small measure of economic stability, perhaps even modest prosperity, might be around the corner, and the President was justified in alluding to it .

But as President Roosevelt had himself said on several occasions (and indeed, as he effectively said again during his second inaugural address), his goals were not limited to simple economic recovery alone – recovery without necessary reform not only courted the very real possibility of another economic depression in the not too distant future, but also potentially encouraged forms of political extremism such as fascism or communism to gain footholds in America just as they were now growing in parts of Europe and Asia. Much of the New Deal legislation, and the various institutions that the New Deal had spawned, had been intended to deliver such reform. However, the experiences of the previous year had shown that the new institutions and the values they offered were not so well entrenched in American society that they were immune from attack from a variety of sources.

In particular, they were seen as being potentially vulnerable to judicial challenge by the Supreme Court, which had already inflicted legal carnage on many of the New Deal's legislative foundations, and might well inflict more in the months and years to come, reversing the accomplishments of the New Deal and making further reform impossible. Roosevelt regarded, the justices of the Supreme Court (none of whom he had appointed) as indulging in little more than legal nit-picking and judicial obstructionism when they issued their various rulings against the New Deal legislation regardless of the damage such decisions might cause the Government or the nation, (the Tipaldo case in particular had infuriated him). Roosevelt even suggested that the ages of the justices might be causing them to be less flexible and open to new ideas than was desirable for judges sitting in the highest court of the land. In the months during the run-up to the presidential election, he and his closest advisers had discussed possible ways of addressing the "problem" of the Supreme Court, and many political observers predicted a "showdown" between the President and the Bench after Inauguration Day.

It was not long in coming. The opening salvo of the President's attack on the Supreme Court was fired on 5th February 1937 in the form of a message to Congress in which he asked for new legislation which would empower the sitting president to appoint additional justices, not only to the Supreme Court, but to other federal courts as well, whenever an existing judge elected to continue in office beyond his 70th birthday. Exercise of the new power would be subject to a maximum of 44 new appointments to the lower courts and no fewer than six new appointments to the Supreme Court, meaning that the Supreme Court could have up to 15 justices sitting on its bench.[124] This new power was necessary, explained the President, to improve the efficiency of the judicial system; he made no mention of presidential exasperation at recent judicial decisions involving the New Deal, nor the fact that the vast majority of judges sitting at all levels of the federal court system had been appointed under Republican administrations.

Immediate responses to the proposals were at best mixed. Roosevelt had some support in Congress, though many southern senators and congressmen, firmly wedded to the notion of the Supreme Court as the ultimate guarantor of

---

[124] Given the ages of the justices of the Supreme Court in February 1937, the proposed legislation would have empowered Roosevelt to appoint six new justices immediately.

individual states' rights (and particularly of the rights of the southern states to enforce segregationist and other racially-biased laws) were opposed. They were joined in their opposition by liberal Democrats across the country, many of whom in other circumstances would have been staunch defenders of the President. Vice President Garner made it known that he himself was not in favour of the new legislation – he is reported to have stood in the lobby of the Senate while the bill was being announced, holding his nose and pointing his thumb to the ground; shortly thereafter he left Washington for a vacation in the South, abandoning his post in the Senate as its presiding officer. Roosevelt is said never to have forgiven him, and Garner's opposition to the President's judicial appointments legislation was one of the reasons why he chose to run for the Democratic presidential nomination in 1940.

The Supreme Court justices themselves, of course, were scarcely likely to be supporters, and some newspapers immediately came out in opposition to the proposals, openly declaring that Roosevelt was attempting to "pack the court". As for the Republicans, a few raised their voices in protest when the proposed legislation was announced (including Herbert Hoover, who declared that it proved that Roosevelt was trying to establish a dictatorship), but they mostly remained silent, watching their political opponents begin to turn on one another. But so strong was the belief in the apparent invincibility of the President's political skills that many commentators, even the New York Times, expected the legislation to pass despite the opposition.

All this ignored the views of the American people. Roosevelt himself was still popular and respected, but many ordinary Americans were not at all keen on the idea of altering the balance of the courts by presidential decree. Not only did most of them actually trust the court system in its present form, but many also thought the reform proposals were similar to the constitutional manipulations of Hitler and Mussolini in Europe. A few weeks after Roosevelt's message to Congress, a Gallup poll showed that 53 percent of people polled were firmly against the President's proposals, and that number was climbing. Emboldened, opponents of the proposals stepped up their campaigns against them.

In response, Roosevelt largely abandoned the argument that the proposals would improve the efficiency of the court system, and began to argue that change was necessary because the Supreme Court was straying beyond its Constitutionally-mandated boundaries of responsibility, usurping the role properly reserved for the executive wing of the Federal Government, and that ordinary men and women were suffering as a result. The Supreme Court, he declared during a fireside chat held on 9th March, had *"...been acting not as a judicial body, but as a policy-making body..."*, and this had to cease if reform was to succeed. He denied he was seeking to pack the court: *"This plan of mine is no attack on the Court; it seeks to restore the Court to its rightful and historic place in our system of Constitutional government."*

The President's staunch defence of his proposals impressed many who listened to him; opinion polls taken shortly after the fireside chat showed a significant swing in favour of the President's position with the result that opponents and supporters were now evenly matched. Nevertheless, there was still very real opposition to Roosevelt's proposals at all levels of government and out on the streets.[125] As the weeks passed, popular opposition to the proposals began to rise once more.

Then, on 29th March 1937, the Supreme Court itself made a significant contribution to the debate, by issuing its rulings in the case of *West Coast Hotel v Parrish* and two other cases involving New Deal legislation. Of the three cases, the Parrish case attracted the most popular attention, if only because it involved a minimum wage law enacted by the state of Washington – in other words, it was very similar to the Tipaldo case of a year before when the Supreme Court had struck down New York's minimum wage law on the grounds that it breached freedom of contract rights. In the Parrish case however, by a majority decision of 5 to 4 (with Chief Justice Hughes voting with the majority), the Court upheld the validity of the Washington State minimum wage legislation. On the face of it, this seemed to be an example of

---

[125] In the meantime, Chief Justice Hughes sent a letter to Senator Burton Wheeler of Montana (an influential progressive Democrat who had early declared his opposition to the proposed legislation) in which he denied Roosevelt's allegation that the Supreme Court was inefficient. Certainly hundreds of petitions to the Court had been rejected, the Chief Justice declared (717 out of a total 867 in the last year alone) because the rejected petitions had been inadmissible due to various legal flaws.

the Supreme Court retreating as a result of political pressure, and the press made much of the fact that the "u-turn" (as it was soon categorised) was the result of a single justice (Mr Justice Owen Roberts) changing his position – in Tipaldo, he had voted with the conservative "Four Horsemen", now he voted with the more liberal wing of the Bench. In fact, Roberts had switched his position before the President had announced his court reform plans, and had done so principally because after the decision in the Tipaldo case had been announced, a previous court ruling that had underlain the legal reasoning in Tipaldo had been overruled. Paradoxically however, while the decision in Parrish made it seem as though Roosevelt was now winning the court reform debate, it also served to weaken the President's arguments as to why court reform was necessary; after all, the Supreme Court now seemed to be approaching cases in exactly the spirit that the President had declared was necessary to ensure the security and stability of the country, so was any reform of the courts needed at all?

The Supreme Court spoke again on 12th April (again, a 5 to 4 majority ruling) in the case of *NLRB v Jones and Laughlin* which examined the constitutionality of the Wagner Act. Ignoring precedents it itself had created only a year or so before, the Court performed another apparent u-turn and ruled that the Act was constitutionally valid. Six weeks later, the Court also approved key aspects of the Social Security Act. These rulings too were seen as evidence of the Court heeding the President's call and seeking to avoid the impression of attempting to make policy decisions.

The following month, one of the Four Horsemen, 77 year old Mr Justice Van Devanter, announced his retirement. At last, a Roosevelt nominee would replace him and sit in the Supreme Court, the strength of the conservative wing of Court would be accordingly diminished[126] and the security of the New Deal legislation and institutions suddenly seemed much more assured.

At the same time, public support for the President's reforms had fallen to 35 percent. Complicating matters still further, Senate majority leader Joseph Robinson, one of the President's key allies in Congress died from a heart attack

---

[126] In due course, there would be another seven replacements over the next eight years.

on 14th July. With Robinson gone, any remaining hopes of shepherding the new legislation through Congress, at least in 1937, also disappeared. At last, Roosevelt conceded that it was time to draw a line under the court reform proposals, and to move on. He asked Vice President Garner (who had by now returned from his vacation) to bring matters to a quiet conclusion in Congress – the result was the distinctly minor Judicial Procedure Reform Act of 1937 which made some alterations to procedures and practices of the lower federal courts, but signally failed to alter the number of justices sitting in the Supreme Court.

Though the President had failed in his attempts to expand the courts, he had undoubtedly brought about a shift in the constitutional balance between the courts and the executive wing of the Government, and in the future the Supreme Court would be more circumspect when asked to consider the constitutionality of major pieces of socio-economic legislation. Indeed, the Court effectively left such pieces of legislation well alone for several decades to come. *"We obtained 98 percent of all the objectives intended by the court plan"* he concluded a year later. The edifice of the New Deal that had been created would now survive for years.

But if there had been a shift in the constitutional balance, it came at a price. The end result of the court reform saga had shattered any illusion that the Democrats were a tightly disciplined body all solidly lined up behind Franklin Roosevelt's leadership, all vehemently supporting further socially aggressive New Deal legislation. The Democrats in Congress demonstrated this in their relationship with the White House. The days when the President could simply issue draft bills and expect to bulldoze them through Congress and into law simply because of the Democrat majority in both House and Senate had receded into history; from now on, dissenting Democrats were willing to openly challenge their leader if they felt it right, or opportune, to do so. Differences of views and values between different wings of the party and particularly between the north-eastern and southern blocks, between the progressive liberals and the conservatives, and between urban and rural Democrats became more obvious. The immediate casualty of this was the New Deal reform programme. While pieces of reform legislation of various types continued to be proposed, debated and even passed, the programme's political momentum had disappeared.

It was of course probably inevitable that the discipline and unity that the Democrats had (by and large) demonstrated during Roosevelt's first term should have crumbled at some time during his second. After all, the darkest days of the Great Depression had now passed, and there was less of a sense of having to "stand together or hang separately" – America's body politic could now once more afford (indeed, now arguably required, if fears of a constitutional dictatorship were to be allayed) a moderately healthy degree of internal dissent, within the governing party, as well as across the country as a whole. The New Deal programme was not universally popular in every respect with every Democrat, and its continued development and expansion was bound to be challenged from within the party sooner or later. However, it was not inevitable that the uprising of discontent should occur so soon into the second term. Had the President not pushed the case of court reform so hard, even after clear signals of mounting opposition, he might have been able to postpone the inevitable for a year or two, and used that time to push through further reforms under the mantle of the New Deal. His failure to heed those signals marks one of the President's rare political miscalculations; throughout his political career, he had generally been keen to be seen as being in step with public opinion. In the case of the court reform proposals, he had been out of step, and he paid a political price for that. From now on, the need to avoid open and politically damaging dissent acted as a political brake on Roosevelt's ability to exercise his executive powers and pursue his own political agenda without regard to the views of others.[127]

---

[127] The need to balance the interests and wishes of the different strands of the party may explain why Roosevelt's administrations, for all the rhetoric about the need for fairness for everyone, did little to assist the impoverished and oppressed African American citizens in the south; any attempt by Roosevelt to use the powers of the Federal Government on the issue of civil rights would immediately have cost him the support of southern Democrats, possibly turning him into a lame duck president for the remainder of his term and almost certainly cost him the presidential nomination at the next election..

At least Roosevelt's personal popularity remained high with the American people. And that was just as well, because by late spring 1937, the economic recovery that had been slowly building since the implementation of the New Deal reforms suddenly stuttered and failed. Economic indices began falling. Henry Morgenthau, the Treasury Secretary was blunt. *"Mr President"* he declared, *"We are headed right into another Depression."*

DARK REALITIES

Chapter 14   The Arsenal of Democracy

"…Britain still fights gallantly, on a "far-flung battle line." We have doubled and redoubled our vast production, increasing, month by month, our material supply of the tools of war…"
Excerpt from a radio address delivered by President Roosevelt from the White House on 27th May 1941, 9.30 pm EST

The Roosevelt Recession

The speed of the economic downturn during the summer and autumn of 1937 took many observers by surprise, including the President and his advisers. During his re-election campaign, Roosevelt had claimed that the Depression was on the retreat thanks to New Deal policies that many people had almost come to believe it as an article of faith, and during the last few months of 1936 and the early months of 1937 the economic picture had indeed seemed increasingly rosy, albeit that a full recovery had not yet been achieved. So confident were the President and his advisers that economic good times were fast approaching that he had agreed, in principle, to proposals by Treasury Secretary Henry Morgenthau and others that steps be taken to start reducing emergency relief for the unemployed, in anticipation that the private sector would continue to create new job opportunities. Both Morgenthau and Roosevelt hoped that this would help to reduce federal and local state spending levels and allow them once more to pursue their long-term goal of balancing the public budget.

However, just as steps were being taken to initiate the relief cuts, the economic outlook suddenly turned dark. Factory orders dwindled. Within a few months, at least 2 million workers, many of whom had only recently managed to regain employment, found themselves out of work once more, and the total number of workers unemployed again rose above the 10 million mark, a figure which evoked memories of the blackest days of Hoover's administration. By the end of the year, overall industrial output had collapsed by 40 percent compared to the previous year. Corporate profits began to fall and kept falling. Unsurprisingly, the economic downturn was reflected in the share prices on Wall Street. The Dow Jones index, which at the beginning of August 1937 had been hovering around 186, stood at 120 by the end of 1937, having fallen as low as 113 on 24th November. A single day's trading (18th October) saw the

Dow Jones lose 7.75 percent of its value, one of the worst crashes on Wall Street since October 1929. It seemed to many people, both on Wall Street and beyond, as though the Great Depression had struck back with a vengeance and before long the recession (the first economic downturn since Roosevelt had assumed the Presidency) was being called the "Roosevelt Recession".

With the benefit of hindsight, it now seems that several factors were responsible for triggering the 1937 economic downturn. To begin with, changes to the banking laws had created stricter reserve requirements for American banks. While this certainly helped to maintain general public confidence in the banking system and lessened the likelihood of future bank failures, the fact that banks were obliged to maintain higher reserves meant that they had fewer funds to release into general circulation by way of business and personal loans. Compounding the problem, the Federal Reserve had for some time been worrying about inflation, partly as a result of the influx of gold into the country from overseas depositors which reflected the apparent success of New Deal economics. Determined to beat inflation down before it really manifested itself, the Federal Reserve (with President Roosevelt's approval) began to "sterilise" gold imports (essentially buying up the gold imports and not allowing them to be released into the market). At the same time, thanks at least in part to the new labour legislation introduced under the auspices of the New Deal, wage demands were rising, as were the taxes demanded by Washington.[128] The net result was that the money supply began to contract sharply and the cost of borrowing began to rise. Domestic demand for American goods and services began to weaken. Faced with these burdens, private sector businesses began to fail and the general economy to retreat once more.

As America slid sharply back into recession during the latter half of 1937 and the early spring of 1938, debates raged within the corridors of power as to how

---

[128] The new taxes included, for the first time, a tax on companies' undistributed profits which had been introduced, not without difficulty, under the Revenue Act of 1936. As early as August 1937, the New York Times was reporting that one effect of the new tax was to cause businesses to reduce their expenditures by cutting their workforces and to curtail or at least postpone planned investments in new plant and machinery.

best the problem should be tackled, with, broadly speaking, the battle lines drawn between those who favoured plans designed to rein in public expenditure and bring the budget back into balance (coupled with a policy of *rapprochement* with the business community generally), and those who felt the solution lay in further large-scale public spending programmes. Worryingly, to some insiders it seemed as though Roosevelt himself was initially uncertain as to which option he preferred. As he procrastinated, he seemed to grow increasingly bad-tempered. This was particularly evident at a cabinet meeting held on 8th November 1937, when he angrily declared that he was *"...sick and tired of being told by the cabinet, by Henry [Morgenthau] and everybody else what's the matter with the country and nobody suggests what I should do."* The problem wasn't that no one was advocating possible solutions, but rather that it was by no means clear which of the options being discussed was preferable. Increased public spending seemed to have succeeded at pulling the country out of Hoover's Depression, but as soon as tentative steps were taken to cut back on the spending, the country immediately fell into recession once again. On the other hand, there were real practical limits to the levels of taxes that could be safely levied and the levels of expenditure that the nation could sustain without suffering long-term political, social and financial damage. In addition, the more fiscally conservative of the President's advisers, including of course Treasury Secretary Morgenthau, kept pressing for a balanced budget, the concept of which appealed to the President as well. Underlying the debate, however, was the simple fact that slashing public expenditure just as the country was slumping back into recession would carry with it a political price that would be too high for Roosevelt to pay. There was never a realistic possibility that Roosevelt would sanction extreme budget cuts in late 1937 or early 1938 as long as the country remained mired in an economic downturn.

Anxious to avoid suggestions that the current economic crisis had its causes, at least in part, in the policies of the New Deal, Roosevelt listened with increasing interest to, and then embraced, arguments advanced by Harold Ickes, and other ideologically committed "New Dealers"[129] to the effect that the current

---

[129] Who now were able to cite John Maynard Keynes' latest work *"The General Theory of Employment, Interest and Money"* (published in 1936) to support their case. Keynes

downturn had little to do with economics, but was due to a politically motivated "capital strike" deliberately engineered by private sector businessmen and bankers anxious to destroy the New Deal and to see President Roosevelt summarily despatched from the White House. There was little or no evidence for the existence of any form of conspiratorially-organised capital strike, but this did not prevent Roosevelt from taking advantage of the suggestion by using it as a political smokescreen, or the more fervent New Dealers from rallying to the President's side to protect him from apparent attack by the forces of *"the modern industrial oligarchy that dominates the United States"*. The appropriate response to this apparent strike of capital, Ickes and his fellow New Dealers argued, was a resumption of large scale spending by the public sector, coupled with measures designed to increase genuine competition between businesses in the private sector. In vehement agreement with Ickes on this point was Marriner Eccles, the Chairman of the Federal Reserve Board, who openly warned Roosevelt that if he went along with Morgenthau's plans to cut public expenditure at that time, the result would be a guaranteed economic slump. During meetings held at the White House on 8th and 10th November, Roosevelt contrived to give Eccles the impression that he agreed that the best course of action would be to increase public expenditure regardless of the effect on the deficit rather than to seek to restrain public spending.

However, only hours after he had spoken with the President, Eccles attended a public talk given to business leaders by Treasury Secretary Morgenthau, during which the Treasury Secretary (with the apparent prior blessing of the President) openly committed the government to the pursuit of a balanced budget. The cynicism of the business leaders in attendance was such that this announcement was greeted with groans and other expressions of weary disbelief; for Eccles, the most important point was that he had clear sight, probably for the first time, of the President's ability to support two mutually contradictory points of view at the same time. It made him wonder, Eccles

---

argued the need for governments to counteract economic downturns by large-scale spending programmes financed by high levels of taxation and government borrowing.

later commented, whether the President really understood what the New Deal was.

From Roosevelt's perspective, the important question was whether the much vaunted but strangely insubstantial conspiratorial capital strike afforded him enough political cover to allow him the luxury of waiting and listening to the political debate within and without his administration as to what should be done to tackle the downturn without the necessity of committing himself, possibly prematurely, to any particular course of action. He judged that it did. Weeks and then months passed without any substantive announcement from the White House of any major new set of initiatives designed to tackle the economic malaise. A special session of Congress was called by Roosevelt on 15th November 1937, but the text of President Roosevelt's message barely mentioned the recession, and instead focussed on the need to introduce further labour protection laws intended to tackle the problems of child and sweatshop labour. These were measures that Congress had found itself unable to pass in the previous session, in part due to the political turmoil arising from the President's attempt to pack the Bench.

Roosevelt took almost no overt measures to tackle the economic downturn of 1937/1938, other than requesting that Congress approve an emergency appropriation of $3 billion in April 1938 intended to provide further funding for the work carried out by the WPA, the CCC and the Farm Security Administration. Essentially, he piloted a middle course between the two extremes dominating the debate within the White House, neither cutting back nor seeking the additional spending that the disciples of Keynesian economics were demanding, but rather allowing the current of economic and political events to carry the nation forward. There were economic and political dangers in both excessive cuts and excessive spending programmes; the option of doing nothing and awaiting events carried at that time the least political danger for the President. Moreover, as the months of 1938 went by, it gradually became clear that the best thing that Roosevelt could do for the economy in 1937 and 1938 was to keep the ship of state on an even keel and allow the economy to right itself. The Roosevelt Recession, despite its sharpness and the fears of many, did not portend another Great Depression[130]. During the latter half of 1938, the economy gradually began to pick up once more, clawing back much of the ground it had lost a year before. Factory orders began to rise and unemployment started to fall once more as companies began to order new industrial plants and machinery and American consumer demand took off once again. By early 1939, America's economic engine was running relatively smoothly once again. Though the number of workers unemployed would not fall back to the levels of pre-1929 for at least another couple of years (not until the US was drawn into the Second World War), nevertheless, by mid-1939, Roosevelt and other politicians could begin to talk once again of the prospect of widespread prosperity with some hope of being believed by at least some of their audiences. If full recovery from the last vestiges of the Great Depression had not yet arrived, it seemed that it was finally on its way.

And this was just as well, for the international situation had been steadily worsening over the years since President Roosevelt had first assumed office. The fascist dictatorships of Europe, and particularly Nazi Germany, were becoming increasingly belligerent, posing the threat of a new European war. War had already broken out in the Far East between China and Japan, and Japan was making little secret of its desire to expand its conquests further into the resource-rich territories of the various European empires, and becoming increasingly antagonistic to American interests in the Pacific. An economically destitute America could not have assumed a key role in the war against the Axis Powers. From the point of view of the preservation of world freedom, America had emerged from the shadows of the Great Depression just in time.

Over There

American isolationism had, if anything, grown more pronounced throughout the 1930s as the war clouds gathered over Europe and symptomatic of this was the widespread demand that the United States should enshrine non-interventionism and neutrality into US law. Support for such measures was not confined to the Republican Party; there were powerful forces within the

---

[130] A better comparison might be the downturn of 1920 which bit sharply when it first arrived but was over within a year or two.

Democratic Party (particularly in the South) who were determined that America should heed the advice of the country's first President and *"avoid foreign entanglements"*. Attempts were made to pass a law amending the US Constitution so that a national referendum would be required before America went to war except in circumstances where the United States had been directly attacked. The proposed new law, known as the Ludlow Amendment, was widely popular: a Gallup poll in September 1935 showed that it was supported by 75 percent of respondents and subsequent polls in 1936 and 1937 showed support for the amendment at 71 percent and 73 percent respectively. Even in February 1939, after the proposed amendment had been defeated, a poll showed that nearly 60 percent of the American population would support its reintroduction.

In the face of such determined isolationism, President Roosevelt (who was no isolationist, but was primarily opposed to enshrining neutrality measures in law because they would to impose limits on the scope of his executive powers) once again had little choice but to follow popular opinion. The Ludlow Amendment may have been destined to defeat, but other neutrality measures were introduced into Congress and the President, despite his personal dislike for their provisions, signed them into law. Most notable were the Neutrality Acts of 1935, 1936 and 1937 which ultimately imposed an embargo on the ability of foreign belligerents to purchase arms and other forms of war material from the United States (though oil and motor vehicles were initially exempt). They also effectively prohibited the making of private war loans or the granting of credit to nations at war, and imposed restrictions on the ability of American citizens to travel on the ships of foreign belligerents. The Neutrality Act of 1937 did, however, permit foreign nations at war to purchase raw materials and non-military goods from the United States, but they had to pay cash, and transport the goods and materials from American ports using their own ships - a practice which quickly became known as "cash and carry".[131]

---

[131] President Roosevelt was not alone in his distaste for the Neutrality Acts; many members of his administration felt the same way. In particular, Cordell Hull, the US Secretary of State, and the State Department generally, were horrified by the new neutrality laws and the implications they held for the ability of America to influence

In the meantime however, the international situation grew ever more desperate.

In March 1935, Adolf Hitler, who had become Germany's head of state the previous year following the death of President Von Hindenberg announced a dramatic expansion of Germany's armed forces in flagrant violation of the Versailles Treaty. Apart from token protests, Great Britain, France and the United States in practice did nothing to prevent this expansion of German military power despite the fact that Hitler had already openly spoken and written about his desire for Germany to expand her borders. Indeed, a few months later, the British effectively sanctioned Hitler's actions (to Hitler's personal delight) in the form of the Anglo-German Naval Treaty of 1935, which allowed the German Navy to expand until it was 35 percent of the total tonnage of the Royal Navy, then still the largest navy in the world.

In October 1935, the Italian fascist dictator Benito Mussolini, determined to build a new Roman Empire, invaded and conquered Ethiopia without a declaration of war. The League of Nations, having been completely impotent in the face of Italian aggression, had demonstrated conclusively it was of no significance in world affairs. Again, Great Britain, France and the United States did nothing of any effect.

April 1936 saw the German military re-occupation of the Rhineland, another violation of the Versailles Treaty, and of the subsequent Locarno treaties of 1925, which had been drawn up with a view to improving Franco-German relations. The re-occupation of the Rhineland might have been expected particularly to incense the French, as it meant that once more German troops were aligned along a substantial portion of the Franco-German border. In practice, the French, beset with political and financial difficulties and divisions, contented themselves with some minor diplomatic sabre-rattling and then acquiesced to the German move. Britain and America followed France's lead.

---

world events. On the other hand, viewed from the foreign chancelleries of Germany, Japan and Italy, the Neutrality Acts just seemed further proof, if proof was needed, that America would pose little obstacle to their expansionist plans. Hitler indeed went so far as to declare that *"Because of its neutrality laws, America is not a danger to us."*

The Spanish Civil War erupted in July 1936, between the forces of the left-wing Republican government and right-wing forces led by General Franco. Before long, Germany and Italy were actively aiding Franco and his forces. 1936 also saw the creation of the Axis by Germany and Italy, and the signing of the anti-Comintern Pact between Japan and Germany, aimed at opposing the international spread of communism. Italy joined the Pact in 1937.

In July 1937 came the formal outbreak of the Second Sino-Japanese War, triggered by an invasion of China by Japan, though there had been intermittent clashes between the two countries throughout the 1930s. The war would see Japan overrunning substantial portions of China before a stalemate of sorts was reached in 1939, but fighting would continue until the end of the conflict in the Pacific in the Second World War.

1938 was a busy year in central Europe. March saw the Anschluss, the forced annexation of Austria by Nazi Germany. In September, Hitler demanded that Czechoslovakia hand over the Sudetenland, an area of the country which was home to many people of historic German descent. There were those who thought that, backed by Britain and France, Czechoslovakia would be prepared to fight but at Munich in October, the British and French governments, in thrall to the supposed merits of appeasing fascist dictators, effectively forced Czechoslovakia to cede the Sudetenland to Germany in exchange for vague declarations from Hitler to the effect that he had no further territorial demands in Europe.[132] Less than six months later, German tanks were roaring across the border to annex what remained of Czechoslovakia, the policy of appeasement was widely regarded as having failed, and the British and French governments finally recognised the reality of the dangers posed by German aggression. Britain and France both began to take steps to strengthen their armed forces which during the years of appeasement had been allowed to fall behind the military strength of Germany. Moreover, recognising that Poland was likely to

---

[132] President Roosevelt had been privately horrified by the appeasement at Munich. That said, there were those (including Winston Churchill, who had of course vehemently opposed the policy of appeasement all along) who felt that the presence of a more robust America on the international stage might have encouraged Britain and France to adopt a stricter response to German aggression.

be the next of Hitler's victims, the British issued promises of military support for Poland in the event that she was attacked by Germany. The stage was now set for the outbreak of World War Two in Europe.

During this period, America continued publicly to cling to its policy of isolationism; behind the scenes, however, following the Munich debacle, Roosevelt and his administration sought to relax some of the more extreme aspects of the neutrality laws, and particularly the arms embargo. During May and June of 1939, strenuous efforts were made by Cordell Hull and others to persuade Congress to relax the neutrality laws, but in vain – the days when President Roosevelt could expect Congress supinely to act as he wished were long gone. His political reputation and power, though in many ways still considerable, had been damaged by events such as the Bench-packing proposals and the Roosevelt Recession, and there were now too many Representatives and Senators who were prepared to defy the President if his wishes clashed with their own agendas. By the end of June, it was obvious that the President simply did not have the votes to repeal the neutrality laws.

The end of peace in Europe, when it came, came quickly. On 23rd August 1939, Berlin and Moscow stunned the western world by announcing they had entered into a mutual non-aggression pact, the practical effect of which was to allow Germany to strike at Poland without having to worry about entering into a long protracted struggle with Stalin's Russia. Little more than a week later, on 1st September 1939, Germany invaded Poland. Two days later, their ultimatum to Germany having been contemptuously ignored, the British and French declared war on Germany. The French declaration of war followed the same day.

The outbreak of war in Europe led to a weakening of isolationism in America. When the First World War had begun, President Wilson had appealed to Americans to be impartial, *"in thought as well as in action"*. In contrast, when President Roosevelt addressed the nation by radio on the evening of 3rd September, while emphasising that America would remain neutral, he added *"...I cannot ask that every American remain neutral in thought....even a neutral cannot be asked to close his mind or his conscience..."* Few listening to the broadcast had doubts as to which side had claim to the President's sympathies, and to a large extent the President's views reflected those of the American people; a nationwide poll in October 1939 suggested that 84 percent of the public supported the British and the French. Only 2 percent of respondents supported Nazi Germany.

This support for the western allies did not, however, translate into a desire for American intervention in the war, a point emphasised by Roosevelt in his September broadcast, during which he publicly disparaged suggestions of the United States raising an army to send to the European front line. Instead, the President continued to emphasise a theme that he had first mentioned a few months before: America should be prepared to assist the British and the French *"by all methods short of war"*, not least because it was in America's own interests to do so. The continued existence of the neutrality laws made this policy easier to state than to pursue, and so a new campaign was mounted by his administration for their relaxation, with a special session of Congress being convened on 21st September to debate the matter. Even now, isolationist opposition to any such steps being taken was formidable, and for weeks the radio waves were filled with denunciations by more extreme isolationists such as aviator Charles Lindbergh, Father Coughlin and others of the proposals to relax the laws. Some isolationists went so far as to allege that the proposals formed part of a secret plot on the part of the President to send American troops to fight *"...on the battlefields of Europe..."* President Hoover, though less extreme in his utterances, nevertheless also made known his opposition, and other leading isolationists such as Senators Borah and La Follette stood up in the Senate to speak vehemently against the revision proposals. But the events in Europe had succeeded in rattling the casual belief of many Congressmen that the width of the Atlantic would pose an insurmountable barrier to potential foreign aggressors. After six weeks of vigorous debate, Congress agreed to relax the neutrality laws, and the President signed the Neutrality Act of 1939 into law on 4th November.

The most important relaxation was the removal of the arms embargo, allowing foreign nations at war (and there seemed little doubt that these would primarily be Great Britain and France) to purchase armaments and other forms of war materials, including fighter aircraft, from the United States. However, purchases would have to be made on the cash and carry basis which had previously applied to foreign purchases of non-military and raw materials. The granting of credits to foreign belligerents, whether by the US Treasury or private individuals remained forbidden. The relaxation of the neutrality laws enabled Britain and France to begin ordering materials of war from the United States, albeit slowly at first.[133]

At almost the same time, concern over the readiness of America's armed services, in particular the strength of her air power, led to demands that the United States should begin to increase its own military spending. America's armed forces at that time were unquestionably weak – her army ranked nineteenth in the world in terms of size, and her air force was considered by some experts of the day to be less powerful than that of Italy. With these concerns in mind, in January 1940, President Roosevelt asked Congress to approve an increase in military spending of $1.8 billion. The German blitzkrieg assault on the western front in May 1940, which led to the fall of France the following month and the expulsion of British forces from mainland Europe, intensified concerns about the state of American military readiness even more. On 16th May (by which time the British and French had begun to place substantial orders for thousands of planes and engines) the President addressed Congress to approve a significant expansion of American military strength. In particular, he called for the creation of a two-ocean navy and for an increase in the production of military aircraft, suggesting that America should produce at least 50,000 planes a year. Pitching his pleas to suit the ears of a still largely isolationist Congress, and despite noting that some of the aircraft would have to be delivered "to foreign nations", Roosevelt's proposals were crafted to suggest that if necessary, a fully-armed America could stand free and alone regardless of what happened elsewhere in the world. This appealed to many isolationist Congressmen, and in the summer of 1940, Congress approved in total a further $7 billion for defence, bringing the total

---

[133] Before the declaration of war, Britain and France had placed orders for some aircraft from the US, but had been reluctant to rely to any great extent on America as a source of arms (partly concerned about draining their foreign currency reserves and also not wishing to antagonise isolationists). President Roosevelt had earlier circumvented the existing neutrality laws by delaying his official recognition of the outbreak of war in Europe for two days, allowing the British and French to take delivery from American ports of materials ordered before 3rd September which, strictly speaking, should have been impounded by the authorities upon the outbreak of war.

defence appropriation for 1940 to over $10 billion. The following year (by which time Roosevelt had triumphed in the presidential election of 1940 and won an unprecedented third term in the White House), Congress was even more inclined to authorise military spending. 1941 saw America spend $13.7 billion on the US Army and Navy, as well as $7 billion in lend-lease aid in order to assist the British, who having proved that they could stand alone in defiance of the Nazi war machine were now placing massive military orders in the United States. America was well on the way to becoming what the President declared she had to become: the arsenal of democracy.

The impact of this flood of dollars on the American economy was dramatic. Factories and other industrial plants across the United States that had been closed, or operating under restricted conditions, were re-opened, and their production capacities enhanced as companies sought to meet the new demand for their goods and services. Even so, the existing industrial facilities were insufficient to meet the new demand, and new factories and manufacturing plants were being built across the country, many on green-field sites. For the first time in many years employers began to aggressively expand their workforces. Unemployment levels began to fall swiftly, helped it must be said by the introduction of military conscription – 1941 saw nearly one million men drafted into the American military service. The official unemployment rate fell to less than 10 percent for the first time since the early 1930s, and it continued to fall. The new jobs meant many people had surplus dollars in their pockets for the first time in over a decade which helped to boost the domestic economy.

Having to pay for the extra defence expenditure dictated the economic policy to be pursued. Increased fiscal deficit and higher taxes were necessary. The expansion of America's productive capacities needed to be managed in order to secure maximum advantage, and eventually Roosevelt would authorise the creation of various organisational agencies to coordinate and direct such matters, including the Office of Production Management and the Office of Price Administration. The new military expenditure, coupled with the economic recovery which was already underway following the end of the Roosevelt Recession effectively delivered the *coup de grâce* to the last remnants of the Great Depression. Economic prosperity did not return overnight everywhere; in the autumn and early winter of 1941, there were still many people labouring under extreme financial difficulties, particularly in the agricultural South. It is not possible to point to a particular date and say *"This is when the Depression ended"*. But gradually, during the course of 1941, the trauma of the Depression years began to recede for most people as America prepared herself for war, though the social and economic deprivations of the Depression were promptly replaced by the nightmare of global war, which finally engulfed the United States after the attack on Pearl Harbor.

Actual war stimulated the American economy even more; by the end of 1944, America was spending more than $90 billion on the war (nearly 50 percent of its gross national product at the time). Unemployment ceased to be a problem. Even as early as the end of 1942, employers were reporting problems of labour shortages, as the armed forces sucked up recruits as quickly as they could be drafted (or accepted as volunteers) and civilian workers once more began to travel around the country, no longer searching for jobs that did not exist but rather seeking higher rates of pay.[134] Despite rising taxes and the introduction of rationing (mild compared to the restrictions then in force in Europe), there was at least on the domestic front, a general sense of economic prosperity for the first time in over a decade. This was largely due to America's abundant natural resources, and the skilled application of those resources by American science and industry – American workers were far more productive during the war than those working in the factories of Germany and Italy. As a consequence, notwithstanding the demands of the US military and those of America's allies, civilian retail spending actually rose in the United States during the war years, a unique achievement amongst all the nations embroiled in the Second World War (in Britain by contrast, civilian retail spending fell during the war by approximately 20 percent, but this was during a time of strict rationing). By the time the Japanese officials signed the instrument of

---

[134] Some unions sought to take advantage of the situation by threatening and holding strikes (in 1943, a strike by coal miners seriously affected war production for a while); but such actions had little support amongst the general public and virtually none amongst those serving in uniform and Congress eventually passed measures (despite a veto attempt by Roosevelt) limiting the ability of unions to call strikes without the support of the majority of their members.

surrender on 2nd September 1945, America was unquestionably not only the world's greatest military superpower but once more also the economic powerhouse of the world. She commanded half the world's manufacturing capability, owned more than two-thirds of the world's gold stocks, possessed the world's largest merchant fleet, produced most of the world's oil, and within a few months (once American industry switched from wartime to peacetime production) also produced most of the world's automobiles and other consumer goods. She was the world's leading creditor nation.[135] It was as if preparation for war, and the struggle of war itself, had unleashed a sleeping giant, a giant that had been comatose during the Depression years, but which had awoken, and now, self-confident and wealthy, stood astride the world. Isolationism was no longer the dominant economic, political or military ideology as Americans relished their country's new role as the unchallenged leader of the western world.

But for many Americans of the time, no matter how much they enjoyed their new-found prosperity[136], their experiences of the Depression years would remain with them for the rest of their lives. For them, whether they articulated it or not, there would always be the sense that economic calamity was possible; and many would feel uncomfortable without having at least some savings to help them through any bad times that might arise. They would try to pass that behaviour on to their children, not always with success. Many remained forever suspicious of the stock market – it is noticeable that Wall Street had to wait until the 1960s before the next true share price boom manifested itself, by which time of course, most of the Wall Street traders and advisers who had witnessed the Great Crash had retired from the scene. Tales of the Depression years – some true, some not - would enter the folklore of America, to be recounted especially when times of economic difficulties returned, which of course eventually happened, but never on the scale and to the extent of the years 1929 to 1941.

---

[135] It helped, of course, that America escaped the territorial destruction that descended upon other nations. None of her factories or industrial plants were destroyed by enemy action.

[136] There remained of course severe pockets of poverty in America, but the new prosperity percolated throughout American society generally to a remarkable degree.

Looking back, it now seems clear that there were several phases to the story of the Depression. First there was the boom of the Twenties, leading inevitably to the Great Crash. There were then the Hoover years when America slid inexorably into an economic abyss. Those were the years when despite good intentions, the Federal Government was unable to alleviate to any significant extent the sufferings of those caught in the throes of economic calamity. The election of Franklin Roosevelt in 1933 marked a turning point. The New Deal policies played a significant part; they unquestionably provided at least some much-needed assistance to people suffering genuine hardship, albeit that the relief provided was not always universal and sometimes caused other problems. Perhaps as important as the relief provided, the policies of President Roosevelt and his administrations also gave ordinary people hope that their lives would eventually improve. But whether the New Deal policies themselves actually halted the Depression, or whether they just helped to alleviate some of its more extreme symptoms is debateable. It is notable that when steps were taken in 1937 to try to cut back the level of federal-sponsored relief, the result was almost immediate recession. The American economy only really broke free of the shackles of the Depression when the shadow of war and then war itself lead to an unleashing of public spending on a scale that dwarfed the spending programmes of the New Deal. There is therefore, a strong argument that it was not the New Deal but the Second World War which finally dispensed with the Depression.

Select Bibliography

Conrad Black – *Franklin Delano Roosevelt – Champion of Freedom* – Weidenfeld & Nicolson, 2003

Hugh Brogan – *The Penguin History of the United States* – Penguin Books, 1985

John Kenneth Galbraith – *The Great Crash 1929* – Penguin Books, 2009

John Steele Gordon – *The Great Game – A History of Wall Street* – Orion Business Books, 1999

David Greenberg – *Calvin Coolidge* – Times Books, 2006

Roy Jenkins – *Franklin Delano Roosevelt* – Times Books, 2003

David M Kennedy – *Freedom from Fear – The American People in Depression and War 1929 – 1945* – Oxford University Press, 2005

Maury Klein – *Rainbow's End – The Crash of 1929* – Oxford University Press, 2001

David E Kyvig – *Daily Life in the United States 1920 – 1940* – Ivan R Dee, 2002

Lucy Moore – *Anything Goes – A Biography of the Roaring Twenties* – Atlantic Books, 2008

Ted Morgan – *FDR – A Biography* – Grafton Books, 1985

Selwyn Parker – *The Great Crash* – Piatkus Books, 2008

Michael E Parrish – *Anxious Decades – America in Prosperity and Depression, 1920 – 1941* – Norton, 1992

Ross M Robertson and Gary M Walton – *History of the American Economy 4th ed.* – Harcourt Brace Jovanovich Inc., 1979

Francis Russell – *President Harding – His Life and Times 1865 – 1923* – Eyre & Spottiswoode 1968

Amity Shlaes – *The Forgotten Man – A New History of the Great Depression* – HarperCollins, 2007

Gene Smith – *The Shattered Dream* – William Morrow & Co Inc., 1970

T H Watkins - *The Hungry Years* – Henry Holt & Co, 1999

Index